Other books by Dr. Aaron Kipnis:

Knights Without Armor

Gender War, Gender Peace (with Elizabeth Herron)

What Women and Men Really Want (with Elizabeth Herron)

Angry Young Men

How Parents, Teachers, and Counselors Can Help "Bad Boys" Become Good Men

Aaron Kipnis, Ph.D.

Jossey-Bass Publishers
San Francisco

Jossey-Bass books and products are available through most bookstores. To contact Jossey-Bass directly, call (888) 378-2537, fax to (800) 605-2665, or visit our website at www.josseybass.com.
Substantial discounts on bulk quantities of Jossey-Bass books are available to corporations, professional associations, and other organizations. For details and discount information, contact the special sales department at Jossey-Bass.

 Manufactured in the United States of America on Lyons Falls Turin Book. This paper is acid-free and 100 percent totally chlorine-free.

Library of Congress Cataloging-in-Publication Data

Kipnis, Aaron R.
   Angry young men: how parents, teachers, and counselors can help "bad boys" become good men / Aaron Kipnis.—1st ed.
   p. cm.
   Includes bibliographical references and index.
   ISBN 0-7879-4604-4 (alk. paper)
   1. Male juvenile delinquents—United States. 2. Juvenile delinquency—United States—Prevention. I. Title.
   HV9104 .K546 1999
   364.36—dc21

                                            99-6184

HB Printing   10 9 8 7 6 5 4 3 2 1   FIRST EDITION

Contents

For Liz
Dragon at the gate. Pot of chili on the stove.
Researcher, reader, chaos mender. Daughter of Oshun.
Aspirin bearer and altar tender. Thank you for making
me a father and teaching me that
Bad Boys really can become Good Men.
You can come back in now, it's done.

Foreword

Angry Young Men is an important book that is especially timely now during our current epidemic of violence by and against boys and young men. It also expresses insights that I believe will continue to be valid far into the future. Aaron Kipnis has seen deeply not only into the souls of troubled boys and adolescents but also into those aspects of the spirit of our culture and our epoch that have turned an unprecedentedly large proportion of our boys and young men into perpetrators and victims of violence. Today more American boys are killing themselves and each other—and being killed by adults—than at any other time in this century and than in any other developed nation in the world. It is vital to the future of our society and our world that we learn what adults are doing wrong, individually and as a society, in the ways we raise our boys and relate to each other, and what we can do to correct our mistakes. Reading *Angry Young Men* is a helpful place to begin in the effort to find answers.

Aaron Kipnis writes with eloquence and passion, and his book is a model of how an author can accomplish the difficult and delicate task of showing the relationship between his own life history and the larger history of which he writes. Just as Freud used examples of his own dreams as a way to illustrate universal themes, so Kipnis uses his own life history to illuminate the universal relevance of his insights.

As a result, his book is both enlightening and moving. *Angry Young Men* is a wonderful book and a major accomplishment. I hope it will find its way into as many hands as possible.

JAMES GILLIGAN, M.D.
Harvard Medical School

Preface

Today, the United States has more boys and young men incarcerated in juvenile halls, jails, conservation camps, boot camps, psychiatric hospitals, recovery hospitals, youth corrections, and adult prisons than any other nation. The majority of these boys are nonviolent or low-level offenders, at least when first encountering these institutions. During my last three decades of work in psychology, I have become increasingly aware that many so-called "boys at risk" are being underserved or inappropriately met by our social, educational, and corrective institutions.

In recent years, various educational organizations and advocates have better focused society's attention on girls' specific needs. This attention to girls was long overdue, and equity efforts on their behalf need to continue. American boys, however, also face some serious "gender-specific" challenges. Although it is often noted that males perpetrate more physical violence than females, the fact that boys and young men are also the primary *objects* of violence is seldom as highlighted in our social commentaries. In 1999 males in the United States accounted for

- The majority of children abused, neglected, and murdered

- The bulk of children in foster care and juvenile institutions

- 70 to 75 percent of student suspensions, expulsions, grade failures, special education referrals, school violence casualties, and all other assault victims

- 75 to 80 percent of the homeless, drug addicts, alcoholics, and suicides

- 80 percent of homicide victims

- 90 percent of persons with AIDS

- 93 percent of workers killed or seriously injured on the job

- 95 percent of prisoners and parolees

- 98 percent of combat veterans

- 99 percent of raped and executed prisoners

Most were boys or young men when they first appeared in these categories, in which young men of color are particularly overrepresented. This book aims to better inform the community about the specific needs of boys at risk and why they appear in the above statistical laments. The male-appropriate therapeutic, social, legal, and educational efforts discussed in this book can create significant change in most crimogenic (crime-generating) environments, institutions, and male behavior. At the dawn of the twenty-first century, however, the majority of our resources remain wedded to nineteenth-century penal and behavioral theories. I believe it is time past due for our treatment of troubled young men to move from the industrial age to the information age.

This book examines conceivable links between young male criminality and physical, emotional, or sexual abuse; lack of mentoring by older males; the inculcation of shame by adults; child poverty and neglect; social and political disenfranchisement; inappropriate, inadequate, and ineffectual education; spiritual impoverishment; father absence; lack of economic opportunity; combat sports; corporal punishment; rigid gender roles; anti-boy bias; the media; easy access to guns and alcohol; substance abuse and the criminalization of drugs; class disparities and racism; and other largely preventable and treatable influences in boys' formative years.

A number of personal stories from my own violent and incarcerated adolescence are presented throughout. Reports from other men who were swallowed by the dark maw of sociopathy in their youth, yet returned to make valuable contributions to their communities, are also included. These accounts are followed with observations about the particular elements that helped us become productive adults instead of career criminals.

The effective programs and innovative approaches outlined in this book are largely drawn from dedicated people working on the challenging front lines of troubled boys' lives. There are detailed suggestions about how adults can create more helpful environments for troubled young men today. Over 500 studies in sociology, psychology, criminal justice, psychiatry, education, and other fields underscore the anecdotal reports.

I believe that whatever damages the lives of boys ultimately puts us all at risk. The behavior of young men can disrupt the entire fabric of our social ecology or help weave it whole. My hope is that the facts, analysis, and stories in this book will inform and inspire parents, educators, helping professionals, policymakers, law enforcers, and concerned citizens to action. There is much we can all do to more effectively heal the lives of the troubled, lost, potentially violent, and angry young men sometimes called bad boys.

Acknowledgments

My editor, Leslie Berriman, is a rare gift to a writer's life. She gently and astutely nurtured this book's development, surgically paring away lesser parts and breathing life into the rest. Alan Rinzler is the emperor of mentors. His guidance in early drafts of the proposal helped chart the book's final course. The whole crew at Jossey-Bass Publishers was consistently helpful, enthusiastic, creative, and professional. My agent, Tom Grady, impeccably handled the business side of things while holding an astute vision of the project.

I am most deeply grateful to Dr. Connie Zweig, Mark Gerzon, Elizabeth Herron, and Bob Chartoff, who read multiple early drafts. They contributed important insights and held the spirit of this project at times when I wavered. Tony Allina, M.D., Rebecca Allina, Hector Sanchez-Flores, Babatunde Folayemi, Jack Zimmerman, Akani Fletcher, Dr. Robert E. Roberts, Ted Ravinette, Dr. Bob Rosenthal, Robert Bly, Dr. Mary Watkins, and Dr. Sara Stark all read various drafts. They made valuable contributions to the manuscript and to me personally.

My colleagues, graduate students, and employment at Pacifica Graduate Institute contributed in various ways, as did our extraordinary research librarian, Mark Kelly. Computer savior Jim Weise nursed me through two hard-drive crashes. Members of the Malibu gang, the Fatherhood Coalition, and the Healing Center Foundation, all contributed valued friendship and encouragement.

Research helpful to this book was conducted or compiled by Dr. Peter Breggin, Ginger R. Breggin, Elliot Currie, Franklin E. Zimring, Mike Males, Wilbert Ridue, Dr. Roger Williams, the RAND Corporation, The Prison Activist Resource Center, Stop Prisoner Rape Inc., Project Return, the Justice Policy Institute, the Pacific Center for Violence Prevention, National Criminal Justice Commission, Amnesty International, the National Resource Center on Homelessness, National Coalition for the Homeless, the Sentencing Project, Boys-to-Men, the Family and Youth Services Bureau, Office of Juvenile Justice and Delinquency Prevention, Certified Male, CURE-NY, the Center on Juvenile and Criminal Justice, Families Against Mandatory Minimums, the National Center on Child Abuse and Neglect, the Fatherhood Initiative, the Prison Ashram Project, the Chicago Theological Institute, investigative reporters of the *Los Angeles Times* and *Santa Barbara News*

Press, the *Drug Reform Coordination Network*, *DrugSense Weekly*, and many others cited in the bibliography. Typhoon Software, a dyslexic's best friend, generously donated their *Spoken Word* speech recognition program with which portions of this book were written.

My daughter, Noelani, helped me understand the unique value of a father in a child's life. My godson, Dominick Howes, gave me the opportunity to become a mentor and thus honor the lineage of the many men who mentored me. My former parole officer, Vincent Price, made it possible for me to survive to tell this tale. Many psychology professors endured me cutting my teeth on their bones over the years. Thank you all; now it's my turn. Hundreds of men have courageously shared the vulnerable depths of their lives with me in various councils and groups. Their stories are the soul foundation for whatever clinical insights I may have developed about male psychology. And I have been enriched and educated by the many bad boys and angry young men who have walked with me, at times, along the way.

Santa Barbara, California   AARON KIPNIS
April 1999

Angry Young Men

1

Bad Boys

There is no such thing as a bad boy.
—Father Flanagan, founder of Boys Town, 1917

On a recent Sunday afternoon five East Side Boys crossed the main street that divides our Santa Barbara neighborhoods. They parked their car near the street corner, a few doors from my townhouse. There they hung out, laughing, talking, working on the car, and drinking beers in the sun. They pumped up the bass on the CD player so high their music vibrated my windows. While reading the Sunday paper, one of my more relaxing weekend rituals, I started feeling irritable.

I went to our balcony window and looked out to see what they were up to. I wondered: Are they checking out my street, planning future burglaries, car thefts, or assaults? My wife walks through their territory on her way to the post office. My daughter often parks her car right where they were congregating. I felt concerned about my family's safety and the security of our home.

It was hard to relax, half expecting to hear the screeching wheels of a West Side Boy's car driving by. Will a bullet shatter *our* window, I wondered? After all, there have been several gang-related shootings nearby in the last year. "Why don't they stay in their own neighborhood?" I blurted out to my wife.

She looked out the window and said, "They are in their neighborhood, Aaron. That's Carlos. He lives down at the Greenwood Apartments with his mother Carla. She's the manicurist at Heads Up where I get my hair cut. Looks like Carlos got himself an old car to fix up. He's just showing it off to his friends. There's probably no room to park it at the apartments."

"Those boys are really OK," Liz continued. "They're just a little wild. Whenever I walk by them in the neighborhood I just smile and say, 'Hi!' They always smile back. Come back from the window, Aaron, you're going to make them feel weird if they see you."

I laughed. Despite having been a wild child myself, at age fifty I had somehow transformed into a bastion of middle-class sensibilities. Several Italian stone-cutter families, who have lived here for generations, populate my street. And there are various working professionals on the block—a schoolteacher, a therapist, an attorney, a loan officer—as well as several blue-collar workers, small business owners, and others I don't know yet. Most of us own our homes. I share many of my neighbors' values today.

In this Southern California seaside community the demarcations of class are sharply drawn. Income brackets visibly graduate from working class on the flats, near the freeway below us, to steadily increasing levels of upper classes on the hillsides and ridge tops above. Between the two is the narrow, middle-class band where we live. The demarcations of race are also quite distinct here. On this border between the Upper and Lower East Side, the residents are predominately white.

One block away is a major thoroughfare. On the other side, a higher density of apartments and rental homes exists, and the neighborhood suddenly changes to predominately Latino and African American. Many who live there serve the affluent in the hills above us. They are their gardeners, carpenters, masons, painters, pool maintainers, nannies, plumbers, housekeepers, and maids. Others run small businesses in the neighborhood. Many members of my wife's African Methodist-Episcopal church also live in the Lower East Side.

I gave a last look out the window and tried to reassure myself. "Hey, they're just kids enjoying a sunny day with no other place to hang out. They're part of my community, as much as Anna, the delightful, retired Italian lady next door who grows ambrosial tomatoes in her back yard every summer."

I went outdoors to take a walk. On the way back, as I passed the boys, I casually looked their way. We exchanged nods. "How you doin'? Good day, huh?" I said.

"Yeah," Carlos replied.

"Hey, watzup," said another, smiling.

My tension eased. I didn't see any "tats" (gang tattoos); they were just dressed somewhat gang style like most teenaged boys in the neighborhood today. But there was a "tag" (gang graffiti) on the stop sign at the corner I didn't remember seeing before. Anyone could have put it there in the last few days. But it wasn't until the boys later drove away that I could fully relax and enjoy the remains of the day.

There are twenty-six gangs in our region, many loosely confederated as belonging to the East or West Side of town. Their tags pervade the area. Over the last few decades I've worked with many so-called "at-risk" boys in juvenile halls, treatment centers, wilderness experiences, foster care, and various clinics. And in that capacity, I usually feel relatively at ease, even "down" (connected) with most of them. Of course, other staff members are usually around. So, it's easy to feel secure.

I like most of those boys and generally feel sympathetic to their situations. They are often victims of rough treatment, neglect, racism, and the insults of poverty. When they gathered outside my home, however, I felt vulnerable and uneasy. I did not feel as understanding as when wearing a professional hat. I have more to lose today than when I was their age. At midlife, I just don't feel so tough anymore. These sorts of fears cause many adults to turn away from young men who do not fit our ideal molds for appearance or behavior. As I thought about it more, my unease felt all the more ironic.

I went out on the deck and smoked a cigar in the afterglow of a sun-drenched day. An ocean breeze stirred our wind chimes and rustled the bougainvillea on the balcony. I suddenly understood more clearly why, when I was Carlos's age, adults displayed so much anxiety around me. I was wild, too. But many people thought I was just "bad." Over the years I've tried to put aside recollections from those days. But the sudden appearance of East Siders, on an otherwise tranquil afternoon, somehow brought these memories to the surface again, like fetid bubbles rising from the muck below an otherwise pristine lake.

Bad-Boy Blues

The outer gate crashed shut with the finality of a head-on car collision. Then came the first deadening click as the lock on my new front door slid in place. Click, chunk—the second lock was secured. Click, click, click—the sound of the guard's hard leather heels striking the concrete floor steadily diminished as he strode away from my seven-by-eight foot, windowless, steel-doored cell. I was eleven years old.

The police arrested me for running away from home after a beating by my stepfather. Incomprehensibly to me at the time, they jailed me but allowed him to remain free. My heart grew cold as I sat alone on a sheet metal cot in the Los Angeles Juvenile Detention Center. As I contemplated my future, the singular thought echoing through my mind was click, click, click, click. . . .

During the next seven years of adolescence, when not in juvenile institutions, I spent most of my time living on the streets of Hollywood or San Francisco's Tenderloin and Haight Ashbury districts. The outcast and the outlawed were my friends and family. I lived with Hell's Angels, drag queens, drug dealers, runaways, dropouts, prostitutes, musicians, artists, and thieves.

I rifled cars and stole from shops. I slept in abandoned buildings and cars. I ate out of dumpsters, "dined and dashed" at restaurants, committed acts of prostitution, sold drugs, and did whatever else I could to survive as a teenager alone on the city streets. Understandably, the police repeatedly arrested me.

During my detentions I witnessed numerous beatings, sexual assaults, bloody suicide attempts, stabbings, desperate escape attempts, and young men driven insane from long solitary confinements that broke their spirits. Because of my rebellious behavior in those institutions, I also spent difficult months in isolation cells.

The other prisoners' enraged screams, threats, pounding on the bars and walls, and cursing filled the air with a frightening maelstrom of discontent. These experiences left indelible impressions on my young psyche that still haunt me on occasions. Even though over three decades have passed since my last arrest, those images remain my most vivid memories of adolescence.

As is still true today, the majority of us in those institutions were there for nonviolent crimes. The horrors I witnessed as a child propelled me into adult life with a drive to find alternatives to the juvenile justice system. This book is one result of that passion. Most conditions that I encountered as an angry young man have steadily worsened since then, as has the incidence of juvenile crime. This leads me to believe that our society has largely pursued ineffective strategies for the care and restoration of youth at risk.

Today American boys suffer higher rates of homicide, suicide, incarceration, functional illiteracy, school failure, child poverty, gang involvement, gun carrying, drug abuse, violent victimization, male prostitution and sexual assault, AIDS, and homelessness than the youth of any other Western industrialized nation. In many categories we exceed others by far. The only other nation with a similar ratio of incarcerated young men is Russia. But then Russia never has been known as the "land of the free."

After my first arrest, a judge made me a ward of the state of California. I remained under the state's jurisdiction, on probation or parole, from age eleven to twenty-three. Most friends from this period died long ago from overdoses, suicides, and the perils of street life. But I survived. Eventually, I even thrived. And so can most boys who are similarly abandoned. They do, however, need some specific help, offered at the right time in the right way. A central principle of this book is my personal and professional belief that the majority of difficult, troubled, angry, criminal, and even violent young men can lead whole and productive lives when given the right opportunities and leadership.

Turning It Around

Unlike most so-called "bad boys," I received a college education. A compassionate parole officer noted that, as a young felon on parole, I might qualify for a rehabilitation grant to cover some college expenses. I had to cajole, campaign, and finally protest to get the money. But I eventually made the case that, by depriving me of a high school education, the state had, in fact, handicapped me. It thus seemed fair the state contribute to my adult education in some way.

Though this support was nominal—a few hundred dollars each semester—it gave an impoverished young man enough of a leg up to make college a possibility. Los Angeles City College's policies allowed me conditional admittance as a nineteen-year-old with only a ninth-grade education. It was the first time I went to the same school two years in a row. From there I worked my way through the California State University system and private institutes, culminating my studies with a Ph.D. in clinical psychology.

While a psychology undergraduate I counseled numerous boys and young men in residential treatment centers, juvenile halls, on wilderness "rites of passage," and in county jail as a public defender's assistant. Over the years, I also held support groups, seminars, retreats, and private consultations for men. In response to the suffering I witnessed over the years, I started conducting research on male psychology in the late 1980s. My book *Knights Without Armor* was the first product of that inquiry.

That book was well received. It generated invitations to teach or speak at universities, learning centers, professional conferences, hospitals, social service agencies, men's retreats, government agencies, corporations, and national television shows. I started receiving requests to train educators and therapists about how to work more effectively with men and boys.

In small groups, in widely varied settings, men of all races and economic status recounted their life stories. The vulnerability, beauty, and tenderness often hidden behind men's opaque exteriors repeatedly struck me. These sensitivities emerged when men felt both safe and supported enough to be authentic about their lives. Many of these groups included felons, combat vets, recovering or not-so-recovered addicts and alcholics, and former gang members. Most of them had been or still were angry young men.

My wife, Liz Herron, a leader of women's groups for twenty years, invited me to co-host communication and conflict resolution seminars for women and men in the workplace. We published *What Women and Men Really Want* based on those experiences. Our Gender Relations Institute facilitated dialogues for about 30,000 women and men in various organizations. In those contexts many more men talked about their hopes, fears, dreams, and confusions with women and their struggles with socially imposed models of masculinity.

After years of listening to men in all these semitherapeutic contexts, certain themes emerged. Many differed from the psychological theories I had learned in training, particularly popular academic ideas about male privilege, pathology, identity, capacity for intimacy, and some that even seem to imply an ontological flaw in men's character. Many of the difficulties men face as adults started when they were quite young, but those problems were often poorly met. And as I talked to more men who, like myself, went through the criminal justice system, it became apparent that most began their initiation into crime, violence, addiction, and alienation when they were boys.

Working Well with Bad Boys

Angry Young Men is about the growing numbers of boys at risk who annually fall through the social net that is supposed to catch youth in free fall. Today that net has a number of large holes in it. The catcher in the rye is asleep in the field. Tragically, most of the boys who slip through the grasp of parents, teachers, counselors, therapists, social workers, judges, and probation officers do not survive. They go to prison, they go insane, they die. And they create a lot of collateral harm when they go down in flames. Instead of dying young like most of my friends, however, or ending up in prison like many others, I stalked a better life with fierce determination. I also had some lucky breaks and a few good people along the way who cared.

Though I still travel about the country a bit, today I am more focused on my local community. As faculty at Pacifica Graduate Institute I teach graduate psychology students. As president of the Fatherhood Coalition, a nonprofit service organization dedicated to aiding fathers and their families, I help implement a variety of programs that support young men in their roles as fathers.

At age fifty I have a beautiful family and home, a stimulating career, good health, and a multitude of loving friends and colleagues. Most of my adult life I've hidden my bad-boy past to all but a few intimates to protect my professional and social standing. Recently, however, I began experimenting with working some of my personal stories into various seminars. When colleagues or clinicians-in-training heard my history projected against the backdrop of my current life, some inevitably asked, "How did you turn your life around?" Following these discussions many urged me to write this book. There is, however, no simple, single answer. I wish there were.

How the gradual transformation from bad boy to good man happened in my life is one of the themes weaving through this book. My hope is that this personal story will support other young men trying to create better lives and aid those trying to help them. I've learned that my work with others often goes only as deep as my willingness to face my own demons. The more authentic I am, the more at ease others feel in working with the central issues most troubling to their lives. This seems particularly true with troubled young men.

Impersonal "professional" personas often leave clients and students feeling separated. Transparency in a therapist or teacher, however, can embolden others to present core issues otherwise too imbued with shame for revelation. Working near the turbulent places of passion and despair in a young man's psyche calls for a certain openness to our own suffering as well. That is one of the reasons I am taking what feels like a somewhat risky approach to this book in the spirit of the mystical poet, Rumi, who advises: "Destroy your reputation." Moreover, Holocaust survivor Elie Wiesel teaches that survivors have a moral obligation to tell their stories to the world.

The repression of personal secrets consumes a great deal of energy in our culture. The consequences of secrets bring many clients into our consulting rooms. A myriad of private behaviors or aspects of personal history, if made public, can deny a person employment, social inclusion, safety, or freedom. In our fragmented culture today many of us long for authentic connection to one another. And, as this book details, alienation is at the core of most male violence. So these are some reasons I've chosen to share my own experiences, alongside what I've learned thus far about what helps boys at risk, what hurts them, and what merely gets in their way. The book presents a variety of emerging programs and perspectives that I believe can best help troubled young men. The inclusion of substantial social science research also illustrates obstacles to healthy young male development in many domains.

Do I come to this topic as an unbiased social scientist, objective and freed from the legacy of my past? No. We're all waist-deep in our personal melodrama regardless of the subjects we research. But I've lived fully in both worlds now: the disenfranchised life of an adolescent outlaw and the privileged life of an educated adult. The pages that follow are my attempt to bridge those worlds.

Our national culture today is a lot like the East Side of Santa Barbara. The divide between opportunity and privilege or exclusion and despair is a double-edged sword that often defends one class and cuts the other. It is harder than any other time in modern history for young men at risk to cross the thickening line that separates them from a good life. This is particularly true for low-income boys and young men of color, as the book investigates throughout. I believe, however, there are many things we can do to assure that boys' lives turn toward hope and community instead of nihilism and destruction.

The book's perspective throughout can, perhaps, best be called one of harm reduction and humane justice. This approach attempts to transform the lives of young lawbreakers through providing essential elements missing from their lives. Many thoughtful citizens think the punishing spirit of retribution reigning over criminal justice policy today does more to harm and disenfranchise troubled young men than restore them to productive citizenry. This book does not minimize the need for dangerous young men to be confronted or contained. It is more concerned, however, with interventions effective in preventing angry young men from becoming violent in the first place and restoring them to lasting health and humanity if they do.

Boys who end up in the criminal justice system often share elements in their formative lives that can be changed if we are willing to make the effort. Many of the critical junctions in my early years are typical for boys whose lives get shunted away from community, toward crime and incarceration. The next seven chapters explore common domains that can twist malleable young men into pathologized (behavior interpreted as mental illness) and criminalized beings. The reader may find some material disturbing.

Just as Dante explored seven levels of hell, *Angry Young Men* investigates seven paths that can lead to prison: (1) Home, (2) School, (3) The Street, (4) Juvenile Institutions, (5) Drugs, (6) Youth Crime and Gangs, (7) The Criminal Justice System. Crossing each of these paths are critical junctions where boys at risk can either be diverted toward community and life by parents, teachers, mentors, clergy, judges, probation, parole, law-enforcement, and helping professionals, or, tragically, be pushed closer to alienation, isolation, incarceration, and death.

Each chapter details the shape of a specific hole in the social net for boys living in the United States today and offers suggestions about how to mend it. The book examines child welfare, foster care, parenting, education, street life, community services, treatment methods and perspectives, adolescent mental health, addiction, public policy, gangs, youth incarceration, prisons, prison after-care, probation, parole and rehabilitation—all through a lens of a "male-responsive" psychology.

Girls are also negatively impacted, in gender-specific ways, by these institutions. This book does not directly focus on girls' issues; however, no minimization of the inequities young women face is intended. Much said may also be useful to those who work with girls at risk. To a large degree, the social world of bad boys and institutions they frequent are male "cultures." The book's attention to understudied and misunderstood aspects of male social psychology does not, however, imply in any way that women's issues, their influence or contributions, are of lesser importance, merely that the focus of the book is limited to boys and young men.

Though not every man in prison today went through the developmental sequence of events in the order presented ahead, most visited these seven domains along the way as boys. Each missed turn at the crossroads of community or prison makes it that much more difficult for a boy to find his way home. For most "bad boys," the First Pathway to Prison begins at home.

2

Living in a House on Fire

My mamma made me run crack to feed her habit.
That's how I wound up here.
　　—Benny, 12, in juvenile hall for drug possession,
　　　second offense

Like the parents of many boys at risk today, mine were teenagers at my birth. They divorced when I was three. My mother, Gloria, won custody, as mothers still generally do. She had only a high school education and no job training. Unfortunately for both of us, she soon became an alcoholic. Although my father regularly sent child support, she wasn't able to cope with the economic or emotional burdens of single motherhood. She put me into foster care the year following their divorce. The government drafted my father, Kip, and sent him off to the Korean War.

From age four to nine I lived in half a dozen foster homes. Today, with a twenty-year-old daughter of my own, it's easy for me to understand how young my parents really were. Even so, being given over to the care of strangers so early in life caused me to feel I had little worth. I took the abandonment personally.

The confusing disorientation of a life lived with strangers, and the irrational childhood belief that "it must be my fault," set the stage for a "bad boy" identity to flourish in the years ahead. The

majority of bad boys experience some similar sense of early abandonment from one or both parents, and often society as well. Foster
children, in particular, are highly overrepresented among unemployed, homeless, and prison populations as adults.

Periodically, my mother moved in with various men and made
abortive attempts to bring me into their households. I liked most of
the guys. But the affairs never lasted long. There were hysterical
departures in the middle of the night and subsequent returns to foster homes.

When I was ten, Gloria married a "nice Jewish boy" from her
hometown in Camden, New Jersey. He turned out to be an inveterate gambler and liar. I fainted at their wedding. It was as though
I had some premonition that he would bring only suffering into my
life. Gloria got me out of foster care, however, and tried her best to
provide a stable home. But by the time I was eleven, I began to
rebel. My new stepfather, "Zombie," as everyone called him, proved
to be both hostile and violent.

Mom was always a little uneven herself. When I was two, I fell
out of a laundry sink full of bath water, where she had left me alone,
and cracked my skull on a steam radiator. It left two parallel scars
still engraved on the back of my head. When I was four, I mysteri-
ously fell out of the back seat of her speeding car and tumbled down
the middle of the freeway. When the police confronted her later,
she told them she just didn't notice I was gone until she arrived at
her destination, miles away.

Gloria often left me in the back seat of her car, which had a broken emergency brake. Once it rolled downhill into the middle of
heavy traffic. Her boyfriend ran out and rescued me. Another time
I accidentally hit the gearshift, and the car rolled away into the side
of a building. She often shared these stories with others as amusing
anecdotes of my childhood. And I would laugh along with her as
she retold the tragicomic stories that defined our relationship. I loved
my mother. She was vivacious, beautiful, and witty. Overall, however, she made me pretty nervous.

Once, in a drunken rage, she swung my thick leather Davy Crockett belt, hitting me in the face with the heavy, solid, brass buckle end. The belt hook embedded just below my eye, which still droops a little to this day. After that, it was difficult for me to trust her judgment.

One night Gloria slapped me hard for some reason, long forgotten. I slipped out my bedroom window in the middle of the night and ran away. A nurse found me in the morning, sleeping in the doorway of a hospital. Mother's handprint was still vividly etched on my face. I was surprised that the obviously concerned hospital staff returned me to her care. I had a fantasy that they would take me away to a better place where little boys were safe. But I was soon to learn that there were no such magical lands for boys at risk for abuse.

Abused Boys

In later years, as I counseled "incorrigible" boys in treatment centers, I came to believe that a primary inculcator of their "bad" behavior was their experience of neglect, physical violence, and emotional or sexual abuse in the home. Boys often express distress more physically than girls do. As some therapists say, "Boys act out, girls act in." Though some boys act out because of neurological or mental illness, domestic abuse is a major factor that turns active, inquisitive, and sensitive boys into angry young men.

Abused children, or those who merely witness domestic abuse, are highly overrepresented among those suffering academic, emotional, and economic failure. They drink more, abuse more drugs, and suffer more juvenile arrests, at earlier ages, than nonabused boys. Abused boys are three times as likely to become aggressive and violent. Abused boys also grow up to become the majority of felons serving long prison sentences and men on death row.

Girls represent the majority of sexually abused children. The majority of children who are murdered, seriously injured, physically abused, or medically neglected are boys. Boys with special needs or disabilities, in particular, are overrepresented in all abuse categories, comprising two-thirds of abused children with disabilities. Protection of boys from domestic violence should be a priority of our social programs. But for the most part, in my clinical experience over the years, violence against males is rarely a leading concern.

One of the many factors accounting for this is that boys are far less likely than girls to tell anyone about abuse. A 1998 survey of 7,000 children found that 48 percent of boys, as compared to 29 percent of girls, said they would never tell anyone if they were abused. Over three times as many girls as boys said they would, at the very least, confide in a friend who might, in turn, tell a concerned adult.

It is egodystonic—not in accord with their self-image and traditional gender identity—for boys to complain about pain. Until I was a middle-aged adult in therapy I never told anyone, except my wife, about my own abuse. As a boy, it never occurred to me that abuse was not the normal experience of childhood. Tragically, in our culture, the problem of child abuse has worsened considerably since I was a boy.

Reports of child abuse in the United States have steadily risen over recent decades. In the latter half of the 1990s alone, reports of child abuse and neglect doubled. Over a million children suffer moderate injuries each year, about 160,000 are severely injured, and over 1,000 children die from parental abuse or neglect. All totaled, 1998 reports of abuse and neglect exceeded three million, up fourfold in two decades. Physical abuse now affects one in fifty American children.

Nearly 80 percent of perpetrators are parents; an additional 10 percent are other relatives. The average age of an abused child is seven. The average age of the abuser is thirty-one; 58 percent of the time the abuser or neglecter of a boy is female. In 1997, the Office of Juvenile Justice and Delinquency Prevention published a study indicating that as a precursor to future incarceration, neglect is as damaging to boys as physical abuse. Therefore, in our analysis of the role of childhood trauma in the etiology of angry young male behavior we cannot really dismiss neglect as a lesser evil.

Children who live with both biological parents have the lowest reported rates of maltreatment (3 percent). Divorced fathers with custody show slightly higher rates, and children living with single mothers, particularly those with a nonbiological male in their home, suffer the highest abuse rates (19 percent). Why do single fathers show lower rates of abuse and neglect of boys than single mothers? The generally better economic welfare of single fathers may partially account for this, since child poverty is also highly correlated with abuse. Children from families with annual incomes of less than $15,000 report maltreatment almost seven times more frequently than children from higher income families. Single mothers with young children living below the poverty line, together with alcoholic and drug addicted parents of both sexes, have the greatest statistical risk of abusing or neglecting boys. My own teenaged parents met all of the above criteria.

Children Having Children

In recent years a great deal of attention has been brought to the issue of teen pregnancy. Welfare reform advocates, who want young parents off the dole, instigate most of the policy initiatives. The bulk of social and educational support, however, has been solely directed toward teen mothers. This movement has also been accompanied by increased calls, by girls' advocates, for incarceration and other punitive measures toward teen and young adult fathers.

The importance of fathers in the prevention of abuse and neglect of boys, however, inspired my local colleagues and I to implement a number of programs through our nonprofit organization, the Fatherhood Coalition. We work in alliance with Planned Parenthood, local schools, community health and social welfare agencies, the district attorney, juvenile facilities, and other agencies to foster

male involvement in both pregnancy prevention and responsible
parenting by

- *Including young men in all family planning and pregnancy
  prevention programs.* A visit to most family planning
  clinics finds young women in the lobby with their male
  partners either absent or sitting outside in the parking
  lot. We can welcome young men, however, by actively
  reaching out to them and letting them know that their
  participation is valued. In 1999, more than half the
  nation's fathers lived outside their child's home.

- *Connecting young men with culturally savvy, adult male
  mentors.* Men can often talk more effectively to boys
  about sensitive issues of sexuality, which are often
  tinged with shame or masked with bravado in
  young men.

- *Offering prenatal and postnatal "Boot Camp for New
  Dads" to all young fathers.* We have "veteran" fathers
  come in as "coaches" with their infants. We create
  an atmosphere that conveys an experience of the
  responsible parenting of young children as manly.

- *Providing fatherhood training at juvenile detention centers,
  continuation schools, and other arenas where there is a
  higher concentration of young men involved in premature
  fatherhood.* Most of the young men in these institutions
  are fatherless or victims of abusive and neglectful
  fathers. I ask them, "Do you want your son to be
  here in fifteen years?"

To a man they say, "No way!"

"So," I reply, "What are you going to do to change your
behavior so you can protect your own children?"

That *always* gives them pause. This encounter produces more buy-in to significant behavioral change than any other approach I've tried.

- *Treating teen and young adult men who impregnate girls as potential resources for the mother and child rather than merely predators to be banished from the family system.* This, of course, is only done in cases where there is no evidence of abuse and with the mother's full cooperation.

- *Offering training to prevent domestic violence to both teen parents, a high percentage of whom were abused themselves.* Children of parents abused as children or who live in homes where domestic violence occurs are at a higher risk—some studies state 70 percent—for becoming abusers themselves. Therefore, we support these programs to protect the welfare of *everyone* in the family.

It has taken years for the Fatherhood Coalition to change the negative sentiments toward young fathers on the part of many agencies that, historically, primarily served only young mothers. Prior to our inauguration of this program, our community had no services for new fathers, even though about thirty-five programs were available for mothers. Such disparities remain common throughout the nation.

We find that when young men are treated with respect, and given the educational and economic opportunities that enable them to help their children, a surprising number rise to meet the challenge. Ultimately, this benefits women as well. Many young men will meet fatherhood—unplanned or otherwise—with pride and commitment once given clear opportunities and support to fully participate in family life.

Most violent, adult male criminals share a common past: They were neglected as children and were emotionally, sexually, or physically abused. This, of course, does not in any way excuse their violence. But the more insight we gain into issues that generate young male anger and violence, the better we are able to prevent or treat it.

Foster Uncare

Coming mostly from young family systems that fail to thrive, more than 350,000 American boys will be in government-run foster care homes this year. Although the foster care system was designed to provide temporary care for abused, abandoned, and neglected children, once committed, many boys remain in state custody for years.

In America today, girls are favored over boys for adoption at least two to one. In fact, even though the general adoption preference is for younger children, prospective new parents will adopt significantly older girls over younger boys of the same ethnic background. One in five foster boys spends more than five years in the system.

Foster care does not ensure the rescue of boys from abuse. In one summer care facility I was forced to chop firewood all day and repeatedly slapped if I failed to work. I was stripped of my clothing and humiliated by a male staff member when I tried to run away. Much more severe abuse, however, is widespread in many foster care arenas.

Los Angeles County has more than half of California's foster kids—about 73,000 (one in seventy children)—the highest rate in the nation. In 1997, dependency court judges approved plans to prescribe behavior-altering medication to about 4,500 of these children. Even more were drugged with parental consent. Moreover, when a Los Angeles grand jury looked into this issue, they found that *nearly half were being drugged with no consent at all*. In Orange County, California—one of the most affluent and conservative counties in the nation—foster boys as young as three were reportedly given drugs several times a day to control their "depression and rage."

Los Angeles County's Mental Health Coordinator says the sheer number of different doctors (over 400) treating these children makes quality control nearly impossible. Unexplained deaths are attributed to the abuse of these medications, as well as drug-induced psychosis, abnormal heart activity, uncontrollable tremors, liver damage, loss of bowel control, and other problems.

Many psychiatrists defend the use of these drugs, saying they can be used safely if they are correctly monitored. But they rarely are in foster care facilities—that's the problem. Psychiatric medication can be a lifesaver for clinically depressed, psychotic, or otherwise *severely* disturbed boys—but most boys in foster care are not.

Foster kids often come into the system with little or no medical history accompanying them. Dr. Kenneth Steinoff, who treats foster kids, says that in many cases, "I don't know who the child's previous doctors were. I have no idea what medications he's been on. You get practically nothing. It's a crime." Dr. Glen Miller, a colleague of mine who works in both pediatric and forensic psychiatry, told me, "I see many links between the medical abuse or neglect of disorders that often plague foster boys and the problems I see in the adult men I treat in prison."

Public defenders assigned to represent foster children can have 1,000 kids on their caseloads, scattered around the county. Logistics alone makes it impossible for them to defend kids against abuse except in the face of the most blatant reports. Accounts in which investigators have found that *all* the small boys in a foster group home were sedated are not unknown.

Various physicians report that foster children are often given behavior modification drugs inappropriate for their age, size, and mental condition; doses of psychiatric drugs exceeding the upper end of recommended adult usage; and dangerous mixtures of drugs, so-called "cocktails." According to Dr. Miller, "In many cases, as children move from home to home and new problems emerge, new medications are simply added on top of the old ones they came in on."

Rarely are attempts made to reduce or eliminate medication that might consequently require greater caretaking and staff involvement. In all too many cases, medical attempts to make boys' behavior more passive and manageable with chemical restraints robs them of their emotional development.

In 1998, a *Los Angeles Times* investigative reporter wrote about a three-year-old boy so dazed and mute that his therapist said he would never leave the child welfare system. He was labeled "retarded and unadoptable." However, a new foster parent learned the boy was receiving massive doses of clonidine. She said, "the amount of medication he was on for a [thirty pound] three-year-old was just incredible. Once we got him off the drugs, his vocabulary increased tenfold and . . . his medical diagnosis went from mental retardation to learning disabled." Learning disabilities are another potential effect of behavioral medication abuse.

The 1997 grand jury report also found that in many foster homes food was bad, clothes were in short supply, and some boys were slapped or even hit by caregivers. Inappropriate mixing of children of different ages also subjects younger boys to abuse by older ones. Many foster care providers make only seven dollars an hour. The turnover is tremendous, with the consequence that few foster boys ever secure a consistent adult in their lives. Many are warehoused with proprietors who merely keep them alive in understaffed environments until they are eighteen.

The abuses in the foster care system of Los Angeles are not unique. What is unique is that child advocates had the courage and resolve to influence the convening of a grand jury to investigate this underworld of the child welfare system. Many American cities appear to suffer worse abuses, but I included Los Angeles here because it's the largest in the nation and also the system I grew up in. Many of these reports ring true to me from my own experience and those of my dozens of foster sisters and brothers along the way.

Take One Home, They're Free

Foster boys need special attention to give them the same chances for a productive life afforded boys from intact families. Many of these boys are abandoned by criminal, alcoholic, and drug-addicted parents. Genetic proclivities toward learning disabilities and mental illness could be overrepresented in parents too disabled to care for children properly. Many boys who end up in foster care are born with fetal alcohol syndrome, narcotic addictions, and AIDS. To ensure that these precious apples fall farther from the tree, government could begin to eliminate obstacles to the adoption of abused boys.

Most public foster care agencies are financially discouraged from seeking adoptive homes for their foster children because government subsidies are based on the number of children in foster care per day. There is no financial incentive to move children into adoption, where care that is both in their better interests and our society's can be provided. Foster care organizations, with staff and facilities to maintain, are instead financially rewarded for warehousing kids.

Consequently, abandoned boys, as veritable commodities, are often cycled through a series of foster homes, group homes, and other institutions as they age. To help turn the growing tide of disenfranchised young men in our culture, more concerned citizens need to offer safe homes for boys at risk for abuse and neglect from their caretakers. For this to happen, however, we would have to change many of our attitudes toward bad boys. Already, however, there are many who would gladly adopt a foster boy given a modest portion of the support available to public agency child welfare— some $12 billion a year.

Another change that can help foster boys is to reduce social workers' caseloads to levels that assure they can, at the least, visit kids once a month to check on their welfare. Also, community-oriented social work, in which staff, as with community policing, are familiar with the residents and resources of one specific area, can help provide more consistent and stable foster care environments.

Every one of my foster homes was in a different community, with a different school and a whole new set of siblings and caretakers. Many of the boys I've worked with have been in a dozen different foster homes, some more than that. But with community care, even if a placement fails, a boy can be placed in new home nearby where he can enjoy continuing contact with known teachers, clergy, counselors, and friends instead of being ripped up by the roots every time he is transferred. And these community resources, as a stable part of the child's extended family, can back up foster parents. Wherever possible, foster parents who work intimately with noncustodial, biological relatives can also expand the continuity and range of support in children's lives.

Abusive, neglectful, and abandoning parents dominate the early lives of foster boys. Such parents are followed by an ever-changing parade of strangers: child protection workers, welfare officials, lawyers, court investigators, judges, psychiatrists, police officers, surrogate parents, foster siblings, social workers, counselors, and teachers. Each new foster home has its own particular rules and regulations. It's confusing for foster boys, who get tumbled around in these whirlwinds of inconsistency, to know the behavioral guidelines in any given situation or how to please the new adults around them.

We put children in foster care to protect them from abuse. It should therefore be all the more offensive to us when foster care facilities fail to protect. These boys are innocent. They are victims of abuse, not criminals—yet. Every effort should be made to get all abandoned boys into a normalized family setting. I remember taking walks in the evening and peering into windows, from the sidewalk, where families were sitting down for dinner. My palpable longing for a real home was extraordinary.

Unintentionally, the well-meaning public servants that administrate our child welfare system lead thousands of boys to the iron gates of our criminal justice system instead of to the pleasures of productive lives. Carefully coordinated efforts in which one committed advocate stays with a foster child's case all the way from home removal to either family reunification or adoption would help enormously. Consistent, integrated care of wards and vigorous oversight of the foster care system could go a long way toward providing security for boys. Most of these boys go through a bewildering and demoralizing process of disorientation from which, both my personal and professional experience informs me, it is hard to recover. This sort of background is a virulent medium for the incubation of antisocial, bad-boy behavior.

Born to Be Wild and Bad to the Bone?

Many evolutionary psychologists theorize that boys are naturally aggressive—biologically programmed hunters in training. But it would be a dangerous theoretical leap to conclude that boys are also innately violent. Theories vary, but in my experience, young male violence generally happens when parents, educators, and other concerned adults fail to direct young male aggression into positive channels and protect boys from abuse.

For the most part, with the possible mysterious exception of innate sociopathy, violence is a learned behavior. That was certainly true in my life. I was a fairly sensitive, inquisitive, "nice" boy who liked to quietly read or play in the backyard with my chemistry set. I did not become violent until others perpetrated violence against me. Once incarcerated, however, I learned quickly that I had to toughen up to survive.

Regardless of their circumstances, the toughening of most boys begins early in life. Our predominant American male self-image is tough, strong, and cool. As noted in my book *Knights Without Armor*, numerous studies show that boys generally receive fewer demonstrative acts of affection than girls do from their mothers, who also wean boys earlier. Boys are touched and talked to less, and are more likely than girls to be held facing outward, toward the world and other people. Coincidentally, boys cry more during infancy. Girl toddlers get a quicker and more positive response when crying for help or complaining of a minor injury than boys. Boys, however, are generally *pushed* toward independence, even to the point of isolation.

In adolescent games, boys are expected to deny pain and never flinch when startled, back down from a fight, or show fear in the face of danger. I learned early on that deviation from this code of behavior made me subject to abuse from other boys who aggressively teased, taunted, tested boundaries, and ranked their status for power, strength, and athletic and fighting abilities. These boyhood "rules" were much more rigidly enforced in the detention centers that I periodically occupied during my adolescence.

Some of the reasons for this young male behavior are probably biological—old genetic "provider" imperatives that are still unconsciously preparing us to hunt large animals in small bands with other males: "Get meat!" But the reasons for most gender differences are more likely social—"protect and defend" norms—that prepare boys to stoically deny pain and remain fearless in the face of danger. The "nature versus nurture" argument over the etiology of gender roles and behavior rages on in the professional literature. It is enough for our purpose here to say that, for whatever reason, boys are often different from girls.

Our culture trains boys to disconnect from feelings in a variety of ways. Most are told, "Don't be a baby, big boys don't cry, keep your cool, take it like a man, chill-out." These numbing-out attributes may be valuable for a soldier or manual laborer, but they are not the ideal basis for becoming a caring and creative member of a peacetime community, a responsive husband, or a nurturing father. Much of the self-reflective activity I've engaged in as an adult has been directed toward overcoming this programming and assisting other men, who often face ridicule for their efforts to do the same.

Protecting Boys

Even though I went to school on several occasions with black eyes from Zombie's beatings, no one ever questioned me. I believe this was true because many adults still unconsciously uphold these toughen-up-the-boys codes. They are deeply embedded in our cultural psyche. This standard is also reflected by the professional literature, which publishes significantly more research about abused females than abused males, even though males represent the majority of victims of violence.

Advocates for women and girls have displayed great courage and commitment in bringing long-overlooked, critically important issues to our social and political discourse. I hope, thanks to those efforts, that it will not take our culture as long to become sensitized to boys' specific needs. We can model women's effective leadership by maintaining a warm, positive, fiercely protective, nurturing, male-responsive environment for boys wherever they are.

Parenting classes, mentoring programs, home visits by health professionals, and anger and stress management for parents can all help prevent child maltreatment. The high incidence of child abuse and neglect by female caretakers points to a need for our social programs to teach anger management to women as assiduously as they do men suspected of domestic violence or child abuse. This can be done in a "blame-free" approach that is sympathetic to the specific stresses that women face, especially when there is turmoil in their homes. In 1998 Congress allotted over a billion dollars to protect women from violence. This official attention was hard won and a long time coming for women. But because children do not vote and boys, in particular, have few organized or effective advocates today, no such largess has yet come forth for their protection.

Bad Boys Love Outlaws

In my mother's home I felt increasingly unsafe as my new stepfather, Zombie, turned the heat up on our domestic cauldron. The only respite from domestic chaos I felt as a child was during the few summers spent with my father. He introduced me to his flamboyant world of gamblers, con men, and outlaws when I was nine. In those years Dad was a professional handicapper—a "tout" who figured betting odds in the horse racing industry. He ran a "wire" service. Gamblers paid him to advise them about what horses had the best chance of winning.

Throughout the year my father followed the horses as they moved from track to track during the racing season. Every summer he was at Del Mar, near San Diego. I spent blissful days at the ocean, body-surfing on a world-class beach. I remember those days as the happiest moments of my childhood. We'd cross the border to watch bullfights and dog races in Tijuana or go to drive-in movies on hot summer nights. Dad would make pastrami sandwiches on the glove compartment door and we'd eat pickles by the jar.

Many people thought my father's lifestyle was inappropriate for a young boy. But the summers I spent hanging out with him lit up my childhood. I loved just being by his side and taking it all in. He occupied a fascinating world of gamblers, gangsters, jazz musicians, and exotic women who welcomed me into their colorful lives. They were, by far, the most interesting and engaging people I met as a boy. My father's world stood out in technicolor contrast to the mind-numbing, cultural vacuum of the low-income, cookie-cutter housing tract my mother and stepfather occupied in the San Fernando Valley. Like myself, many bad boys today experience the outlaws in their environments as the only alluring avenue of escape from a world without hope.

Early in life I received a positive imprint toward those on the fringes of our culture. For better or worse, my childhood identity became wrapped around an outlaw core that would persist for many years to come. Sadly, as it is for boys everywhere, my summers all too quickly ended. For me that meant a return to the monochrome world of life with Gloria and Zombie.

Runaway to Jail: First Offense

One night, in my eleventh year, I ran away from my mother's home again, this time to escape my stepfather's violence. He said it was "all my fault" that he had so many problems with my mother. I thought I could simply fix things for them both by leaving. But that just made him angrier. With Zombie on my tail like a hound after a rabbit, I tore through the neighborhood and climbed over a twelve-foot fence surrounding the Budweiser brewery. I hid in some bushes most of the night. Plant security guards discovered me the next morning, sleeping in a parked car. Though my face was obviously bruised, the police charged me with "incorrigibility" and took me to juvenile hall. Click.

On the morning after my first despairing night in juvenile hall, foreshadowing hundreds of nights to come in locked cells, a guard brought me out to the day room where about 100 boys sat on wooden benches in front of a black-and-white TV. The majority of the boys were Latino, with a number of African Americans, Caucasians, and few Asians. I later learned from the chaplain that I was the only Jewish boy there.

The "barber" shaved my head bald. A trustee issued me the uniform that every inmate wore, a white T-shirt and worn-out jeans. In exchange for a purloined cigarette or match he'd give out better quality clothing that fit. But I had no contraband, so he doled me out misfit seconds from the bottom of the pile. Despite our differing backgrounds, our uniformly shorn appearance sent a message to me that we boys were now all part of the same outlaw tribe. I was startled when I saw myself in the mirror for the first time. My new countenance was grimly reminiscent of other European Jews: those interned during the previous decade's Holocaust.

One of the boys there was a thirteen-year-old named Peter. He was overweight, had blotchy skin, and wore thick glasses. I thought he was rather funny looking. But after a few weeks we became friendly. Peter was originally from Louisiana and spoke with a curious lilt. His family moved to California, which, in those days, still had a number of small farms. After a neighbor caught him having sex with a ewe inside his barn, he was arrested for sodomy.

Peter was an expert "hambone" player who would entertain us with rapid rhythmic slaps against his thighs and chest. But this unusual behavior, plus his odd appearance, speech, and the nature of his crime, made him subject to ridicule in this hard-edged, urban juvenile detention center. Jails are extremely conservative places. Their behavioral protocols tend to be rigid and narrow. Like the Jewish "Kapos" who turned against their own in concentration camps, those who have suffered society's intolerance can become equally hostile toward others' deviations from the norm.

Other boys taunted and hit Peter. One night, after I'd been there for a while, a gang of older boys raped him in the shower. The rest of us, I am still ashamed to say, continued showering, acting as if nothing unusual was happening. None of us wanted to be known as the one who attracted the guards' attention and thus risk suffering a similar fate at the hands of the same gang.

There was a toilet at one end of the day room in full view of the guards and everyone else in the room. The extreme lack of privacy made defecating difficult for me. But eventually, if you have to go, you have to go. The next day, I noticed Peter had been sitting on the toilet in the day room for a long time. He looked pale, which was understandable considering what he had been through the night before. Suddenly, he pitched over and landed hard on the floor with a sickening thud. Blood streamed down his legs and began pooling on the floor.

Apparently, while sitting there in plain view, Peter reached beneath his groin and sliced his testicles with a razor blade. He then just sat there on the toilet, bleeding in front of the guards and all us boys. Many of the boys thought it was hysterically funny. I was horrified. Unconscious, he was taken to the hospital. The next day the authorities released me, on probation, to my mother's home. I never did find out if he lived or died from his suicide attempt. But the immutable fact that juvenile hall was an extremely dangerous and degrading place for children became indelibly stamped on my soul.

The punitive atmosphere of juvenile hall had its desired deterrent effect on me. I was highly motivated to avoid future incarcerations. Despite my loathing of jail, however, I was to spend several years of my coming adolescence behind bars and my entire youth and young adulthood as a ward of the state, under the critical eye of probation and parole officials. Deterrence simply does not work for most angry young men. But, as I discuss throughout this book, there are many sorts of interventions that do.

Today, My Son, You Are a Man

After my return from spending several months in "Juvi," my mother never hit me again. But more severe beatings from Zombie replaced her sporadic outbursts. For a time, I suffered his abuse as the price of my freedom. But one day, I reached my limit.

Early one Saturday morning, Zombie attacked me for failing to get out of bed to mow the lawn. He came into my room yelling at me. When I sleepily told him to "bug off," he jumped on the bed and began slugging me in the face. My experiences in juvenile hall, however, had toughened me up. I'd also learned how to stick up for myself in the street fights that often occurred in our working-class neighborhood. I learned that even the older boys, who went after my lunch money as I cut through alleyways on the three-mile walk to school, would leave me alone when I started fighting back. For the first time, I was undaunted by his rage.

That morning, yanked straight from sleep into a violent assault, I suddenly reached a boiling point. Having grown stronger and more confident about my fighting ability, I hit back, swift and hard. Zombie was stunned. He instantly became frenzied. His face turned red. He began bellowing and punching me in earnest. I weighed about 100 pounds and he weighed over 200, so there was clearly no chance of me winning the fight. But I didn't care. I felt he had to learn that, from now on, there would be a price to pay for hitting me.

A running battle ensued. We tumbled out of the bedroom into the living room where my mother tried to break it up, screaming and swinging a hammer at us. To this day I don't know whether she was aiming the hammer at her husband or me. I wasn't so sure at the time either, so I broke free and ran out the door with Zombie in hot pursuit.

I ran into the garage. Like many boys, I kept a variety of special things in a secret hollow among the storage boxes: a raven's wing, my marble collection, fishing lures, some firecrackers, pages from a *Playboy*, and a hunting knife my father gave me. Zombie chased me around the pool table (a prize Gloria won on a game show) screaming, "I'm going to kill you, you little punk!" When he picked up a pool cue and swung it at me, I believed he meant it. I plunged into my secret space and grabbed the knife. Brandishing it I cried, "Go ahead, take your best shot, Zombie. But if you miss I'm going to stick this knife in your fat belly." Standing there with blood streaming down my face I was suddenly perfectly calm.

I had no shred of doubt in my mind that I was ready and able to kill him. He must have seen it in my eyes somehow. A resolute look can communicate a great deal, man to man. He put the pool cue down and backed away. It was the one and only time in my life that I was completely prepared and resolved to kill another human being.

The experience of repeated abuse alone can drive boys into sociopathic behavior. Had I killed Zombie, however, my life would have been destroyed as well. I'd have spent the rest of my youth incarcerated. Few survive that experience with their soul intact.

I was lucky that he backed off. Having caused a grown man to back down from a violent attack, I felt a new sense of power. I had proved my "manhood" to my stepfather. To assault me now he knew that he would risk the same consequences he could incur for hitting another adult male—a man.

Don't Mess with Me!

For many bad boys, violence toward an abusive "caretaking" adult paves their road toward long-term incarceration. Sadly, by the time they commit a violent crime little is available to most boys but even more abuse from the criminal justice system. One study indicates that over 60 percent of all murders by teenaged boys are against adult men who were abusing them or family members. In a cycle of violence that affects generations, boys who were abused by their mothers as children are also more likely to abuse their spouses as adults. And women abused by their spouses are, in turn, more at risk for abusing their boys, thus completing a grotesque circuit of family violence.

Even though crime rates dropped in the mid to late 1990s, violence toward boys remained at epidemic levels in America. Our adolescent male homicide rate averages fifty times that of Japan's and twelve times that of most other industrialized societies. Boys who present a hard-edged, violent posture to the world around them are not necessarily "looking for trouble." Many angry young men develop a menacing demeanor as an unconscious defense designed to keep the violence in their world at bay. Often, it is merely a sociopathic facade covering an inner experience of profound anxiety.

The fundamental organizing principle of most gangs is rarely hate. Though elaborately disguised, it is more often *fear*. Sociologist Rafael Ezekiel conducted an in-depth study of white, racist youth groups. He told me that almost every one of the boys he interviewed was fatherless, poor, and undereducated, lived in a decaying neighborhood where they were often an ethnic minority, and had little hope for the future.

Males throughout the world tend to enforce their physical boundaries though looks, gestures, and postures. The more threatening the environment, the more stereotypical these nonverbal signals tend to be. Urban gang graffiti is a modern extension of this "marking" behavior by males who feel threatened by, rather than welcome toward, the potential intrusion of other males into their territory.

The rest of the short time I lived in my mother's home, I marked my territory through hostile looks and by remaining continually armed. Gloria took the hunting knife away one day when I was out of my room, so I stole her butcher knife from the kitchen and hid it inside my box spring mattress. Every night I took it out, put it under my pillow and slept with my fingers wrapped around the handle. For weeks she complained about the loss of her favorite knife.

During the day I kept hidden in the lining of my jacket a switchblade that I had bought from a Mexican boy at school. Zombie knew I was armed with a knife, moreover that I was resolved to use it. He never hit me again. The resolution I made—never again to suffer abuse by others, regardless of the cost—helped keep me alive during the incarcerations I faced in the years ahead. Now, as an adult, I find myself equally resolved to help protect other boys from abuse.

How We Can Help Protect Boys from Domestic Abuse

- Provide better support for single mothers in achieving economic self-sufficiency and education, understanding that economic stress alone can contribute to their higher incidences of abuse and neglect of boys.

- Assure that *both* parents are mandated to anger management programs or drug and alcohol treatment programs where applicable when there is violence in the home, regardless of the perpetrator's gender.

- Dedicate more public resources to protecting foster children, knowing they do not have the political power to lobby on their own behalf.

- Support male-involvement programs to assist fathers in developing the emotional, technical, and financial capacity to be more involved with their children's lives.

- Initiate aggressive adoption campaigns, including economic incentives and professional support networks, for all America's children currently abandoned to institutions.

- Require professional training and supervision programs to examine anti-boy biases that exist today in some arenas and increase male-positive attitudes to assure that boys enjoy equal protection and opportunity.

- Require high schools and marriage-license grantors to provide all teenagers and newlyweds with parenting instruction. Also, require all divorcing couples with children to attend joint child-care planning before granting a divorce.

- Implore teachers, doctors, coaches, counselors, clergy, parents, and neighbors to speak directly to children who appear abused or to contact authorities. Whenever safe to do so, talk to adults who are abusing their children in public.

- Abolish the notion that any adult should be allowed to strike any child, for any reason.

Some costs are involved in better protecting child welfare. But as we will see, the investment in protecting boys is considerably less than the resources needed to contain the criminal behavior of angry young men who, as a result of child abuse, do not properly develop. Broken homes, poverty, neglect, abuse, parental substance abuse, and criminality all contribute, as they did for me, to boys becoming abandoned to the wasteland of the juvenile justice system. Abusive homes pave the First Pathway to Prison. Another factor that most "bad boys" also have in common is early difficulty in school.

3

Slipping Through the Cracks at School

Why should I stay in school? I'm not learning nothin'
that'll help me on the street.
—Jessie, 14, during a life issues discussion
   at a Los Angeles junior high

Today, in addition to teaching psychology at Pacifica Graduate Institute, I periodically conduct seminars for other schools, such as the University of California at Berkeley, Harvard Medical School, and the University of Wisconsin. No matter how warmly I am welcomed, however, I often feel like an infiltrator from another planet—"Badboyia."

I was not a great student during my primary and secondary education. After a particularly bad year in the eighth grade my father, Kip, took me aside and said, "Son, I predict one of three things will happen by the time you are eighteen: (1) you will be a drug addict; (2) you will be in prison; or (3) you will be dead." He was right about the first two. Only remarkably good fortune prevented the third from becoming inevitable. My formal education ended in the ninth grade, making me an unlikely candidate for higher education. Luckily, I found my way to a city college.

As a teacher of higher education today, I notice that few bad boys make it to the ranks of my students. In fact young men of all backgrounds are a steadily declining minority of new college and graduate students. The reasons for this trend are complex, but some factors stand out.

Disciplining Boys or Breaking Their Spirits?

There were a number of reasons I failed in the two dozen or so schools I attended prior to dropping out. Like many boys I was restless in the classroom. I was bored and distracted. I interrupted the teacher and acted out, goofing around with other kids. I was a wise guy, the one who asked tough questions or responded to queries with a sarcastic retort. I was a dreamer who wrote poetry and short stories, often not paying attention in class.

Consequently, teachers often sent me to detention or "social adjustment" classes. Though I didn't show it, I usually felt ashamed for being singled out and punished. If I was tardy, talkative, or missed detention, I was sent to the vice principal's office for punishment. That, however, only made me feel even more rebellious and defiant.

In his book *Beating the Devil Out of Them,* domestic violence expert Murray Straus notes, "It is virtually certain that part of the link between corporal punishment and crime occurs because 'bad' children [who] are hit go on to have a higher rate of criminal activity than other children." Despite the evidence, the institutionalized practice of disciplining boys with paddles, belts, rulers, and other implements widely persists, both in school and at home.

In the seventh grade, I received over 100 welt-raising swats from the vice-principal's hickory paddle, delivered with the full force of his athletic strength. After receiving the hundredth swat, boys got the privilege of signing his paddle. While other kids were out playing ball after school, I was in "social adjustment," meeting other boys who had signed the paddle. They became my first gang, "The 100s."

"Social adjustment" consisted of writing 500 "I will not _____ " affirmations. There, we also received more swats for infractions such as breaking room silence or failing to complete the assignments on time. Insidiously, the assignments were often impossible to finish in the time allotted.

The posture the social adjustment "teacher" made us assume was to bend over, grasp our ankles, and then raise our heads so we looked straight ahead. Then, wham! A good swat could knock a boy halfway across the room. Florid bruises remained for days thereafter. When swats came daily, the hematomas overlapped one another.

During these "classes" I became friends with Denny Slayter, the class clown, Chuck Mendez, a tough Chicano who "ruled" the schoolyard, and other bad boys whom I met there. In the bathroom one day, the three of us showed off the vivid palate of colors on our behinds and upper thighs, as though they were merit badges or other hard-won symbols of achievement. We began to wear triple pairs of underwear to soften the blows. But that didn't make much difference.

Eventually, our pain thresholds increased. This only incensed the social adjustment teacher. As a measure of our "manhood" we prided ourselves on not showing any reaction when hit and derided one another if we failed in our stoic display. Sometimes, despite our resolve, tears just leaked out. It was good training for turning restless and mischievous boys into cynical, angry, and violent young men. After detention, we were so wound up, we sometimes took vengeance on the community. Vandalism and fights with other boys after school were frequent after these sessions.

One day, our gym teacher broke Andy Lipinsky's tailbone with his paddle. After that, and the ensuing lawsuit, they stopped swatting kids at my school. Years later, the state legislature made corporal punishment illegal in California.

Today, however, in the half of our states that still permit it, boys still receive two to three million applications of corporal punishment a year. The majority occur in Southern states, where, coincidentally, there are also higher incidences of gun violence at school.

In fact, states in which teachers are allowed to hit children have the most student violence and higher murder rates overall.

Thousands of boys punished at school require medical attention. But this is one of many arenas in which authorities apply different standards of protection for boys. Although corporal punishment may effect short-term changes in bad boys' behavior, it ultimately does more to fuel young male anger and aggression than assuage it.

Have Boys Become a Second-Class Gender?

The ecology of neglect toward boys at school is evident in many other arenas, as revealed by various studies. This list is not intended to minimize the inequities that girls face, but rather to highlight some areas where boys are not faring as well.

- When both girls and boys are equally misbehaving, boys receive more frequent and severe penalties.

- Boys, particularly low achievers, receive eight to ten times the reprimands of their female classmates. These reproaches are more likely to occur in front of class-mates, whereas girls are more frequently taken aside in private.

- Boys are removed from classrooms and serve more detention than girls. They receive 71 percent of school suspensions and are expelled at even higher rates.

- Boys are victims of the majority of school violence.

- Boys are referred to special education four to one over girls. They represent over 70 percent of students labeled as learning disabled and 80 percent of those sent to programs for the emotionally disturbed. Minority males are highly overrepresented in these categories.

- Boys drop out of school four to one over girls.

- Boys receive more F's, have lower grade point averages, and fail to graduate more often than girls.

- Girls continue to outperform boys in reading and writing by much greater degrees than boys *ever* outperformed girls in math and science.

- Boys are in fewer clubs, student governments, and school newspapers than girls.

- Boys are the minority of valedictorians, academic scholarship winners, new college students, and those going on to graduate school.

Combat sports, such as football, also proliferate in school. Annually, over 300,000 high school boys are injured, 14,000 are hospitalized—many with permanent disabilities such as paralysis—and several are killed playing football. Sports with the highest injury rates are largely reserved for boys. Annually four million visits to emergency rooms result from high school sports. The promise of full-paid college scholarships, gargantuan professional sports contracts, the adoration of cheerleaders, and praise from older men all tell boys that a willingness to face violence, suffer injury, and endure pain is the formula for success.

Boys as young as ten are now using steroids to pump up their muscles for combat sports. A 1998 survey of Massachusetts's middle schools found almost 3 percent of students using the drugs. Since a cycle of steroids can cost several hundred dollars, the study's author suspects coaches and parents of buying the drugs for the child athletes. About 500,000 adolescent boys today take steroids to pump up to a masculine ideal of performance beyond the natural limits of their bodies.

One of the potential side effects of steroid abuse is drug-induced psychosis, so-called "roid rage," in which boys become uncontrollably aggressive and violent. It can chemically transform serious athletes into bad boys. Other damaging effects range from severe acne and atrophy of the testicles to heart and liver damage. Some boys may feel confused when they are rewarded for violence that entertains others but punished when they are wild off the field. One out of five NFL players—the role models for high school players—have criminal histories, many for violent crimes.

One of my university students was a full-scholarship football player. In his paper for "The Sociology of Men," Luther wrote, "I've come to realize that the real price of my education is the destruction of my beautiful, young black body for the amusement of my classmates who get their checks in the mail from Daddy. I keep my grades up, because one of these days I'm going to blow a knee or something and that'll be it. I've got to get something else going for me other than knocking heads. But for now, that's the only way I'm going to stay in college." A professional football player's average life span is merely fifty-four years.

Violence 101

Today, many of us ask why boys seem more prone to violence and acting out than previous generations. I believe the socially tolerated abuse of boys and young men, in many arenas, is one cause of unarticulated, young male rage. Our schools have come to tolerate a social ecology of punishment, neglect, and even outright abuse of some boys. Highly publicized school shootings have desensitized many teachers to more common forms of violence and made them less likely to report it or intervene in other ways. Director of the National School Safety Center, Ron Stephens, confirms that today, "School officials seldom report if no blood is drawn."

As numerous surveys of domestic violence bear out, violence against males is substantially underreported. Boys tend to believe that complaining about injuries from assault is not manly, whereas most girls are encouraged to ask for help. Many boys also fear that "informing" will subject them to retaliatory assaults. Statistics on school safety are therefore deceptive when it comes to boys. In 1995, almost half of all boys surveyed in grades nine through twelve reported involvement in a physical fight during the previous year. Yet official school statistics cite a rate closer to only 10 percent, in itself an unacceptably high incidence of victimization.

Although I was involved in numerous school fights, several of which drew blood, authorities were never called in response to a single incident. I never received a single session of counseling to help me extricate myself from the violence at or near school where most fights occurred. In a strange quirk of male culture, I instead became friends with several of the boys who fought with me.

After battling Denny Slayter on the basketball court one afternoon, we wiped the blood off one another with paper towels in the school bathroom, laughed about the whole thing, and were fast friends thereafter. During the time (ages twelve to fourteen) that my identity was transforming from wimp to wild boy, I never felt there was a single adult I could go to at school for help or guidance. After I refused to back down when Chuck Mendez, who "ruled" the schoolyard, challenged me on the football field, he invited me to join his gang. The idea of inclusion and protection by a group, any group, sounded good. I joined.

Today, some school safety guidelines list behaviors typical of half the adolescent boys in school as predictive of students most at risk for violent outbreaks. Because bad boys are referred to programs in which the staff usually has the lowest level of training, the poorest tools, and most dilapidated facilities, our highest risk students tend to become the least well cared for.

Few teachers are trained or equipped to deal with boys who act out. Boys sense this. Teachers legitimately fear both personal injury and lawsuits for using excessive force. Yet the small incidents that lead to most fights, such as pushing, scuffles, name calling, and "mad dogging" (stare downs), tend to settle down when a serious adult male shows up in the immediate vicinity.

A Father's Place Is in the School

Social research increasingly confirms that one thing the majority of boys at risk have in common is an absent or abusive father. In the late 1980s, at Arlington High in Indianapolis, students were so out of control that the school could no longer hold large events like dances. For years this school, where one-third of the students came from fatherless homes, was a troubled, dangerous place. Things began to change, however, when a new principal, Jacqueline Greenwood, simply asked for help. She told the fathers, "Come to the school any time that you can and be with your kids. We need you to get involved."

In response to this call, one student's mother, Mrs. Linda Wallace, said to her husband, "Those are big kids and no mother can yell at them and make them behave. But maybe a father could." She printed a T-shirt emblazoned with "Security Dad." Her husband, Anthony, saw looks of surprise the first night he showed up at a football jamboree wearing the shirt. Students smiled and waved: "Hi Mr. Wallace—how're you doing?" Whenever students started to get unruly and he moved in their direction, other students would say, "Hey, that's Lena's dad. Be quiet. Sit down." When he asked them to move out of the aisles, they did so without a fuss.

His wife recalls, "He talked to them with respect and they listened. He treated them like they were his own kids. It was fantastic." After more fathers joined the "Security Dads," the school was able to reinstitute events previously canceled out of fear of violence. Also, about two dozen fathers got together to patrol the school during classes to increase security for all students.

"What works is that father image," said Ron Cheney, another father who joined the group. "So we don't need to say very much. Just being there is what counts. With a [police] officer they think, 'Hey, I must be in trouble.' With us, they smile and say, 'Hey, what's up?' And we love it."

One student said, "It's much happier to have fathers around, rather than guards (noon goons). Our dads are like real people.

They don't intimidate us. Where parents are involved, our lives are a lot easier. It's like a family."

In 1997 the U.S. Department of Education found that better grades and behavior both result when men are more involved in school activities. The power of a father's presence to lift his children's academic performance transcends class, race, ethnicity, and his level of education. The rate of suspension, expulsion, and repeating grade levels is also lower for "father-involved" students than those for whom only the mother is involved. The success rate declines much further when neither parent is involved.

Over the years, in our consultations with couples and families, my wife, Liz, and I have noted that fathering often complements mothering. Frequently, mothers seem more concerned with the emotional life, safety, and health of their children. Fathers often appear more focused on encouraging achievement, discipline, motor skills, and independence.

Neither approach is better or worse. Together, they are a balanced parenting "meal" that better nurtures children. Of course, not all couples fit these tendencies, and sometimes when these differences are present, they create conflict between women and men vying for the preeminent approach to parenting. But for single parents of either gender, it's often tougher to balance a boy's needs for consistent discipline and fierce direction with tenderness, nurturing, and protection.

In the same way that women want men to open doors to arenas where women have historically been excluded, men need women to assist them in moving into women's traditionally held domains. For example, in the past, because most fathers felt unwelcome in the delivery rooms of maternity hospitals, they were seldom present at the birth of their children. The prevalent myth of past eras was that they just didn't care. But when obstetricians' attitudes toward fathers started to change in the 1980s and fathers were actively welcomed, they showed up in droves. Now more than 80 percent of married fathers are present at the birth of their children.

In the same way, when fathers feel invited into the schools, they fill a personal need to play a role in their children's lives from which they have historically felt excluded. In the wake of more schools' recognizing the value of father involvement, their numbers are increasing. In California, the "Dads Club" and "Dads in Action" are getting rave reviews from school officials. Nationally, "Mad Dads" and other such groups have similar positive impacts. The fathers in these programs often report that their school involvement also improves relationships with their own children. Even the busiest executives somehow find a few hours a week do their stint at school, and many do more.

Sadly, however, even with burgeoning male-involvement initiatives such as our Fatherhood Coalition, more than half the fathers in two-parent families and over 80 percent of divorced fathers have no significant involvement in their children's schools. Although father involvement can help restore order to rowdy schools, teachers remain the primary resource for pointing boys toward smoother roads than those paved with the rough, hot bricks of societal blame upon which most boys at risk chafe and fry.

Gender Balance in Schools

Teaching is a difficult profession. Teachers make much less than prison guards, whose jobs require much less education. Today, however, the teaching profession is equally stressful and, in some schools, almost as dangerous as law enforcement. There are many institutional problems that prevent teachers from providing the quality of education many wish they could.

Failing schools reflect a failure of our culture. Many schools are crumbling and out of date, often lacking adequate textbooks or even basic teaching supplies. In California, graduation rates have steadily fallen over the last twenty years. This drop is coincidental to changes in the state tax code. In 1978, Proposition 13 gave a huge tax break to existing property owners, largely benefiting elderly voters, and gutted the primary source of school funds. Subsequently, our state slipped from the top 10 percent in education spending to the bottom 10 percent. Now, one third of our boys fail to graduate with their class.

Most teachers are dedicated, capable, caring people. Few have blatant prejudices toward any specific group of students. Many teachers today, however, are ill prepared. In California over 31,000 are learning on the job, unqualified for a state license. Many have less than a minor in the subjects they teach, particularly in schools serving low-income communities. Only 13 percent of teacher's aids even have a college diploma.

Teachers have low accountability for creating success in their students. A greater focus on teacher training, mentoring on the job, and continuing education could help. As with most jobs, teachers' salaries should be tied to their performance.

But all logistical barriers to good education aside, I believe the last few decades of gender-focused educational research has also caused some anti-boy bias to creep into the unconscious attitudes of some educators. Our schools hold many double standards for boys and girls today. For example, educators have been rightly concerned about girls' lower performance in math and science. Many gender-focused surveys, however, fail to also highlight that boys lag much further behind girls in reading and writing and have lower grade averages and higher dropout rates.

A 1997 survey of community colleges in Washington indicates that male students fail three to one over their female counterparts, who also now outnumber them by the same ratio. In several educational surveys female teachers admit that they feel more comfortable discussing gender-related issues with female students and that they often feel more disturbed by male students' behavior.

One common fallacy in gender equity philosophy is the belief that any identified disadvantage for girls corresponds to an advantage for boys. When gender equity programs emphasize girls' math or sports deficits without spotlighting boys' reading and writing deficits, it's spurious for them to claim that schools are *only* "failing at fairness" toward girls.

In higher education today, there is a paucity of research on male psychology, sociology, and learning theory. In the United States, there are over 15,000 courses focusing on women's issues and needs. These women's studies classes are needed and valuable. Yet there are fewer than 200 men's studies courses, similar to those I've taught at various universities, that examine the specific needs of boys and men in our rapidly changing world. These inequities aggravate an already bad situation for boys and young men in school.

Nationwide, males now number only 44 percent of college admissions and 41 percent of graduate students. At the institute where I currently teach, men are merely 25 percent of our graduate students. This three to one ratio is not uncommon in graduate programs for helping professionals today. To Pacifica's credit, they outreach to males as part of their commitment to diversity. This overt concern for male students or their subsequent underrepresentation as youth educators, counselors, and therapists, however, is rare on most campuses.

Contrary to past studies, recent surveys indicate that greater numbers of girls report receiving positive feedback from teachers than boys. The girls reporting the highest levels of teacher attention also have the highest levels of college participation. Minority boys, however, who report the lowest attention rates from teachers, have significantly lower college participation.

Other issues prevent many minority boys and girls from getting the educational skills they need. We are approaching a time where computer competency is tantamount to literacy. Yet schools in which two-thirds of students are minorities are much less likely to be hooked up to the Internet than predominately white schools, whose students are also three times more likely to have a computer at home. Economically disadvantaged schools also have the highest male dropout rates and the lowest male reading scores—as much as four whole grade levels/years below affluent schools. "Classism" and racism readily compound the gender issues that cause many schools to underserve boys.

Instead of Suspension

Although they may improve school safety, zero-tolerance regulations are also having a severe negative impact on boys at school. Parents find few educational alternatives after a student is expelled from school because of truancy, drugs, tobacco, alcohol, weapons, bad language, fighting, acting out, or sexual harassment. Even five- and six-year-old boys have been suspended for kissing a girl on the cheek as boys' behavior becomes subject to ever greater degrees of scrutiny and punishment. Even though boys report similar degrees of "harassment" from girls, boys receive the most punishment for teasing, name-calling, and other behaviors that upset girls. Since adults, not kids, commit the vast majority of drug abuse, sex crimes, weapons carrying, and violence, we are now holding school boys to higher standards of behavior, greater scrutiny and punishment, and lower standards of legal protection, than adults.

At least 15 percent of eighth-grade boys, nationwide, were suspended or expelled from school in 1998. Boys of all ages are suspended or expelled at two to three times the rate of girls. Black students are significantly more likely to be suspended or expelled than Asian, white, or Latino students. Students from lower socioeconomic backgrounds of all ages are two and one half times more likely (17 percent as compared to 7 percent) to be suspended or expelled from school than economically advantaged students.

Regardless of economic class, however, black males are suspended at higher rates in *every* economic grouping. In many urban schools, up to one-third, and in some, as many as *half* the black male students are suspended or expelled during a single school year. Does this statistical indicator of racial imbalance in school suspension/expulsion rates indicate overall worse behavior from

African-American males? These are the same young men who disproportionately fill our juvenile institutions and prisons. Or does it indicate a widespread racial and gender bias toward culturally specific African-American male behaviors? My contention throughout this book is that the behavior of young men in general is becoming increasingly pathologized by our culture. This trend intensifies significantly, however, for boys who are members of racial, cultural, and economic minorities.

At the risk of perpetuating stereotypes, I notice that some young African-American men are, in fact, more boisterous, challenging, and outspoken in the classroom. The communication styles of some are imbued with speech that is encoded with subcultural dialects. Though culturally congruent for the boys, their speech can feel alien, even offensive, to the largely white, middle-class, female sensibilities of the majority of teachers. An African-American colleague of mine puts it this way: "We are all two 'mens,' one for white society and another among ourselves." African-American boys resist adopting the language style of the dominant culture, their historical oppressors, to a much higher degree than African-American women. From one point of view this could be interpreted as resistance to cultural assimilation, or cultural pride.

That does not make these boys wrong, however; it merely makes them different. These differences are often not as great a problem, however, for male, African-American teachers, under whose tutelage both grades and behavior of African-American boys often improve. Unfortunately for those boys, however, only about 2 percent of our teachers are African-American men. Even fewer Latino male role models are present in our schools. Coincidentally, Latino boys, who fail to see their own faces reflected in their teachers', have the highest dropout rates in the nation.

Of course, wild boys have to be taken out of classrooms at times. They distract other students and sidetrack teachers. If suspended from campus, however, their punishment is often more a vacation. They are free to roam the streets and are motivated to talk friends into cutting class to join them. That's what I did on the many occasions I was kicked out of school for smoking, fighting, or missing detention.

With in-school suspension, however, boys get up, go to school, and get their classwork. There, they can receive one-on-one tutoring and counseling, something many failing boys need to succeed. An alternate form of suspension would be to send bad boys to programs designed to help them overcome problems, instead of dumping them on the streets or shipping them to other districts. Counselors and social workers could also work more closely with other school professionals to ensure that every bad boy has a real chance to succeed in school.

Some schools are responding by holding regular "councils" in which students have an opportunity to speak about their lives. These facilitated dialogues encourage openness and nonjudgmental listening skills by allowing one student to speak at a time while others simply listen. They build community and make education more relevant to the students' real life experience. It's hard to sit still in class when your life is lousy and no one seems to care. Youth councils show promising results as a proactive approach to reducing disruptive behavior at school.

My wife and I periodically hold "gender dialogues" with students. Boys sit on one side of the room and girls on the other. We then teach them a process in which both sexes have an equal opportunity to discuss topics such as

• How it is both hard and special to be a boy or a girl

• What their questions or conflicts are with the other sex

• What they want in the way of behavior and understanding from one another

• What they appreciate or admire about the other sex

These sessions have been highly productive. Both educators and students tell us this process feels more helpful than just instituting sexual harassment rules and suspending the boys who break them.

What impresses us most is high school students' capacity for mutual empathy and openness beyond that of many adult professionals with whom we have held similar encounters. Recently, we adapted the process to talk about racial differences. The preliminary response is encouraging. Youths possess a vital capacity to create mutually supportive communities, given the opportunity to do so.

We Don't All Learn the Same Way

Much of the research on boy-friendly curricula is happening outside the United States in places like England and Australia, where Father Martin Wallace, headmaster of an all-boys school, notes, "Boys are not without special needs: They just have different needs [compared] to girls. A lot of the disadvantages boys suffer have to do with social skills, self-image, and self-understanding. To begin with, we need to let our boys know we like them; that they are worthwhile human beings. In the justified push to adapt curriculum to encourage girls, boys have sometimes felt pushed aside, their needs forgotten. Sometimes, they need to hear a few positives about themselves."

I was never perceived as a boy with special needs. Rather, the general response seemed to be that I was just bad. The more adults treated me like a bad boy, the more I began to think of myself that way. Eventually, rather than be crushed by shame, I began to take pride in the role. Other bad boys, like Chuck, Denny, and their gang, accepted me just the way I was. Soon, I really believed I was bad. After a while, so did everyone else.

Though I had only finished ninth grade, I found it easy to maintain an A grade point average in the university. I failed in secondary school primarily because my home environment lacked a supportive atmosphere for study and because the structure of the classroom did not account for my more restless learning style. I was punished for failing to conform to the rigid standards of a classroom that insisted I be silent and still.

It wasn't till late in my adulthood that I learned that I suffered from dyslexia, a learning disorder, and a related attention deficit disorder. As a result of the learning disability I never could learn how to spell or write legibly. Had computers with spellcheckers not come along while I was in graduate school, I don't believe I ever would have obtained advanced degrees.

This handicap negatively affected all my schoolwork and, as a child, caused me to feel confusion about my intelligence and ability. That, in turn, had a negative impact on my self-esteem. On multiple choice intelligence tests I always tested high, but my grades were mediocre, and my conduct was "unsatisfactory."

My caretakers must have felt frustrated when they were told that I didn't apply myself, was unmotivated, and even that I was lazy. But try and try as I might, I could not learn how to spell. Yet my verbal expression and comprehension skills were strong. My mind often raced ahead of teachers who, at times, almost seemed to be speaking in slow motion, thus contributing to my sense of boredom and frustration in the classroom.

Since our culture ubiquitously socializes boys to be more autonomous, we're often less interested than girls in pleasing the teacher. When frustrated by repetitive verbal drills or bored in class, boys like me often get labeled as having social adjustment problems, conduct disorders, or even moral and cognitive defects. But for many reasons it's often harder for boys than girls to sit still in a classroom.

Stillness, neatness, conformity, quietness, politeness, attentiveness, and *verbal* skills—historically regarded as more feminine virtues—are highly emphasized in most classrooms. But boys, whether by nature or nurture, are often active, challenging, disorderly, assertive, irreverent, questioning, boundary testing, and, perhaps, a little more physical and *visual* in their learning style. Consequently, teachers tend to perceive boys as having more personality and behavior problems than girls. Instead of regarding spirited boys as disruptive, defiant, or deviant, a male-responsive view sees them as full of energy that needs firm direction.

Boys' language skill deficits are often deeply tied to shame. One boy I worked with was a twelve-year-old named Eddy Speers. Eddy was new to the school, and teachers noticed that he was always silent. Though capable of speech he refused to speak in class and was referred to me for his "behavioral problem." After our first session, however, it was apparent that his difficulty was not attitudinal. Eddy suffered from a severe speech impediment; he was a stutterer.

In his halting way Eddy told me that at his last school he had been ridiculed for his speech. "They called m-m-e Ma-ma-machine Gun Eddy," he sheepishly confessed.

As we talked, I observed that his speech gradually improved. I noted that to him, and he informed me "that it's much worse when I have to speak in front of other people, when I feel put on the spot in class."

Eddy didn't really have a behavioral problem; he had a verbal skills challenge. Though not a speech therapist, I had been a public speaker for years and was able to work with him, over a few playful sessions, on performance anxiety and fear of ridicule. We used a microphone to give him a feeling of power with his words. I also referred him to a speech specialist available through the school district. Within a few weeks he started speaking in class. In fact, after about six months it was hard to shut him up. Boys stutter about six to one over girls, comparable to their significantly higher incidence of dyslexia and other learning disorders.

Read or Bleed

A 1997 study by the U.S. Department of Education states: "In recent years, literacy has been viewed as one of the fundamental tools necessary for successful economic performance in industrialized societies. Literacy is no longer defined merely as a basic threshold of reading ability, but rather as the ability to understand and use printed information in daily activities, at home, at work, and in the community. As society becomes more complex and low-skill jobs continue to disappear, concern about adults' ability to use written information to function in society continues to increase." Being able to read also remains the primary foundation to being able to fully participate in a democracy.

A higher percentage of American boys now score in the lower ranks of literacy than in any other industrialized nation. Of the various language disadvantages that boys suffer, the gravest social consequences follow their failures in reading. Language skill deficits for boys are closely tied to failure in all academic, economic, and social arenas.

There is a clear, causal link between academic failure in boys and their involvement in the disruptive, violent, and criminal activities that channel them out of educational institutions and into the criminal justice system. Failure in reading tops the list of self-esteem-busting events in school boys' lives. A 1997 survey by the Dyslexia Foundation found that about *70 percent of boys in juvenile institutions suffer from learning disabilities*. Even more disturbing, 80 to 90 percent of all convicted felons are high school dropouts. Cristy Kraemer, a literacy specialist with the San Juan Unified School District in California, confirms that "Reading and behavior are really connected. A kid that's feeling really unsuccessful is often less obedient in the classroom."

By middle school, most girls are developmentally twelve to eighteen months ahead of boys. Their language skills generally exceed same-aged boys by far. When boys fail at verbal skills, in the presence of girls whom they often want to impress, the embarrassment can be unbearable. Bad boys in particular often feel sensitive about their verbal deficiencies. The way many boys deal with not being able to perform as well as girls is to act out in other ways that display their strength and self-confidence.

Richard Fletcher, at the University of Newcastle, believes, "When teachers express concern that girls are not interested in physics, while ignoring boys' lack of interest in languages, a clear message is conveyed that physics is valuable while languages are not. The recent push for a girl-friendly curriculum implies that the existing offerings are boy-friendly. This is not true and we can expect that addressing boy-shy subjects will be just as complex as encouraging girls into math and physics has proved to be."

English is a subject that boys often do not like. Many perceive reading, especially reading or writing about subjects that feel irrelevant to "boy culture," as uncool or unmasculine. An article from research funded by the U.S. Department of Education notes that "Boys who are encouraged to engage in activities normally preferred by girls may need adult help and support to cope with teasing and rejection by their same sex peers."

In 1998, Education Secretary Richard Riley expressed his frustration about the reading meltdown in America: "Prisons are full of high school dropouts who cannot read," yet Congress "continues to dilly-dally and dawdle rather than enact a bill to build a corps of reading tutors."

Although I repeatedly failed at handwriting, spelling, and other written language–based tests, in college I discovered how to learn in new ways. Computers allowed me to write my way through graduate school and even develop a successful writing career. Most of the solutions to my academic problems as a child were simple but overlooked. These oversights remain true for many other boys today.

I recently had a consultation with a twelve-year-old, Max, who was kicked out of school for being disruptive in class. After two terse sessions, he revealed that he was frustrated and bored because he could not see what the teacher was writing on the board. He was too embarrassed, however, to admit that he could not see.

Male pride gets in the way of many boys asking for the help they need. Once Max got glasses, his classroom disturbances ceased. About a quarter of adolescent boys have vision defects that can affect their ability to read well. But most of the problem is in the approach to learning itself.

All the energy going into debates about differing educational approaches to reading tends to divert attention from significantly helping the 40 percent of American fourth graders who read poorly. This is a group that is disproportionately poor, male, and composed of ethnic minorities. Not only are boys in lower economic ranks over-represented by poor reading, the reading gap steadily widens between boys and girls as their economic class descends. Nationally, two out of five children cannot read well enough to keep up in school. In California, only 36 percent of third graders read at grade level.

In Inglewood, California, the Bennett-Kew elementary school's student body largely comprises students from low-income families. This school, a mile away from the epicenter of major social upheavals and gang activity in South Central Los Angeles, defies all expectations. Bennett-Kew is nationally recognized for consistently, over the last two decades, scoring well above the national average on standardized reading tests. Their rankings are roughly double that of students in my Santa Barbara district.

What's the secret at Bennett-Kew? Principal Nancy Ichinaga says it is simple. "We have an unfaltering commitment to teaching every child to read in English by the end of first grade, no matter what color they are or where they come from. Many of their parents can't speak English. That doesn't matter. Those are just excuses. If a child isn't learning, it's not the parents' fault—it's the school's."

The Cotswold School is a coeducational secondary school in Leicestershire, England. As an experiment the school assigned fourth-year boys and girls to separate English classes. They also created a curriculum of texts, poetry, and discussion materials tailored to what they believed would most interest boys or girls. Class sizes were reduced to about twenty-one per class—key to success with many struggling U.S. students—and some intensive writing and reading support was instituted for the boys.

According to statistics for the United Kingdom, only 9 percent of fourteen-year-old boys get grades in the range of A to C for English. After two years in the gender-segregated classes, however, the number of boys in the high-scoring range increased almost 400 percent. The girls did better, too: 75 percent scored in the A to C range, compared with 46 percent the previous year, now merely double instead of five times the boys' rate. Marian Cox, head of the English department at the school, reported, "[Boys'] behavior, concentration, and reading levels all improved significantly." She observed that boys could relax and express themselves more without girls present, and girls reported the same. Cox noted that "Some of these boys had never read a complete book before, apart from an adventure game or instruction manual. But they found they enjoyed it." Subsequent to the study, several boys planned to pursue English studies at higher levels.

Of course, cautions should arise in discussions about providing different reading materials or classes for boys and girls. Will stereotypes be reinforced? Will capacity for understanding the other sex diminish? Will one gender get shortchanged? These are all worthy concerns. But before we try to meet curriculum agendas of gender-equity advocates, we should first assiduously assure that boys take to reading with a passion.

As an informal experiment, I encouraged a few English teachers to take boys out on the football field and read to them while walking around. They would then sit for a while, discuss the material, and then walk and talk some more. The teachers reported that their boys' reading comprehension and verbal skills increased while their behavioral problems noticeably declined. Once the boys' bodies were liberated from the stultifying atmosphere of the classroom, their minds apparently became liberated as well. A more controlled study is needed to test this theory.

In my male psychology courses I often show *Dead Poets Society* as a training film about how to get boys to fall in love with language. In it, Robin Williams plays a passionate, irreverent poet who teaches English literature through activating bored boys' emotional and physical bodies. In my experience, when boys are allowed to let their feelings and physicality stay connected with their mental learning process, they are *never* bored or restless.

Same Sex, Different Story

So are same-sex schools the answer? Rhode Island professor Cornelius Riordan notes that black and Latino boys do better in all-male Catholic high schools with mostly male teachers than do demographically matched boys in mixed-gender Catholic schools. Boys in single-sex schools have better test scores, are more likely to take academic courses, and feel more secure in their environments.

Same-sex schools can increase boys' academic performance and reduce behavioral problems. But despite the advantage for boys, I do not believe that segregated schools are the ultimate answer for boys or girls. Economic and political barriers make a massive reorganization of our beleaguered coeducational school system impractical and, in my opinion, undesirable as well. Ultimately, boys and girls need to learn how to work together as partners in learning, even though that may be distracting, difficult, and challenging to their self-esteem at times.

Students learn life skills at school along with academics. We must prepare them to live in a diverse world. But occasional same-sex classes, in arenas in which boys or girls feel most challenged, can support students at a time when they are more developmentally challenged than many other times of life.

Given all of the above, what can we effectively do now to help boys learn how to read?

- Acknowledge that development of language skills is often slower for boys than girls; structure learning so that boys do not fall behind.

- Identify and remediate learning problems early on.

- Introduce reading materials most likely to capture boys' interests.

- Assign some writing exercises relevant to boys' daily lives, such as a journal that is then reviewed more for content than form.

- Use frequent visual and physical interactions to integrate boys' reading skills.

- Understand that when boys feel verbally outclassed by girls, they may act out as a defense mechanism against shame. They need to be encouraged and supported.

- Use one-on-one tutoring, wherever possible, with boys who have difficulty concentrating and customized approaches designed to meet individual needs.

- Reduce English class sizes, thus allowing teachers to give boys additional time and attention.

- Use the arts, trade classes, and even sports to stimulate reading and writing. That is, make reading a key part of nonacademic courses to which boys may be attracted.

- Encourage, train, and support more males—especially energetic, fierce young men—as reading teachers. Boys can thus directly experience, through their teacher's role-modeling, that better language skills are not a threat to their self-image, but rather can complement and enrich their masculinity.

Educate or Medicate?

It is ironic that in a nation trying to teach children to "just say no" we medicate ever larger numbers of boys to bring their behavior into accord with classroom norms. Normalcy, however, is a very fluid concept. In one era it was normal for children to labor sixteen hours a day and marry at age fourteen. In our era, most children go to school for at least twelve years. In one era it was normal for girls to wear pretty dresses and only become mommies. In our era they are also astronauts and executives. Only twenty years ago, diagnostic manuals referred to homosexuality as a mental disease. Today it is largely considered a lifestyle. So normalcy in the classroom might also be seen as a relative, cultural, and temporal concept.

For example, many of the criteria used to determine a diagnosis of attention deficit disorder (ADD) and attention deficit hyperactivity disorder (ADHD) are actually typical behaviors for many boys. The "symptoms" include rambunctiousness, contrariness, poor impulse control, trouble staying on one task, fidgeting, noisy play, difficulty waiting one's turn, interrupting teachers, leaving one's desk without permission, talkativeness, trouble finishing schoolwork or chores, and oversight of small details. In fact, this is exactly the way many highly creative people act when forced to perform repetitive and boring tasks.

For many boys, the persona called for in the classroom is ego-dystonic. Though this may not make me many friends among teachers, I feel compelled to write that it may be, at times, both developmentally appropriate and *completely normal* for adolescent boys to challenge the environment of today's coeducational classroom. Developmental psychologist Jean Piaget wrote that it is the "duty" of a boy "to revolt against all imposed truth and to build up his intellectual and moral ideas as freely as he can."

Many boys do not want to be the teacher's pet. It's egosyntonic (in accord with their traditional identity) for them to challenge authority as part of their developmental process. Competition and confrontation are healthy, normal ways of testing the worth of new knowledge. We need teachers who welcome confrontation and who can work effectively with the assertive energy of challenging boys and increasing numbers of "nonconforming" girls as well.

I am concerned by the number of my college students who left high school with little or no capacity for classroom debate, believing their role instead to be to just passively take notes. New knowledge, however, does not come that way, nor does creativity or the joy of learning. I am also troubled by how few of my graduate students—though often extremely bright and highly educated—display the ability to write in their own authoritative "voice," often choosing instead a cautious reiteration of others' ideas.

Rather than educators' taking a hard look at teaching style, values, and the structure of today's classroom, various drugs are increasingly being used to quiet "overly active" boys. Why do so many educators today appear to assume that if girls fail, the fault is with the institution, but if boys fail, the fault is in the boy's character?

By various estimates, over 5 percent of American boys now regularly receive behavior modification drugs to help them conform to what could be interpreted as a more "girl-normed" school environment. And increasing numbers of assertive girls—those who do not conform to traditional, quiet, and cooperative female role expectations—are given drugs. If current rates continue, we could be drugging one in ten students by 2002.

As schools increasingly fail to meet the needs of spirited boys, professionals keep widening the diagnostic criteria for ADD and ADHD. These "mental illnesses" are now the number one childhood psychiatric disorder in America, affecting at least two million children. Other industrialized nations, however—most with better schools and student achievement than ours—do not diagnose remotely near the same incidence of learning disorders in their boys.

Ritalin is the primary drug being given to "hyperactive" school children today. The educational process, for some boys, seems to benefit from taking it. Ritalin is methyl-phenidate hydrochloride. It is an amphetamine-like drug, a stimulant widely sold on the street as "speed." Many boys sell their prescriptions to other boys who use the drug for recreational purposes. In 1999 it was selling on the street for $5 to $10 a tablet.

Gene Haislip, of the Drug Enforcement Administration, says that the potency of Ritalin ranks "right up there with cocaine." In fact, it is pharmacologically very similar. When I first raised concerns about Ritalin in *Knights Without Armor* a decade ago, Haislip was strongly recommending that our government restrict and curtail its use. Since then, however, despite the warnings of many other informed professionals, its use and abuse have grown dramatically.

- After steady growth for many years, the amount of Ritalin produced and used in this country further increased over 500 percent during the latter half of the 1990s.

- U.S. doctors write over 11 million Ritalin prescriptions a year, over five times those in the rest of the world combined.

- One in thirty Americans between the ages five and nineteen now have a prescription for Ritalin.

According to the *Physicians' Desk Reference*, however, there is no definitive test to diagnose ADD. Physicians and psychiatrists rarely spend as much as one hour determining whether a child should be drugged. Diagnosis is based solely on subjective observations of the child's behavior. The American Psychiatry Association agrees that "There are *no* laboratory tests that have been established as diagnostic in the clinical assessment of ADD." A 1998 brain imaging experiment on a small study group may hold some promise for definitive diagnosis. But at this time, none exists.

Some boys and their families do suffer significantly from the consequences of severe learning disabilities. For them, medication is often experienced as a God-send, the only thing that works. As a person in recovery from substance abuse, however, I believe that powerful central nervous system stimulants should only be used to control behavior or ameliorate learning disabilities *when all other attempts at treatment have failed.*

According to experts, such as Dr. Peter Breggin, author of *Talking Back to Ritalin* and other valuable related books, stimulants like Ritalin should *not* be used if a child has symptoms of marked anxiety, tension, and agitation. These drugs are not intended for "children who exhibit symptoms secondary to environmental factors and/or primary psychiatric disorders." They are not designed to treat emotional or behavioral problems. Yet increasingly these are the very reasons for which drugs like Ritalin are prescribed. The potential serious side effects of Ritalin tend to be downplayed by those who advocate social control through behavior-modifying medications. Some of these effects are

- Suppression of growth; one study suggests some atrophy of the brain as well

- Greater agitation, irritability, abnormal gait, tics, spasms, and seizures

- Social withdrawal and flattened (zombie-like) affect

- Insomnia, drowsiness, nausea, dizziness, blurred vision, and headaches

- Hair, appetite, and weight loss; anorexia

- Heart palpitations, hypertension, and chest pain

Even though Ritalin can make spirited boys quieter or more attentive in the classroom, a clinical fallacy has been propagated in the field of learning disability treatment. Since no tests can determine ADD, some psychiatrists think that if Ritalin makes a boy more "tractable," he must, therefore, have had the disorder. But normal kids given the drug also become more attentive. Most of us get more focused when we take a little speed. That's why I drink coffee in the morning and why so many "normal" students use various types of speed—from caffeine tablets to amphetamines—to cram for exams.

After more than a decade of unrestrained proliferation, Ritalin is now widely abused in secondary schools and colleges. Students crush the tablets and snort it like cocaine. Some college students fake learning disabilities to get prescriptions. Ritalin may even be a "gateway" drug to other addictions. Several studies indicate that adults who used it as children are three times more likely to abuse cocaine but show no similar increased use of alcohol or marijuana. In other words, in street parlance, these drugs can make children accustomed to the "need for speed."

Increasing numbers of teenaged boys are being charged with felonies for selling Ritalin. The number of emergency room visits attributed to Ritalin abuse, for children aged ten to fourteen, jumped tenfold from 1990 to 1995, from 40 to 400. This rate matched cocaine overdoses for that group and included several deaths.

With all the dangers they present to a growing mind and body, why are drugs being pushed to ever larger numbers of spirited children? For the answer to this question we must look not to the children, but to ourselves. Ritalin treats our need for control more than it does the educational, mental health, or social needs of children. For example, we don't give passive children drugs to make them *more* assertive in the classroom. Nor should we. We don't give unimaginative children marijuana even though some artists have claimed it enhances their creativity. No, we drug spirited boys to control their behavior in schools and institutions that have forgotten how to reach boys and how to teach them with out chemical binds and gags.

Many boys need a strong classroom presence that can contain and direct their aggression with caring firmness. Highly spirited boys need one-on-one periods or small-group instruction, realistic expectations, clear behavioral limits, frequent changes in activity, and opportunities to burn off excess energy. In many schools today, academic demands have become so great that physical recreation is reduced to fifteen minutes a day. Many schools have no functioning outdoor equipment. Some host no physical activity at all.

Parents, teachers, and mental health professionals long for a silver bullet that will cure the growing problem of agitated children. Adult frustration with difficult children is fueling this unprecedented expansion of classroom behavior management with drugs. The decision to drug most boys is primarily economic. It costs considerably more focused time and energy for parents and educators to work with spirited boys than it does to medicate them. Behavioral medication is expedient. Teaching children, however, that powerful drugs are the way to solve behavioral problems or cope with learning discontinuities may not be the best lesson we could offer.

Much of boys' problems in school are related to the funding priorities and structure of our schools. Educators simply lack the needed resources to work intensively with time-consuming students. Instead of being met with "tough love," boys at risk are increasingly pathologized, kicked out of school, transferred to marginalized "alternative" or continuation schools, and, finally, criminalized in "prison-preparatory" juvenile institutions.

Some Recommendations to Make Schools More Helpful to Boys

- Engage parents, especially fathers.

- Keep expectations high for *all* students.

- Relate demanding academic work to career training linked to the marketplace. Create more alternative, continuation schools that teach life skills and other survival tools.

- Give teachers the latitude to innovate. Move beyond numbing memorization and silent cooperation. Develop gender-specific ways to work with boys, such as team learning, in areas where boys fail to thrive.

- Foster an atmosphere that creates a web of close relationships among teachers, students, parents, business, and community programs for youth. Encourage home visits by teachers. Try to make the school a tribe that boys want to belong to. Boys like tribes.

- Assure that every student has textbooks, supplies, and equipment for every subject as well as computer access in the community during and after school.

- Provide summer, intersession, and after-school programs for any boy who does not meet grade-level standards.

- Recruit "bad-boy literate" young men, from groups overrepresented by school failure and underrepresented by educators, for teacher training programs.

- Stop kicking salvageable boys out of school and onto the streets. Instead, provide in-school suspension programs with boy-friendly curricula and teachers/ counselors well trained to work with noncompliant boys.

Given the right opportunity, most troubled boys are fully capable of learning and changing their lives in a positive direction. Once the mark of Cain is upon them, however, it's very difficult for most to move beyond their bad-boy imprinting. They need the dedication, direction, and support of healthy, caring adults who can point them toward a better life.

Inadequate schools for at risk boys represent the Second Pathway to Prison. It will take a major investment in teacher training and the creation of boy-friendly curricula to change current trends. Education, however, is cheaper by far than incarceration. When, through suspension, expulsion, school failure, or dropping out, boys fall through the safety net of the schools, they often wind up on the street.

4

Mean Streets

*Hell, I'm still safer on the streets than I ever was
at home.*
—Joseph, 14, street hustler in a youth shelter
    after being beaten by a customer

As a boy's social velocity takes him beyond the orbit of home
and school, the community becomes the next level of con-
tainment and direction for his life. The community net may con-
sist of after-school programs, church and temple involvement,
sports, youth activity clubs, work, and mentoring. These and other
opportunities are provided by adults to engage boys positively during the hours they are not with their teachers or parents.

For all too many boys, however, the streets become the next arena
from which to glean formative information. For the purpose of this
book *the street* is defined as an informal community, outside established organizations committed to youth welfare, where there is little or no mature adult guidance for boys. The street is an institution
as deeply embedded in our national fabric as any other social arche-
type. There, angry young men learn the ropes. Left to their own devices, the very energies for which we value responsible men in times
of adversity can run wild, like uncultivated plants in the garden.

In many other cultures, towns have a square where young people
gather to talk, play, be admired, and flirt. But there, in the villages

of Greece, Kenya, or Mexico, are also adults who, while socializing among themselves, are also keeping an eye on the youth. In many villages, children are accountable to *all* the adults. It was once largely that way in America as well.

Many of my parents' generation remember that if a boy was acting out in front of a neighbor or shopkeeper in their community, chances were that person would confront the boy and also inform his parents. That kind of community cohesion is becoming rare in our mobile, fragmented, and, all too often, fear-based culture. Many adults today legitimately feel they risk litigation or even violence if they directly engage another parent's child.

Adults on our streets today are likely, at best, to ignore and avoid, or, at worst, to prey on boys rather than lead them toward productive lives. Most low-level drug dealing and minor property crime takes place on the street. Those two activities cause the majority of young male incarcerations today. Crimes against persons are also propagated in this undisciplined atmosphere. Most initial police contacts happen here. Gang induction, child prostitution, and victimization by violence are also products of this province.

Life on the Streets

When not behind bars, I spent most of my adolescence living in or near street life. I was usually broke. Survival took up a good portion of each day. I regularly looked for work but was repeatedly refused because of my age, few skills, and the lack of an address or phone number. Also, using only public bathrooms for hygiene, it was difficult to stay impeccably clean. I imagine my appearance got somewhat scruffy over time. The hungrier I got the more I fantasized about stealing as an immediate way to get food or money. Like most low-level offenders, I was not particularly violent. But I wanted to survive. So, I started committing petty thefts.

Armed with a coat hanger, I'd walk the streets of the Hollywood Hills late at night. Many cars were unlocked. Others I'd open with the hanger, sticking it down between the window and the door frame to catch the locks. Rifling cars produced a steady stream of spare change, an occasional item I could sell on the street, and often a place to sleep.

Though I always tried to wake before dawn, I preferred sleeping in underground garages where I could hear people approaching in the morning if I overslept. The few times someone discovered me, I bolted and ran, hopping fences and working my way through the tangles of poison oak, manzanita, honeysuckle, and sage that filled the rugged canyons below.

I was always quickly away and never caught. But for many years I was haunted by exhausting dreams about endlessly running away from pursuers. Once I snagged a doctor's bag, an item that suddenly elevated a petty theft to a serious felony. A junkie on the boulevard paid $20 for it, enough to support me for a week. Generally, however, these thefts were insufficient to even provide me with steady meals.

Survival Sex: The Prostitution Solution

I never planned to get involved with prostitution. I simply drifted into it as I got more desperate. Hustling gay men proved to be the only steady income I could produce as a homeless fifteen-year-old. I "turned" my first "trick" at 4:00 A.M. in a Hollywood hotel. A man bought me drinks in a bar till 2:00, fed me steak at an all-night diner, and then took me to his room. He was a dumpy, pasty white guy with a wife and kids in the suburbs. So were many of the others along the way.

One day I met a guy on the Sunset Strip who took me to a large abandoned house in the hills. There, about ten gay men were squatting. They had turned the gas on at the street and were cooking a pot of stew over a gas log in the fireplace. The only furniture consisted of some mattresses lying around and a stained, threadbare couch rescued from some alleyway. I shared their meal. Gary let me sleep on the couch.

Because "you dance with whom you came" I "belonged" to Gary. The other guys left me alone. But there was a high-strung guy, Patrick (Patty), who kept asking for sex when Gary wasn't around. But Patty was a jerk and also had nothing to offer. So, I just kept putting him off. After all, sex was my only coinage at the time. I tried to only spend it for survival.

After a week or so Patty got agitated about being refused. Then he got aggressive. I fought him off, giving him a black eye. A few nights later I was at the After Hours club, where I often hung out and danced. During a break, I went out to the alley to cool off. A couple of dealers, who regularly sold drugs at the club, suddenly attacked me. Patty had told everyone that I was a police informant, doubly dangerous because I was a minor. The first part wasn't true. Though today I work professionally with law enforcement at times, I had nothing but contempt for the police at that stage of life. But I was banned from the club and the house, exiled to the street again.

A man who worked for Bank of America picked me up and took me to his apartment late that night. After being coerced into having sex with him, I became so distressed that I tried to slash my wrists with a razor blade in his bathroom. This was my third suicide attempt, having unsuccessfully overdosed with pills twice in recent years. I was unable to cut myself very deeply. I remember feeling like a coward. The bank teller discovered me bleeding in his bathtub; even those superficial cuts made quite a mess. He was furious. It was about 3:00 A.M. He taped up my wrists, made me get dressed, put me in the car, drove me back to Hollywood, and pushed me out of the door. I spent the rest of the night sitting in a twenty-four-hour diner drinking coffee.

On the Road

Broke, bruised, depressed, and no longer feeling safe in Hollywood, I hitchhiked out of town the next morning. I caught rides up Highway 101 along the California coast, generally heading for San Francisco. A couple picked me up in Big Sur, took me in, fed me, tended my cuts, and shared their infinite supply of excellent pot. He was a burly, heavily bearded sculptor. His willowy, long-haired wife grew herbs, vegetables, and marijuana in a large organic garden. This was the first of many times in my life that I was blessed by unconditional compassion emanating from counter-cultural strangers. I worked around the house and garden for a few days, gained strength, and moved on.

A week of bumming my way up the coast brought me to San Francisco's Tenderloin district. After a few homeless days, two Hell's Angels offered me a place to crash. I moved into their single, $20-a-week room in a hotel near Turk and Eddy Streets. Betty, a teenaged runaway from Indiana, was also there. We slept in shifts, generally using the room at different times than the bikers.

Betty was also hustling for survival. We walked the streets and worked the clubs from about 10:00 P.M. until 2:00 or 3:00 in the morning. Sometimes we'd hang out together. But just like Hollywood, the straight and gay trolling grounds were on different streets, so we mostly had to go it alone. Then, unless we were spending the night with a trick, we'd come home and crash. We often held one another in the bed for comfort.

The two bikers were running a scam that kept them on the street from 3:00 A.M. until dawn. They had a key that opened parking meters. They would raid them in the small hours, coming back to the hotel room in the late morning to wrap coins after their breakfast. I'd get up then, hit the streets, and come back sometimes to sleep in the afternoon when the bikers were usually out.

I don't know why they let me live there. I found, as I made my way along the underground corridors of our culture, that outlaws were often unexpectedly kind. While the churches and synagogues barred their doors at night and my middle-class relatives just did not care, it was usually the poor, the outcast, the freaks, and the downtrodden who offered me a hand. They asked for little. More often than not, they asked for nothing in return.

My first night in San Francisco I slept in the bushes above the Union Street parking garage. It was a cold night. A raggedy alcoholic bundled up in the same hedge told me, "Hey, this is no place for a kid." He gave me a musty blanket he'd bundled under his head for a pillow and dug into his pocket for 50 cents. He told me to buy a bowl of soup in the diner across the street so as not go to sleep hungry. That was probably all the money he had. The blanket was half his personal property. Like Blanche, in A *Streetcar Named Desire*, I survived primarily because of the kindness of strangers. The generosity of this bum in the bushes touched me deeply. In my current good fortune the memory of him assures I do not forget those with less.

The bikers got busted one night. Cops came in the middle of the night. Betty and I were in the bed. They searched the place and hauled away coin wrappers as evidence. They asked us if we knew anything about an extra parking meter key. We said no, we just used the room to sleep when the guys weren't there—the truth. The cops left us there. Why they didn't haul us in, I'll never know. Betty took off for parts unknown the next day. I never saw her again.

Making the Scene

I couldn't afford the next week's rent on the room so I moved in with two gay men down the hall, Jackie and Johnny. They taught me tricks of the street-hustling trade. It seemed like a good deal at the time. In addition to $10 or $20 in my pocket, sometimes a decent meal or a bath in a comfortable hotel also came along. Ten bucks equaled twenty chili-dogs or a week's rent-share for my Tenderloin firetrap. It wasn't until years later, when a friend's sister told me she made $500 a night hooking, that I realized my innocence was so cheaply sold. In a strange twist of "equity pay," boys don't command nearly as much for their bodies as girls. One day, as winter began to cool the streets, Jackie went off to Mexico. I hopped a Greyhound bus with Johnny and went back to Los Angeles in search of warmer nights.

I stayed away from the After Hours club. Patty had ruined my reputation there. But Johnny introduced me to new haunts in the arts and theater district of West Hollywood. The 8727 was an underground gay club on Melrose Avenue. Outside, nothing advertised its presence but the address. Inside, the flame of Hollywood gay culture burned with bright intensity.

We hustled a little but mostly just hung out. Night after night I reveled in the scene. Actors came in after the theaters closed. Intellectuals lit up the night with articulate debate. Drag queens preened occasionally, adding a campy hilarity to the night. And there was a steady stream of food, drugs, and lodging. The occasional payment of sex assured the older men who paid for it all that I was a player.

I spent nights drinking bottomless cups of coffee, chain smoking cigarettes inside and marijuana outside, dropping bennies (benzedrine) like M&M's, and talking with everyone about anything and everything. The richness, tempo, and depth I missed in school were abundant in the coffeehouses. I learned about art, music, poetry, literature, dance, cinema, sex, radical politics, and the engaging psychology of those living outside society's norms.

Like a vampire, I left before the full sun of first light, lest it somehow return me to the demon hells of depression stored behind the manic mask I wore in those nocturnal parades. The amphetamine-drenched nights heightened the mystical quality of dawn as I often walked to the boulevard for breakfast awash in beauty.

Abandoned as I was by straight culture, gay men kept me alive. But they also took their toll. Some tricks abused me, cheated me, gave me disorienting drugs, pressured or threatened me. I often felt afraid of things getting out of control. On two occasions, "gay bashers" (men who beat homosexuals for sport) assaulted me.

Ironically, I never regarded myself as gay. Men have never sexually attracted me. Many adolescent male hustlers self-identify as heterosexuals. But since few women seek male prostitutes, street boys, gay or straight, work the gay clientele. In Los Angeles today, just as in my time thirty-five years ago, women still work the straight crowd on Sunset while boys walk the streets of Selma or Santa Monica, a few blocks south.

The gay scene was the most interesting subculture around till LSD hit town. The whole bizarre milieu intrigued me in some perverse way with a strange charm. It's taken a lifetime, however, to recover from the shame and sexual confusion resulting from some of these experiences as a teen prostitute.

The Tolerated Sexual Abuse of Boys

During my street years I met numerous kids selling sex for food, lodging, or drug habits oft incurred to medicate the pain they felt as discards. It wasn't until I began working intensively with male clients, however, that I began to understand these experiences as sexual abuse.

Most people would immediately regard a homeless, teenaged girl prostitute as a victim of predatory adults. But I never thought about my life that way, in part because no one else ever framed it in that light. Like many victims of child sexual abuse who blame themselves, for years I felt that any deviance in my experience must have been my own. Although it is essential for people in recovery to take responsibility for their actions, it is also important for abuse survivors to understand the impacts predatory sex can have on their psyche. For most men and boys, however, this topic is so taboo and shame-laden, they rarely find forums supporting forthright discussions about the impact of uncomfortable, early sexual experiences.

Today, there is a serious drought of compassion for males. Cynicism abounds. I've conducted seminars in a number of mental health institutions with blatant double standards of care for young men. Recent research confirms, however, that at least one-third of all child sexual abuse, perpetrated by both women and men, is against boys. Yet many sex-abuse treatment programs still predominately focus on female victims and male abusers.

In California, legislators did not even make the statutory rape of boys illegal until 1993. Yet various studies and the stories many young men tell me indicate that sexual abuse creates as many psychological problems for boys as girls. When working with male clients I am still surprised at how often sexual abuse emerges from their personal histories. Few report, however, that anyone previously showed much concern about it.

To remedy this lacuna in psychological treatment theory and training, clinicians, educators, and other helping professionals may need education that better sensitizes them to the often silent suffering of boys. To even speak of males as victims, however, rubs against the dominant cultural grain. To get needed male sensitivity training on the agenda of our mental health and educational institutions, our culture must confront its apathy toward the often hidden vulnerability and pain of angry young men.

Today, thousands of boys continue to walk the nation's streets with little support from social services. It isn't until they become bad boys, until they attract the interest of the criminal justice system, that most of these boys get any significant attention. For many of them, by the time they get into juvenile justice, it's too late. What does it say about our society that we cavalierly abandon thousands of boys to prostitution, drug addiction, AIDS, and the violence that accompanies life on the streets?

Why Are So Many Boys Homeless?

More than any other issue, poverty is the key element pushing increasing numbers of young men onto the streets. Now, with welfare reform, more mothers with children are also homeless. As their mothers' benefits shrink below the capacity to maintain a home, more children of both sexes are put at risk. Boys and men, however, are still the majority of the homeless.

In The Grapes of Wrath, John Steinbeck wrote that during the Great Depression, "it was obvious to all but the most dense that vast and uncontrollable economic forces were responsible for the millions thrown into poverty." But today, as most policymakers enjoy wealth and privilege, the injuries of class do not seem so obvious. Though

Americans enjoy one of the highest levels of affluence in the world, an equally extreme moral and spiritual poverty seems to sanction the disenfranchisement of millions of citizens. Disenfranchisement, like shunning, excludes those deemed offensive to societal norms through incarceration, narrowed economic and educational opportunity, and revocation of rights normally accommodated enfranchised citizens.

The National Law Center on Homelessness and Poverty estimates that about 760,000 Americans are homeless on any given night. One to two million experience homelessness sometime during the year. About thirteen million American adults today were homeless at some point in their lives. So I am not alone in my own experience. But I don't take much comfort in the company. It's getting worse. More than half report their homelessness occurred in the last decade. Homelessness is expected to keep expanding at 10 to 30 percent a year, and the death rate for homeless people also keeps growing.

According to the U.S. Conference of Mayors, children under the age of 18 account for 25 percent of the urban homeless. Single men—40 percent of whom have served in the armed forces—constitute 47 percent, and single women are 14 percent of the homeless. High rates of addiction plague the homeless, particularly the young men, 20 to 25 percent of whom also suffer severe, persistent mental illness.

Every night there are about 150,000 homeless youth nationwide. One out of four report a history of abuse and neglect at the homes they left. More than half report that their parents told them to leave or just did not care what they did. One in five homeless youth has attempted suicide. For gay youth, the rate leaps to an astounding 65 percent. Of course, only those who failed in their attempts get counted here. Overall, adolescent boys have the highest "successful" suicide rate in the nation—four to five times that of same-aged girls. In 1999 about 3 percent of homeless persons under age twenty-five were HIV positive. For homeless young men alone, the rate leaps. By some estimates, one in ten male prostitutes are infected.

Many youth become homeless because of family poverty. In our affluent nation over 20 percent of American children live in poverty. Our "war on poverty" parallels our similar "success" in Vietnam and the "war on drugs." American youth in the mid-1990s were 50 percent more likely be poor as in the mid-1970s.

Forty percent of the homeless were once foster children, a history that also correlates with becoming homeless at an earlier age and remaining so for a longer time. Eighteen months after discharge from placements, one in four former foster kids reports having been beaten, seriously hurt, or incarcerated; a third have not completed high school; and half are unemployed. Many young men are also discharged from jails and prisons without any housing or employment waiting.

Incarceration frequently severs boys' few threads of continuity with jobs, housing, social support systems, and family. As a result of insufficient shelter beds for youth in general, and admission policies often biased against single young men, few are housed in emergency shelters. Shelter Services, an organization receiving a major chunk of national shelter funding, refuses to provide housing for boys over the age of ten. Youth shelters, when available, however, are not merely interim safe housing. They also frequently function as sites for drop-in crisis counseling, legal aid, and health services for street kids. Without safe and simple access to these services, these children needlessly suffer.

According to the National Coalition for the Homeless, "Homeless adolescents often suffer from severe anxiety and depression, poor health and nutrition, and low self-esteem. Furthermore, homeless youth face difficulties attending school because of legal guardianship requirements, residency requirements, proper records, and lack of transportation. As a result, homeless youth face severe challenges in obtaining an education and supporting themselves emotionally and financially."

Perhaps because I longed to create some illusion of normalcy in an otherwise bizarre life, I made one abortive attempt to attend Hollywood High when I was sixteen. I enjoyed being around regular teenagers, but just maintaining my life took most of my energy.

There were no school programs to help students living independent-
ly. After a few weeks I dropped out again. Today, however, more programs for homeless youth are coming on line. A graduate student
of mine, James Crank, runs just such a program, EAGLES, in my
old neighborhood. Male prostitutes, gay, lesbian, transgender, and
homeless youth come from all over the city to attend this public
school. There, sensitive adults warmly accept them as they are, while
providing as many services as possible to aid them in their education, safety, mental and physical health, and their interactions with
the broader culture.

Homeless boys and young men benefit most from programs
that meet immediate needs first and then help them address other
aspects of their lives. Programs that minimize demands for strict
adherence to "normative" behavior models and offer a range of support services are consistently the most successful in helping homeless boys regain stability. Educational outreach, job training and
living wage employment, transitional living programs, counseling,
affordable housing and health care, all specifically designed for and
directed toward homeless boys, are sorely needed.

The child welfare system could make a greater effort to prevent
boys from ending up on the street—if for no other reason than to
save us taxpayers money on the inevitable social costs that follow
homeless boys throughout their lives. The documented costs of
increased rates of hospitalization, mental health services, welfare
dependency, substance abuse, violence, AIDS and other diseases,
crime, and incarceration for this population far exceed the investment needed to create zero tolerance toward child homelessness.

Violent Streets

Today guns are increasingly the great pacifiers for boys who legitimately feel threatened by street violence. In 1998 and 1999 there
was an unusual rash of highly publicized school shootings. This drew
a lot of attention to violence at school. Sadly, however, most media
and legislative responses merely advocated changing laws to try

more teenaged boys as adults so they can be sent to adult prisons for longer and harsher sentences.

Now, in New York, a fourteen-year-old who takes a gun to school can be sentenced to prison for four to seven years. No such laws affect adults, however, who bring guns to school, work, or any other arenas, except those strictly prohibited such as courtrooms or airplanes. Additionally, zero-tolerance regulations at schools were strongly reinforced, thus resulting in dramatically increased expulsions of boys. As a nation, however, we did little soul searching to ask ourselves why so many children today feel the need to be armed.

Although many think of gun carrying as an urban, street gang–related problem, the Justice Department reports that one in five suburban, adolescent boys owns a gun, and even more say they have been threatened with a gun or shot at on the way to or from school. Apparently, there are violent streets in the suburbs too. And tragically, as we now all know, affluent suburban students with good grades are quite capable of horrendous gun-related school crimes. Many suburban and inner-city boys who tote and use weapons seem to have something in common — a profound feeling of isolation, alienation, and a perceived lack of protection from others who attack their emotional self-esteem or physical safety. Another thing these boys have in common is easy access to handguns and high-powered assault weaponry.

According to the Centers for Disease Control and Prevention, nearly 20 percent of all ninth- to twelfth-grade U.S. students periodically carry a weapon to school. Typically, boys carry weapons four times more often than girls do. Weapons include guns, razors, knives, chains, and clubs. In a 1995 survey, one in twelve students reported carrying a firearm for fighting or self-defense in the previous thirty days. This was almost double the 1990 rate. The rate declined somewhat by the decade's end.

In my interviews with kids, the majority of them say they carry weapons to school because they feel threatened. A local fifteen-year-old boy, Ramón, says, "You need to be 'strapped' [carry a gun]. If someone 'draws down' [pulls a gun] on me I've gotta pull my 'gat'

[gun] too. Otherwise, wind up in the wrong place, you wind up dead, too."

Paradoxically, in any community, schools are still the safest places for boys to be, even allowing for the underreporting of violence toward boys mentioned in Chapter Three. The majority of violence toward boys is from adults, not other kids. Adolescents are 14 percent of the overall population yet 30 percent of all victims of violent crime. Adults kill more children every week than are killed by other children in an entire year at U.S. schools.

A great deal of weapons carrying at school is an attempt to assure street safety on the way to and from school. Considering the inordinate amount of weapons carrying by students, the death and injury rate at school is remarkably low. Most students still respect schools as safety zones. So when we kick increasing numbers of boys out of schools and onto the streets, we practically ensure an increase in the level of youth violence and victimization. All too often boys are now suddenly transported from school, safety, and hope to the streets, danger, and despair.

A U.S. Department of Justice study of inner-city schools shows one in three boys shot at, stabbed, or otherwise injured by a weapon in transit to or from school in recent years. Forty percent of them said their male relatives carried guns on the street. Many weapons-toting boys are emulating the adult male culture where they live. In a nation where there are now more guns than people, gun control could be a good idea. Adolescents today are easy targets for adults to blame for society's ills, leading one researcher, Mike Males, to name them *The Scapegoat Generation*. Trying selectively to force gun control through the schools, singles out the primary victims of gun proliferation—children—instead of focusing on the primary perpetrators of violence and gun culture: adults.

In the seventh through ninth grade I usually went to school armed with a switchblade. Sometimes, when I felt particularly threatened, I would also hang a length of lead pipe on a strap inside my coat. I never used either of these weapons against another kid; however, I threatened to do so on occasion. The threats caused both violent kids and my abusive stepfather to back down. Guns today are as easy to acquire as switchblades were in my era. Had gun access been so easy then, I would have bought one without hesitation. Chances are high that I would have eventually shot someone, most likely Zombie.

Where do kids get their guns? They purchase them on the street, mostly from adults, or steal them from adults' homes and cars. Why do they want them? Primarily, because street violence causes many school-aged boys to live in fear. Angry young men rarely admit that they are afraid. But when we get them alone in our councils with supportive adult males, they frequently confess that they literally live their lives "under the gun."

According to the Centers for Disease Control and Prevention, the majority of homicide is linked to handguns.

- Homicide is now the second leading cause of death for all young people aged fifteen to twenty-four.

- Homicide is the leading cause of death for African-American and Hispanic youth in this age group.

- One out of four homicide victims are younger than twenty-four.

- The rate of death by homicide among fifteen to twenty-four-year-old males in the United States is ten times Canada's, fifteen times Australia's, and twenty-eight times that of France or Germany.

- Handguns kill thirteen children a day in the United States.

- Handguns kill thirteen people a year in Sweden.

Expulsion Adds Propulsion to Juvenile Crime

Under the federal Gun-Free Schools Act of 1994, public schools are required to expel any student carrying a firearm to school for a full year or lose their federal funding. Of course, any weapons on campus are of serious concern to us all. I want my own daughter to be safe. But if we can't even keep weapons out of prisons, it's unlikely that increased policing alone will eliminate them in schools. Expelling increasing numbers of boys, however, without offering educational alternatives is a sure recipe to transfer more already at-risk boys into the criminal justice system.

Instead of education, counseling, or other support to prevent violence, the most common antiviolence strategy used by schools in 1998 was suspension (78 percent) and expulsion (72 percent). Guns, however, represent the minimum of weapons-related expulsions. According to the Department of Education, in 1997 about 16,000 students were suspended, expelled, or transferred to continuation school for having guns. This was out of 74,000 suspensions and expulsions for weapons and over 600,000 such actions for all other causes. Increasingly, traditional "boy toys" are being classed as weapons under zero-tolerance regulations, including slingshots, yo-yos, pocket knives, and pocket folding tools. In our local district these lower level incidents have increased over 700 percent in the last decade alone. They now account for about 80 percent of all expulsions.

The mother of a local fourteen-year-old boy expelled for bringing a peashooter to school says, "I can't teach him at home. I have a job here. We have a home here. How can we move [to another district] that easily?" Her son and his friends used the plastic tubes to shoot inanimate targets after school.

In response to this incident Ray Franco, the board vice-president for our school districts, said, "We shouldn't be throwing kids out of school. We should be locking them in school." Our last governor, however, vetoed a $32 million bill to set up community schools for bad boys while simultaneously promoting much more costly legislation designed to expand prisons for this same population.

What many of these boys really need is a regular opportunity to talk openly about the serious issues that trouble them and distract them from education. They need adults to express concern and support. After several months in a community school youth council, Ramón, who had advocated carrying a gun, said, "I'm talking now to homies from the other side. I'm not packing [carrying a gun] anymore. We are just trying to be cool with each other." That underfunded school, however, has had to move three times in four years and still has no permanent home. These kids don't miss the message that they are of the lowest priority.

Given the violent culture in which so many American boys live today, boys need to learn conflict and anger management skills as much as reading and math. It's a lot to ask of schools and community programs, but families and our culture are unusually fragmented today. Children need more support outside the home than ever before. They need regular, safe opportunities for self-expression.

Shane Gerzon is an athletic young white man who recently taught at predominately African-American schools in rural Mississippi. He told me, "It was rare to ever see *any* man in the classrooms there. So not only was I a minority there as a Caucasian, I was even more so as a male. Most of the playgrounds were so old there they were condemned. For fear of litigation no students were allowed to play on them. The boys often became unruly after repetitive mental drills all day. They had no way to burn off their physical energy. So, they would be wild in the streets after school. But none of the teachers seemed to make that connection.

"After school I coached a soccer team. And lots of other boys came down to the field just to hang out. I made a better connection with them there than I ever could in the classroom. I think if we paid some unemployed older guys to hang out with these kids and coach them after school, we could practically eliminate juvenile crime. They were all starving for male attention and structured physical activity."

Whatever the approach, schools and after-school community-based programs remain the last lines of defense for boys at risk for initiation into street life. If we want to reduce crime and violence, we may do better to highly concentrate community resources on adolescent boys at risk instead of building prisons, at which point, for many, it is then too late.

Sentenced to the Streets

In addition to boys being sentenced to the streets by escalating expulsions, suspensions, dropouts, and school failures, between five and fifteen million children of working parents are home alone after school. More than half of all juvenile crime occurs between 2:00 and 8:00 P.M. During the few years I lived in the homes of my working parents, I hung out at the railroad tracks or drainage basins with other wild boys after school. There was nowhere else to go except home, alone.

It is not just homeless boys who populate the streets. Many boys live in homes that are essentially crash pads with family members only marginally involved in their lives. Unsupervised children swell the ranks of boys on the street. There, male loiterers are much more subject to suspicion and arrest than females. Boys near the street generate significantly more police contacts for noncriminal activity than do more socially integrated boys. They are much more likely to be arrested and incarcerated for the same crimes that divert more affluent and sheltered youth into mental health treatment. Boys who are "hangin' with the homies" know they are targeted more than other citizens. Often, a negative encounter is their first experience with police. This can make them cynical about justice. Inequity, in any arena, tends to breed contempt for the law.

Most of the street kids I knew lived in terror of the police. Many of us suffered abuse in police custody. Few would approach police if victimized by crime ourselves. We legitimately feared that we were more likely to be arrested than assisted. A Hollywood vice officer raped a homeless girlfriend of mine, Angela, in his police car the night of her sixteenth birthday. In wasn't till many years later that a police commission finally held several officers at that Hollywood substation accountable for their sexual abuse of homeless kids and prostitutes over the years.

When we create opportunities for alienated young men to come into positive contact with public safety officials, however, it can go a long way to bridge the divide between angry young men and the law. Police officers who demonstrate that they regard young men as a part of the community they "protect and serve" can win their respect. After all, boys on the street have the highest victimization rates of all citizens.

In community law enforcement, cops walk the street and live in the same neighborhoods they patrol. They get to know the people there. They know the boys by name and where they live. Positive community policing can go a long way to forging strong alliances with bad boys while better ensuring public safety at the same time. Midnight basketball games, often sponsored by police organizations, are very successful in creating a context where bad boys and police officers can begin to forge positive and productive relationships with one another. When a pilot program in Arizona kept basketball courts open until 2 A.M., juvenile crime dropped about 50 percent. The cost of the program was 60 cents per boy.

A graduate student of mine, Brent Blair, runs summer workshops where police officers and gang members act in Shakespearean plays together. They become a community of creative artists, and, at least for a few months, largely transcend their antagonistic roles. Most bad boys are hungry for positive attention, especially from older males with strength and power. Cops fit that bill. These sorts of activities are as legitimate a form of crime prevention as enforcement. Some boys, unconsciously, act out just so some strong man *will* show up in their lives, even in a negative role. Bad boys often respond well when any powerful adult shows a genuine interest in their welfare. Many long to come in from the cold.

Back to the Street

My second major homeless period started after I turned seventeen, and the California Youth Authority released me as an emancipated minor. I rented a cheap apartment in the same part of Hollywood I'd worked as a prostitute two years earlier. About six months later, however, I lost my job as a county clerk and started washing dishes at a trendy French restaurant on the Sunset Strip.

I was stunned by the quantity of food wealthy diners left on their plates. This was my first ongoing encounter with affluent adults, or, at least, their leftovers. Steaks that skinny women hardly touched, half-finished lobster tails, mounds of salad, whole baked potatoes, and piles of vegetables filled the plates sent back to me for cleaning.

I lined my coat pockets with plastic and stuffed them nightly with leftovers. That fed me during off-work hours as well as my unemployed roommate and other kids I knew living on the fringes of Hollywood. I was appalled that the restaurant wasted so much expensive food. I realized then that wealthy people lived in an entirely different universe of privilege.

One of my most visceral memories from the street years is one of persistent hunger. I'd go into fast food restaurants and finish food left on tables, glean garbage cans, and retrieve discarded sand sharks from fishermen at the Venice pier. Shark stew was pretty good. Even a small shark, combined with vegetables plucked from a supermarket dumpster, would feed a lot of kids.

I had a whimsical moment, years later, while visiting my publisher's home near Beverly Hills, following the release of my first book. Earlier that day, a limousine provided by a television talk show had driven me around town. As I relaxed, sipping Perrier and listening to jazz in the air-conditioned embrace of the limo's plush interior, I felt strangely amused as we passed through the same streets where I once struggled.

In my mind, I waved to that skinny boy on the streets and told him to take heart, that the wheel of life kept turning and many delightful surprises were ahead. He just had to persevere and keep hope alive. That evening, my publisher told me he had occupied his exquisite home for over thirty years. I realized that he had once been on my Wednesday night trash-picking route. But not wishing to spoil an enchanting dinner with a sordid tale, I just kept this story to myself, as with most of these memoirs, until now.

Even with the free food gathered from the restaurant, a dishwasher's wages were insufficient to pay rent and other expenses. But I didn't want to go back to hustling. I was fiercely heterosexual at this point, with a girlfriend, April, living in a Bahai faith foster home nearby. And, in part from encountering so much sexual violence in jail, the thought of sex for cash now felt humiliating and repulsive. So, I closed that door. But I still needed more money. "Opportunities" to sell drugs, which I had previously declined, started looking more attractive.

Some Recommendations to Help Keep Boys Off the Streets

- Provide shelters for all homeless youth with the educational, medical, and vocational support needed to stay off the streets.

- Challenge the biases that bar homeless young men admittance to many shelters.

- Train social workers how to reach out to homeless young men on the streets where they live.

- Ensure that all young men leaving foster care, juvenile institutions, or jails have the resources needed to transition from institutional to independent living.

- Implement primary prevention, treatment, and diversion programs, wherever possible, to keep boys in the community in the first place.

- Support mentoring programs that can connect young men at risk with caring, capable, and responsible adults.

- Increase entry-level employment opportunities for young men in jobs with upward mobility and a living wage.

The cost of any or all the above is considerably less than that of criminalization. Poverty and the streets immutably intertwine to create the Third Pathway to Prison. When boys fall through the safety net of the community and crash onto the streets, the next step for many is a juvenile institution of some kind.

5

Juvenile Injustice

I wish someday I could walk down the street without
looking over my shoulder. I want to get out
[of the gang] but I just don't know how.
—Ramon, 16, street gang member in a boys-to-men
program

Throughout my childhood and adolescence, as I bounced among family, friends, foster care, the streets, and institutions, I never lived in the same place for one year. The cumulative effect of this chaos gradually instilled a belief that nothing was stable, the world was unsafe, everything was subject to change, all relationships were conditional, and no one could really be trusted.

Although these experiences created paranoid tendencies in my thinking, they also led me on a spiritual quest for enduring values. As circumstances worsened, I began to look within for places of refuge. My first transcendental experience occurred at age fourteen in a solitary confinement cell in the subbasement of the Cook County (Chicago) Juvenile Detention Center.

The events that had led me into that desolate underworld below the bright streets of the city began a few years before the experiences described in the last chapter, when I spent a summer in Chicago with my father, my stepmother Marie, and my year-old half-sister Swann. Marie was twenty-one then, having married my father two years earlier when she was nineteen and I was twelve. Marie was pretty, voluptuous, and during those first few years, very seductive. She liked to talk to me about her sex life with my father and to wrestle around on the floor with me wearing only a nightgown.

She presented a confusing mix of erotic attention and irritable demands that I serve her around the house when my father was at work. She often complained to him about me not working hard enough and having a "bad" attitude to boot. Before his marriage, my father and I enjoyed a positive relationship. But Marie's complaints began to take their toll. His attitude changed.

My father increasingly felt that he had to choose between his new wife and baby and his teenaged son. This is an oft-repeated syndrome in the lives of many boys, who suffer higher rates of abuse and home banishment from step-parents, particularly those with new children of their own, than they do from biological parents.

Tensions mounted through the summer, culminating with an event in the fall that significantly changed my life. Frustrated with Marie's complaints, my father agreed to discipline me. He cut up some old leather belts, nailed the strips to a sawed off wooden broom handle, and wound wire around the wood and leather, creating a makeshift cat-o'-nine-tails.

I thought he was just trying to scare me, but he insisted on giving me ten lashes. I stood there, defiant, as he flayed my back. My stoic response enraged him, just as it had my social adjustment teachers. He got carried away, hitting me harder than first intended. The whipping drew blood from the welts. Though he had spanked me a couple of times as a child, this was the only time in my life that he hit me in anger. Recently, he told me that he wept for over an hour afterwards. The resulting emotional distance between us then hurt much more deeply than the wounds.

Afterwards, I pretended to be contrite, but I began stashing food, money, and warm clothing in the garage. A few days later, instead of going to school, I jumped on a Greyhound bus with my girlfriend, fifteen-year-old Sandy. We had just enough money for a ticket to St. Louis. So that's where we went. We slept in a derelict building, on a tattered mattress amidst a debris-littered floor. We huddled together for warmth as the first snow of the season fell on the street outside the broken windows of our new home. But we were happy.

We panhandled and performed petty thefts to survive. Sandy charged a man, who approached us on the street, for the gifts she gave me for free. I felt ashamed that we were so broke. But we were basically starving, so I was grateful for the money. After a week on the streets the police picked us up for loitering. We had destroyed all our identification. But there was an interstate, all-points police bulletin out on Sandy. Within a few phone calls, the police figured out that we were those runaways from Chicago.

Caged

The police charged me with violating the Mann Act (interstate kidnapping) and statutory rape. But since I was a minor, and because Sandy convinced her parents that she was a willing conspirator, the authorities dropped those charges. They just held me for being a runaway. I remained in the St. Louis Detention Center for about a week. The guards gave me a thin mattress on the floor in a cell with four young men, who filled the double bunk beds on either side. They began taunting me. The oldest one said that as soon as the lights were out they were going to take turns "fucking me in the ass" while I "sucked their cocks." Each one of them was larger than me.

Being raped by a cage full of urban psychopaths was not an experience I was looking forward to. I tried to act unfazed, making whatever attempts I thought might garner their good will. I tried to make them see me more as a brother gangster than "fresh white meat." I made some progress during the day, to the point where their behavior became less hostile and belittling. Toward the end of the evening one man was almost apologetic about their plans. He explained that they had all been in youth prison for several years and were just being held there for a hearing the next day—and they had needs. . . . "You'd understand if you been in the Missouri pen like us," he said.

I felt a foreboding despair but silently resolved to fight. I figured that at best I would be raped and, at worst, badly beaten, maybe killed. Miraculously, I was spared those fates. Thousands of other boys are not so lucky. Just before lights-out, our cell door suddenly opened. Three deputies charged in. They made all five of us strip. Then they conducted an exhaustive search of the cell and our clothing. They found a few cigarettes and matches hidden in personal items belonging to the other men.

Possession of contraband is a serious offense in the nether world of juvenile justice. The breaking of institutional rules can add to a boy's incarceration time, without any due process hearing, or send him to solitary confinement. A thread of hope—winding like Ariadne's lifeline to Theseus, lost in the Minotaur's dark maze— glimmered in the impending doom. I said, "That's mine," hoping, like Br'er Rabbit longing for the briar patch, that they would punish me with solitary confinement. No such luck.

The guards knew the cigarettes belonged to the other men. But I insisted, "They belong to me." The others didn't deny it. The guards left in disgust. The other prisoners were grateful that I, now a "stand up guy," took the rap. They left me alone that night. The next day, they went to court, were loaded into a bus, and were sent back to youth prison. A week later St. Louis shipped me, in handcuffs on an airplane, to the Chicago Juvenile Detention Center.

Chicago Blues

Sandy went home. Her parents reconciled whatever issues they had with her. I spent the next four months in "Juvi." Beatings by guards, for slight infractions, were frequent. They hit us hard with the flat of their hands in ways that hurt but did not leave significant bruises or break bones. I contracted severe bronchitis. It went untreated. Forced every day to run in circles in the gymnasium, I would sometimes collapse with a racking cough. The guards told me to continue running or I'd be sent to solitary confinement—the ultimate punishment in jail.

Nights were terrifying. The dormitories housed about 100 boys each, sleeping in cots side by side and head to toe. In the deep of night, various predatory activities occurred. Some boys were raped. Others boys received "blanket parties," during which a group would beat a boy under a blanket so he could not identify his attackers. Some of the older gang boys slept with tightly folded blankets on their chests, held in place by T-shirts or towels, as armor to protect them from being stabbed.

One night, I awoke to some boys trying to set fire to a heap of toilet paper they had piled on my bed. I had no idea why. I didn't even know them. They fled as I let loose a blood-curdling scream that erupted from some previously untapped depth within. After that, I slept on the floor under my bed. For years afterward, a part of my psyche remained vigilant in the night.

When I was in my early twenties, my first wife, Satri, would sometimes try to rouse me early for work. I would often break out of sleep with a scream and fists flailing. Fortunately, I never hurt her. But she was badly shaken the first few times it happened. After the first occurrence, she learned to wake me from a distance. It took me about twenty years to grow out of this posttraumatic stress response.

On rare occasions I still jump up suddenly from sleep when my wife, Liz, gets up in the night. I'm occasionally startled when she walks into a room when my back is toward her. And to this day, like gunslingers in the old west, I pick the restaurant seat with my back to the wall and my gaze toward approaching people. But the more extreme responses have waned as I keep reminding myself that, today, I live in a safe and loving environment.

One day, as I was sitting in the Chicago Juvi's day room, watching TV with a few hundred young hoodlums, I accidentally poked the guy in front of me with my foot. He stood up, all six feet of him. His pumped-up jailhouse muscles rippled across his torso. He punched me so hard in the nose that I flew into the benches behind me. A melee ensued. Guards hauled me off to solitary confinement to serve a month in the "hole" for fighting.

Life in the Hole

The windowless cell was in the basement of the cold, damp concrete tomb in which Chicago housed its discarded youth. I could almost touch both walls simultaneously by outstretching my hands. The cell was slightly longer than the steel cot bolted to the floor. A stainless steel, lidless toilet was alongside the foot of the bed.

Three times a day a guard opened a slot at the bottom of the solid steel door. He slid a paper plate of food and a paper cup of Kool-aid through the door. A cardboard spoon accompanied the meager meals. That flimsy spoon seemed so ironic to me at the time. They didn't want to give me an implement with which to hurt myself, since suicide attempts are rampant in solitary. Yet they created an environment of sensory deprivation that was psychologically the most brutal experience of my life.

There was no light in the room. A naked light bulb further down the dimly lit corridor bleakly illuminated the room through a small, thick, Plexiglas observation port in the cell door. If I looked out at just the right angle, I could see a clock on the wall under the light. So by keeping track of meals and checking the clock I could figure out whether it was day or night. I don't know why that felt so important, but I didn't want to lose psychological connection to daylight. I found the perpetual twilight of my cell unnerving.

The lack of any reading material or any other distraction was tortuous. For days, an agony of loneliness and boredom, intense as intractable physical pain, filled my every waking moment. The only relief was frequent masturbation and the meals that I ate as slowly and methodically as possible, prolonging every mediocre bite. I ate the canned corn a kernel at a time and rolled the two slices of white bread into little dough balls that I could chew on throughout the day.

One day, a few weeks into my confinement, I felt I could not bear another single hour. I began carving on my arm with the edge of a plastic comb that I sharpened on the concrete floor. The pain helped distract me. My cough worsened. When it racked my body, my nose kept spewing blood. Since there was no towel I used my T-shirt to staunch it. I could have used toilet paper but didn't want to run out of my limited supply. That had already happened when, to amuse myself, I used up the last roll by braiding it into paper twine that I then wove into little funny animals. When it ran out, a week passed until I received a new roll.

Laundry, however, was exchanged once a week through the same slot in the door that the food and toilet paper came through. I sent the blood-stained T-shirts though the door like messages in a bottle. I hoped they would land on some distant shore where someone cared about a teenager with declining health locked in a basement.

Sometimes Escapism Is Not So Bad

Someone finally determined that I genuinely needed medical care. All my senses were heightened as I was taken, in handcuffs, to Chicago General Hospital. Outside it was fourteen degrees below zero. Though sunlight blinded my unaccustomed eyes, the glittering crystals formed by breath in the winter air delighted me. Everything looked beautiful. After months in jail, every aspect of the outer world was novel. The simplest icicle overwhelmed me as an exquisite wonder.

The doctor determined that the blow to my nose had caused a deviated septum. When I sneezed or coughed hard, broken cartilage kept opening blood vessels. They cauterized the inside of my nose, gave me antibiotics for the bronchitis, a shot for anemia, and topical treatment for the now infected, self-inflicted wound on my arm. I remember the doctor telling me that I was lucky I hadn't contracted pneumonia in my weakened state. He told me to stay warm, rest, and drink plenty of liquids.

The guard took my comb away when he returned me to my cold, damp, solitary cell with its bare metal cot and one thin blanket. The bleak contrast to the sensory richness of the trip to the hospital made my solitary confinement all the more unbearable. I instinctively knew I had to find a new way of coping with sensory depravation—or go insane.

Set into the wall was a round, stainless steel button that flushed the toilet when depressed. When staring at it I noticed that if I fixed my gaze unblinkingly, the surrounding visual field would begin to fade. After a while, the entire cell would disappear into a gray haze until, eventually, only the silver button remained. Then the button itself would disappear as patterns of light, colors, and other visual effects swam into my vision. Hours would pass this way as I sat watching whatever was playing on my mental TV.

Like Alice through the looking glass, I stumbled into another world. Or perhaps, as do countless prisoners in isolation, I had a psychotic break. Either way, I learned from this self-taught meditation that no matter how inescapable the agony a hopeless soul feels in the underworld, some avenue of escape exists from the binding terrors of the maze. A few years later I learned that meditation could be more than simply an escape from pain. It proved to also be a path toward healing, renewal, and a spiritual life. Most prisoners, however, find little respite from the torture they experience behind bars. The mere thought of prisoners spending *years* in solitary confinement today, regardless of their crimes, is like a steel knife scraping on the slate of my psyche.

Prisoners of Our Imagination

Many believe that the need to keep expanding juvenile institutions is inevitable. But prisons, juvenile or otherwise, are not an indelible fact of life. Our culture invented penitentiaries. Our evolving society has modernized many other archaic institutions to meet the needs of a changing world. The time is overdue for the leaders of a new era also to revise our juvenile justice system, much of which is still guided by nineteenth-century beliefs. The crumbling cell I first occupied in the Los Angeles Juvenile Hall had been built in 1903.

The bulk of public moneys, however, continue to go toward punitive restraint, a practice that has little or no efficacy in reducing violence. Many fear that humanistic treatment of young offenders reads as "soft on crime" or encourages lawlessness. Politicians pander to voters' fears, urging more police and prisons, as though this will magically solve the deep-rooted economic and social problems that cause most violent crime.

A year of imprisonment costs $30,000 to $36,000 per boy. Though not a direct comparison, in contrast, a year at Harvard costs about $24,000. Troubled boys and young men need facilities designed for rehabilitation and restoration of a sense of human worth, an institution somewhere between a university and a prison. Recovering bad boys need opportunities to give back to their community instead of returning from abusive lockups with a desire for revenge against a culture that subjected them to torture. Numerous learning and behavioral studies demonstrate that punishment is the *least* effective means for creating lasting change in people. Positive reinforcement for new behaviors has the greatest efficiency.

Rehabilitation programs could move youthful offenders out of remote, isolated institutions into secured environments near populations that can provide educational and social services, community volunteer programs, and regular interactions with family members. There is much we can do. But first we must change our attitudes about the intrinsic worth of young males and their capacity to exhibit real and significant change, once given the chance to do so.

Homes on the Range for Wild Boys

In my early twenties, while a psychology student at Sonoma State University, I worked full time, for a few years, at the Lane Ranch Children's Center. Boys referred from the courts were released to us from locked institutions into our unlocked, residential treatment houses. Many of these boys were violent. All were deeply troubled. As I spent time counseling them, I learned that adults and peers had sexually, physically, and emotionally abused most of them. As children, several had been tortured with implements, burned with cigarettes, and given alcohol, heroin, and other illegal drugs.

We didn't medicate the boys. Wherever safely possible, we weaned boys off the drugs they brought with them from other institutions. We chose instead to work with their problems through intensive staff interactions, good diets, exercise, mentoring, independent living, social and job skills training, education, and regular opportunities for recreation.

The parents of one ten-year-old boy, Doug, whom I counseled, made him take LSD in an attempt to "improve" his behavior. Since police seldom search children, criminal adults sometimes use their children to carry hidden guns and to hold and distribute drugs for sale. One of our boys was a heroin courier at age seven. The caretakers of some boys had used them as prostitutes. It was hard to bear some of the hideous stories they told me once they felt safe enough to speak openly about their lives. Their recollections were often far worse than any of my own. Most troubled young men have an intense need to tell their stories. Through merely being heard and understood by a sympathetic listener, many calm down and begin to change in positive ways.

In 1998 and 1999 I hosted public dialogues with social workers, teachers, police, government, clergy, and the bad boys of our region. They were called "Boys to Men: It Takes the Whole Village." We brought in gang members from the East Side and the West Side. We invited the boys locked up in boot camps and juvenile hall, who came under guard. And we invited the mentors, counselors, and educators who experienced the most success in aiding positive transformation in the lives of these troubled young men.

Each adult brought one boy who had successfully made the transition from the juvenile justice system to our community. We paid the boys honoraria to address the entire group. With their mentors

close at hand, they went to the podium one by one. With more eloquence than I could have ever imagined they informed the professional community about what had changed their lives and what
they thought other boys like them needed from the community.

One young man, a former local gang leader, now a gang diversion program leader, said, "I had no heart. Anyone [who] tried to
show me love, I put my walls up. Babatunde [my mentor] is a strong
man. He gave me a chance, guidance, love, a job. He gives me focus, showing me how to be a man, walk the walk, and be a father
to my son. If I didn't have my son I'd be in the joint. All I knew was
drugs. I'm trying to break the cycle. Everything I do in my life now
I do for that little man [my son]."

Another told the assembly, "I grew up in the 'life.' My dad was
a gang member. I'm only seventeen but I feel thirty or forty. My fear
is getting out of the gang. I want to make something out of my life,
get a good job. I'm afraid I'll end up six feet deep. I want to be able
to just walk down the street without looking behind my back."

Each boy who spoke that day said it was the first time that people in authority had *ever* listened to him or indicated that he had
anything of value to offer. Everyone was moved. Did these conferences help lower gang violence in our community? I don't know.
But they did open up lines of communication between groups that
seldom talk to one another.

The incarcerated young men saw their former cohorts being
honored and valued for trying to get their lives together. Many of
the boys who spoke had previously been in the same institutions.
Several incarcerated boys said that the success stories they heard
gave them hope. Many were previously unaware of the programs
available to them once they left jail.

Often, the abuse my boys at Lane Ranch had experienced in
locked institutions was more severe than what they'd experienced
in the parental and foster homes from which they'd been removed.
From our combined experiences, over time I realized that the institutions mandated to help at-risk boys frequently do more damage
than they assuage. In jail, avoidance or escape from violence is often

impossible. In some cases it's difficult to say which is worse for a troubled boy, a bad home or a good jail. Our society, however, desperately needs substantial alternatives for the hundreds of thousands of boys stretched between these two demoralizing choices.

Residential treatment centers are a step in that direction. Unlike most foster care, the counselors in these homes for low-level juvenile offenders generally have more supervision. They know their boys are at risk for further incarceration. They attempt to implement comprehensive treatment plans accordingly. But treatment homes are generally underfunded. And there just are not enough of them, by far, to meet the pressing needs of our growing population of disenfranchised young men.

Undertrained, overworked, low-paid, idealistic psychology undergraduates, like myself at the time, fill the ranks of these staffs. The burnout rate is extremely high. And the atmosphere of many treatment homes is depressing. The buildings are often ugly, old, low-rent bargains with holes in the sheetrock, worn and stained carpets, and rooms furnished with Salvation Army rejects. Child psychiatrist Bruno Bettleheim suspected that boys in an environment furnished with garbage might also think of themselves as discards. To the astonishment of his colleagues, he furnished his treatment homes with antiques and fed the boys on fine china and silver. Counter to conventional wisdom, they responded with dramatically increased respect and care for their surroundings.

Understandably, I never cared much for the environment of the homes where I worked, even though they were among the best. So when summer break and other vacations came around, I got out of the house with the boys whenever possible. For several years, I led a wilderness experience program. This "Rites of Passage" approach, designed under the tutelage of Dr. Robert Greenway, became a model for many other treatment centers over time.

Many of these young men (age eleven to seventeen) were so institutionalized that they had never even cooked a meal for themselves. Through hiking, camping, fishing, cooking, fire building, finding our way cross-country with a compass, shelter building and more, these boys learned essential living skills. They learned how to cooperate. Most developed a sense of pride in their new abilities.

We told stories around the fire at night. There, they opened up in ways they never did in the therapy groups at the home. In the parlance of psychology, we established a "therapeutic alliance." In other words, we became friends and allies. We created little tribes based on the foundations of our shared experiences in the woods, which, to some degree, sustained themselves back in the group homes.

Much to my disappointment, over time I had to return some boys to locked institutions. Most of the boys, however, went on to get jobs in the community. A few went to college. Major transformations can take place when caring adults treat a young man with value instead of as a troublesome nuisance or a piece of trash. Most of those previously written-off boys made it to a productive adult life. Several studies show that even a few hours a week of focused, positive attention from teachers, parents, or other adults can make a significant difference in a bad boy's behavior. Most incarcerated boys, however, never get the opportunity to live in a treatment home. As inadequate as they often are—and there is much we could do to make them more productive—they are significantly better than a neglectful home or an abusive, demoralizing juvenile jail.

When Jerome Miller took over as Massachusetts Commissioner of Youth Corrections he was appalled at conditions and the treatment of youth there. He ordered an end to corporal punishment and proposed many other reforms. Many of the guards, however, resisted. So he just closed *all* youth corrections in the state. The inmates were paroled or placed among 200 community-based treatment programs. Subsequent to this dramatic action there was *no increase in the recidivism rate* for juveniles. The funds saved from youth corrections paid for all the rehabilitation-oriented programs with no increased cost to the state. Perhaps we should try this elsewhere. Intensive supervision in the community is a proven, viable alternative for the majority of boys sent, instead, to jails.

Criminalize or Hospitalize?

After four months in the ulcerated bowels of the Chicago juvenile prison, authorities released me to my father's custody, with an admonition that I never contact Sandy again. My father had left the horse racing industry and was marketing hairpieces. For the first time in my life he was upwardly mobile. We left Chicago and moved to the middle-class outskirts of an upper-class neighborhood, Bala-Cynwyd, Pennsylvania. I lasted two weeks at Bala-Cynwyd Junior High.

My classmates shared last names with familiar products and companies like Maytag or Du Pont. They'd go to the deli for lunch and have shrimp cocktails, cheesecake, and other exotics beyond my wildest means. I felt out of place. And I certainly looked that way with my California "pachuco" look: hair cut into a D.A. with a waterfall and sideburns, Pendleton shirt and vest, "chino" pants, and Cuban-heeled spit-shined boots.

Even though my course work was OK, the principal soon kicked me out of his upper-class public school for refusing to wear a tie. Dad's business folded. He sent me back to California to live with Marie until he wound up things on the East Coast. Marie demanded I leave. I obliged. With no other options, I hit the streets of Hollywood, as described in Chapter Four.

One night, in the latter half of my fifteenth year, the police picked me up for being on the street after 10:00 P.M., a curfew violation. I was on probation and "living alone without adult supervision," also against the law. So after a night in the Hollywood police substation, a judge remanded me to the Los Angeles Juvenile Hall—again. Since I was dressed as a hustler, the guards sent me straight to the observation unit. The "O" unit was for mentally disturbed inmates. In my opinion, however, any boy who spends more than a few days in one of these institutions becomes mentally ill with, at the least, posttraumatic stress disorder (PTSD). Psychological "treatment" primarily consisted of having my behavior observed by unknown persons behind one-way mirrors and seeing some sort of therapist for about half an hour once a week.

The man in the white coat asked many questions about my sexual fantasies. He always wanted to know how often I masturbated. His approach to therapy seemed odd, even then, since the only fantasies I had were about how to escape from jail. I spent several months there, with no hope of release. I remember feeling outraged at being indefinitely incarcerated again in an environment that was substantially more abusive and weird than the worst indignities of the street.

The citizens of "O" were more violent and sexually aggressive than the main population. One day, two older boys used a ping-pong table to trap me into an unobservable corner. They demanded a blow job. One thing I learned in jail is that inmates in every institution could easily find ways to commit rape or assault outside the view of understaffed guards. I went berserk for the first time in my life.

I threw the ping-pong table across the room with the heretofore undiscovered strength of long-stored rage. I then fought both the boys off me, bloodying one's face in the process. It took four guards to wrestle me to the ground. They put me in restraints and strapped me to a metal cot in solitary confinement.

Years later, in my work with men who've committed violent acts, I try to remember that there are sometimes reasons that men resort to violence. Solitary confinement is widely regarded as one of the worst forms of psychological torture, just short of the intentional inducement of pain. Humans are social animals. It is dehumanizing to deny an individual all human contact. Dehumanization results when authorities regard certain behaviors as indicative of moral inferiority and use such judgments of "less than fully human or civilized" to justify the abrogation of international human rights.

Some men meet injustice and violence against themselves or those they love with violence of their own, just as some nations go to war when attacked. This, of course, doesn't justify violence. If therapists carefully review violent clients' narratives, however, they may see that their acts were not "senseless." When patients know that their therapists understand the meaning and message of their behavior—the ways in which their violence may be a defense against a violent world—the patients often become more responsive to treatment.

Some days after the ping-pong incident, the authorities transferred me, still bound in restraints, to the UCLA Neuro-Psychiatric Institute. NPI was a state-of-the-art mental hospital on the campus of the University of California. Some doctors there were running a study on youth violence and needed subjects. My name came up.

The Twenty-First Century Snake Pit

Today, many prisoners are mentally ill and in need of treatment. In Los Angeles County alone, on any given day over 3,000 inmates are mentally ill by any clinical evaluation standard. Their numbers steadily climbed in the wake of widespread cost-cutting closures of California state mental hospitals over the last few decades. This makes the Los Angeles County Jail now the largest mental institution in the United States, as well as the largest homeless shelter.

Abuse of mentally disabled prisoners is widespread. In 1998 a handcuffed mentally ill prisoner was asphyxiated and died after Los Angeles deputies reportedly hog-tied him. In the prior year seven deputies had killed a mentally ill traffic violator after he allegedly resisted a strip search. The investigative reports that followed determined that eight other deputies in that jail formed a vigilante group called "the posse" to discipline mentally ill prisoners who they believed were being "coddled." Their discipline consisted of beatings with fists and flashlights and stomping the prisoners hard enough to leave boot prints on their bodies.

In response to these incidents county sheriff Chief Lee Baca admitted that serious reform is needed. The jail is understaffed and overcrowded, and deputies receive less than half the training they used to get. Reports of this nature are common around the country today.

Many county jail prisoners have not been convicted of a crime. They are often the indigent, who cannot make bail while awaiting trial. Although there are some parole violators and convicted felons awaiting transfer to state prisons, most convicted prisoners in county lockups are serving short sentences (less than one year) for minor crimes. When I was a prisoner in the Riverside County Jail, as discussed in Chapter Seven, I witnessed the rape of a naïve nineteen-year-old man who was merely being held overnight for unpaid traffic tickets.

The average cost for comprehensive, outpatient mental health care is about $4,000 per year. Incarceration costs five to eight times that. Without treatment, most of the mentally ill get worse. In jail, however, these patients—mostly young men—receive no psychological treatment for their disorders. Over 15 percent of inmates nationwide are mentally ill. Half of them—seven times the general population—suffer from schizophrenia.

Conditions are such that the mental health of most prisoners steadily declines in jails and prisons, thus further affecting society when authorities return them to the streets. Unless we are willing to create a totalitarian society where all mental patients are locked up for life, this climate of neglect represents a significant threat to public safety. Several judges have handed down opinions stating that this neglect violates mental patients' Eighth Amendment rights to be protected from cruel and unusual punishment. But in today's punitive atmosphere, little significant reform is taking place.

If our policymakers perceived criminality more as an illness than a mark of Cain, it would be treated more as an epidemic. In an epidemic, we must discover a cure for any disease we cannot contain or risk infection ourselves. In the past, lepers were confined in colonies set apart from the rest of the society. There was no cure for their disturbing illness. In a similar manner today, we shut away troubled young men in prisons, primarily because we have failed to find a way to cure them. But when treatment of a physical disease fails to help, health professionals don't blame their patients, they mobilize to find new treatments. Once found, they create campaigns to ensure that all people can receive its benefit. In this way the World Health Organization virtually eliminated smallpox from the planet.

In the nineteenth century, when doctors realized that more birthing women were dying in hospitals than at home, they reexamined their medical practices. They made new discoveries about how infections spread. This made hospitals safer for women giving birth and for all other patients. Like "birthing fever," the "violence virus" is spreading fastest in the very institutions designed to halt it. To better treat young male violence, we must also try to understand the ubiquitous cultural climate that nurtures its growth.

Violence Is Crazy

If we look at most violence as a disease—even further, a virulent, contagious one—then our current epidemiological approach could appear to be rooted more in the Dark Ages than the third millennium. In the past, for example, many perceived alcoholism as a moral defect. Now, most clinicians perceive it as a disease. Consequently, we have developed more effective treatments. We can properly view much violent and criminal behavior in similar ways.

Violent behavior is usually part of an addictive system. Violence is rarely "senseless." There is usually a raison d'être for violent behavior. People use violence to produce specific external and internal reactions. It has a function. People often use violence to right wrongs in a dysfunctional attempt to create homeostasis in a system. Like most addictions, when left untreated, its use tends to increase over time.

Violence has quasi-biological and psychological aspects that manifest exactly like a drug in many ways. It has numinous, intoxicating, and archetypal dimensions. People who use violence often feel powerful, even godlike. Paradoxically, however, violent behavior is almost always an expression of weakness and failure. Violence, like drugs, alcohol, sex addictions, and other obsessions, tends ultimately to destroy persons engaged in it, and the life support systems around them as well.

Violence is a disintegrative system. The more violent the behavior, the more disintegration takes place. Violence is energetic. It has a force, a direction, a flow. One of the keys to curing violence is to redirect the energy and concurrent "rush" that often accompanies violent actions.

Many hide violent tendencies, as we hide other addictions, homosexuality, AIDS, or other characteristics that we may believe are socially unacceptable. We carry individual and collective shame about violence, and we fear reprisal for acknowledging our problems with it. For me, writing this book presented a challenge for those very reasons.

Violence is self-propagating. It is especially virulent in environments where people lack opportunities to assure their self-worth, economic security, and physical safety. Violent behavior is a normal response to certain types of dysfunctional situations. History shows us that the more inhumane a culture becomes, the more violence it generates, either internally or externally. The same is true in a community, family system, personal relationship, or institution.

Our nation breeds increasing numbers of sociopaths (people devoid of a conscience) every year. Though some may be born that way, I believe that sociopathy, for the most part, is a learned behavior in which addiction to violence becomes the only way people know how to feel fully alive or powerful. Violence is often a provocative response to a seemingly indifferent world—an attempt to get a reaction, any reaction, from distracted and inured adults. When young men see a world around them in which it appears that no one cares for them, some think, "Why should I?"

Indifference and neglect are regarded by many therapists as one of the most devastating forms of abuse toward the "unseen and unheard." If our only response is to put young offenders in jail, how will they ever learn to care? If we want them to behave humanely, someone in their world must model that humanity for them to imitate.

A Finely Feathered Cuckoo's Nest

In my life, that humanity was displayed during my first few hours at NPI, where I received an extensive and cordial intake interview by the hospital's psychiatric staff. I explained the reason behind my violent outburst at juvenile hall and assured them they had nothing to fear from me. A staff member immediately removed my restraints. A doctor led me to a clean, well-lit room with a window. My door had no locks. Shortly thereafter, another person brought me a set of clean "street" clothes.

A friendly crew served lunch, cafeteria style, with a selection of appealing and ample dishes. Though there were strange people muttering, staring into space, and walking about oddly, there was no violence by the staff or the inmates. The environment was unusual, but atmospheric tension was low, especially compared to the predatory violence of Juvenile Hall's "O" unit. In fact, it was the first time in many years that I felt safe.

The doctors talked to me often. They treated me humanely, as a patient with an illness instead of a criminal with a moral defect. There were engaging groups, individual therapy sessions, physical activities, and arts and crafts.

Many of my fellow patients were fascinating. A renowned physicist wound up there after trying to kill himself with an overdose of pills. The attempt wrecked his nervous system. But he was still able to speak in an impaired way. He taught me about the magical world of quantum mechanics. His introduction to that field created in me a scientific curiosity. It also stimulated research for my master's thesis, many years later, on parallels between quantum states and higher states of consciousness.

I became friends with a teenaged girl, Melissa, a child prodigy violinist. She wandered aimlessly around the unit playing her violin and occasionally had wild outbursts. But sometimes she would sit down and talk coherently with me for hours. After a series of ECT treatments (electro-convulsive shock therapy), she lost portions of her memory. She didn't know who I was anymore. I hoped to avoid that fate and tried to behave myself.

The various treatments going on captivated me. I questioned all the patients about their drug treatments, what went on in their therapy sessions, and the details of their lives that had driven them crazy. The seeds of my future career in clinical psychology were deeply implanted in the rich, nurturing environment of the hospital.

The staff impressed me with how carefully they treated each patient. They regularly monitored and adjusted the patients' medication. Wherever possible, they attempted to reduce or even eliminate medication. One elderly man was so bombed he could not move or speak when he arrived. He recovered all his faculties over several weeks, as they weaned him off the multiple-drug regime he received in an elder care facility. That created a lasting impression on me, out of which my current concerns about the growing abuse of psychiatric medications for social control were born. The NPI staff relied, as much as possible, on treatment and therapy to help restore their patients to health.

Mentally disturbed prison inmates, on the other hand, like foster children and spirited boys at school, are frequently warehoused and managed with psychoactive drugs. These drugs are often poorly administered, causing dependency, distress, irreversible damage from side effects, and, in some cases, death. A few years ago several prisoners in the California state prison at Soledad died because prison officials allowed the temperature in their cells to rise over 110 degrees. They were under the influence of heavy doses of antipsychotic medications that made them vulnerable to heat stroke. Guards ignored the prisoners' cries for help. A simple fan, pan of ice, or adequate ventilation would have saved their lives.

Fortunately, I was sent to an ethical facility like the NPI instead of a penal snake pit.

As a child, I had occasionally visited my grandmother, who spent over twenty years in Camarillo State Mental Hospital, stupefied by massive doses of tranquilizers and antipsychotic drugs. Naturally, with those images in my mind, I was disconcerted to become a mental patient myself. Much to my astonishment, however, not only was I well cared for, but after a few weeks of treatment the doctors gave me unsupervised passes out of the hospital every afternoon.

They allowed me to roam freely anywhere within the confines of the sprawling UCLA campus. Having always been an avid reader, I spent hours in the library. I wandered through the corridors of the science building looking at brains in formaldehyde and other wonders. I started feeling at home at the university. Thirty-five years later I now spend much of my time teaching psychology. Boys often emulate their environment as they grow up. They look around them for models of adult behavior. If all they experience is punitive authority and violent institutions, it's less likely they will achieve much difference in their adult lives.

After a few months, my doctor told me that they were releasing me. The staff concluded nothing was really wrong with me, psychologically, so there was no good reason for me to be at the hospital. I begged them to let me stay. It was the first time I had felt safe and well cared for in many years. The doctor told my father, "All this boy really needs is a safe home, an education, and some counseling." Over the years I have often repeated that admonition to parents and teachers on behalf of other angry young men.

Crazy Boys

Two-thirds of all juvenile psychiatric hospital inpatients today are committed for conduct disorder or oppositional-defiant disorder (ODD). Once in treatment, however, some clinicians note that many of these ODD boys act "normal." That is, the symptoms of their mental "disease" disappear once their environment is changed.

Young, male anger and acting-out are often more situational than intrinsic to, or indelibly representative of, adolescent manhood. Incorrigible, bad-boy behavior is often in reaction to dysfunctional, bad-adult behavior. It rarely comes out of a vacuum. For example, as with many categories examined in prior chapters, the majority of conduct-disordered boys were also abused as children.

One day, a thirty-eight-year-old single mother, who made her living as a graphic artist, brought her son to me for a consultation. Andy was sixteen. He was having trouble at school and was openly hostile toward his mother. The beginning of the session started with Margie telling me how frustrated she was with Andy's behavior. While she spoke, Andy just sat there, sullen and withdrawn. She told me they had been to sessions with several therapists, but they had all been "unable to get him to change."

One by one she listed all the issues she had with Andy, from how he dressed (like a Gothic punk rocker) to his choice of friends (bad boys). When I gave Andy an opportunity to speak, he said, "Why bother?" I told him that it was his time; he could use it as he liked. We all sat in silence for several minutes. Margie started urging him to say something, but I asked her to hold off. He blurted out, "See. She never lets me just be!" He then angrily related how frequently she criticized, insulted, slapped, kicked, swore at him, and even hit him with various objects that she threw. He was embarrassed to admit this, saying he had never told anyone else. Margie was less than two-thirds his size and weight. He could have broken her neck with little effort. But though he cursed at her a lot, he had never hit her back.

Instead of making Andy the focus, I talked to Margie about *her* anger for the rest of the session. She justified her rage by saying she was so "frustrated" with his "negative" traits that she didn't know how else to "change him." But finally she admitted her anger was out of control. I referred her to anger management classes and reminded her that I was obligated to notify child protective services.

Andy was astonished and visibly relieved about the outcome. Suddenly, he was no longer the identified problem. We met alone a few times after that. Margie did enter a support program for single mothers. A few months later she called to let me know Andy's "conduct disorder" had improved, along with his school performance.

As Chapter Three details, restless behavior in the classroom is normal for bad boys whose educational needs are not being met. The authors of a definitive book on conduct disorders note that defiance toward adults is often "a fundamentally healthy reaction to a pathological environment." Some investigators believe that as many as 9 percent of adolescent males today meet the diagnostic criteria for conduct disorder. That's about six million angry young men. As more normal, understandable responses to unhealthy situations have become defined as "symptoms," over one out of ten American boys are now classified as mentally ill. Our trend toward increasingly pathologizing male behavior follows, yet exceeds, a national trend, as every new edition of the American Psychiatric Association's *Diagnostic and Statistical Manual of Mental Disorders* (DSM) encompasses ever broader and newer categories of mental illness.

In addition to the psychiatric, social control of about three million "ADD and ADHD" children, as previously discussed, over a million more are being drugged with antidepressants and other mood- or behavior-altering drugs. Although these medications have legitimate uses for significant disturbances, they are all too often used in place of good parenting, quality education, intensive psychological treatment, and integrated child protection services. The volume of pediatric psychiatric medication prescriptions steadily increases as more professionals enter the field in need of clientele. Moreover, few studies have been done on the effects of many adult psychiatric medications now being used on children. Pharmaceutical companies are pushing hard, however, to expand these lucrative, fresh markets for the behavioral medication of children.

Historically, the field of juvenile mental health research has been chronically underfunded. Children and adolescents under the age of eighteen represent about one quarter of the total U.S. population. The proportion of the National Institute of Mental Health's total research budget allocated to juvenile mental disorders, however, is consistently less than 25 percent, thus creating proportional shortfalls as much as $38 million per year.

A "Report Card on the National Plan for Research on Child and Adolescent Mental Disorders" notes, "Our nation continues to waste needlessly its most precious natural resource: our children and youth. We are permitting more than 12 percent of our children and adolescents to suffer from mental disorders, often for life. And we are doing far too little to develop the scientific knowledge needed to treat or prevent their illness or lessen its enormous human and financial costs."

One force driving the dramatic increase in labeling boys as mentally ill is the economic self-interest of the mental health profession. Crazy boys have become big business. In 1973, when incarceration and hospitalization rates for boys both began their dramatic growth toward today's unprecedented levels, only 10 percent of mental health facilities turned a profit. Now the majority make good money. From 1980 to 1985 alone, juvenile admissions to inpatient private psychiatric hospitals, treatment "camps," and locked psychiatric wards rose over 500 percent. Since then the rate has continued to rise substantially.

Despite whatever genuine help these institutions may provide, they also represent another link in a growing juvenile male control web. In the same way that low-asset boys are increasingly identified as the problem for schools or society, asset-rich boys are now more frequently identified as "the problem" in their families.

Diagnoses for psychiatric illness is much higher for boys from middle- and upper middle–income families. Diagnosis for delinquent behavior is much higher for low-income boys. More than two-thirds of boys in juvenile institutions are minorities. Over two-thirds of juvenile mental health inpatients are white. Insurance companies pay as much as $16,000 per month to keep an insured bad boy in a hospital. Taxpayers pay $3,000 a month to keep an uninsured boy in a juvenile jail where over half the inmates have been previously diagnosed with mental disorders and three-quarters are currently suffering symptoms of mental illness.

Parents—not courts—request most private hospital commitments for economically advantaged boys. Social, educational, and law enforcement officials—not parents—instigate the majority of incarcerations for low-income boys. A number of investigative studies indicate that at least half of mental hospital commitments for boys are inappropriate. They are often boys who just don't get along with their affluent parents or who fail to embrace their values.

Juveniles are generally admitted for far less serious problems than are adults; yet they spend, on average, twice as much time on a psychiatric ward. And as in all other arenas for pathologized boys, those in psychiatric hospitals have significantly fewer legal resources, advocates, and rights to challenge their commitments than do adults.

Today Tom Sawyer and Huckleberry Finn would undoubtedly be institutionalized. So would Wild Bill, Kit Carson, Jim Bowie, and many other heroes of American independence and settlers of the West. Young men who braved the new frontiers were often too restless for "modern" culture. They did not fit well into the social molds of eighteenth- and nineteenth-century urban life. The very stuff that helped make America an independent nation—rejection of tyranny, creativity, questioning of authority, love of wildness, breaking away from old traditions and values—are highly pathologized in young men today. Young men tossing tea into the harbor today would go straight to jail.

A major study by the Carnegie Corporation found that, by age seventeen, a quarter of American adolescents have "engaged in behavior that is harmful to themselves and others." The California Wellness Foundation notes that the state spends *$2 billion* a year on police, courts, and jails, just responding to juvenile crime. But funds allocated for the prevention of youth violence are merely *$116 million*. Most states have similar ratios in their use of prevention as compared to punishment funds. We can do better.

Some Ways to Make Juvenile Institutions More Helpful to Boys

- Provide substance abuse treatment, therapy, education, parenting education, and literacy and vocational training in all locked juvenile facilities to help break generational cycles of poverty and violence.

- Reduce caseloads of probation officers so they can provide intensive supervision and integrated support services for young men returning to the community.

- Establish citizen oversight of locked institutions—similar to police review boards—to assure zero tolerance toward the abuse and neglect of boys behind bars.

- End solitary confinement and corporal punishment in all juvenile institutions.

- Provide rights for juvenile mental patients against involuntary commitment and medication equal to those granted adults.

- Increase public awareness about how expanded criminalization and pathologizing of young male behavior is skyrocketing the rates of hospitalizations and incarcerations.

- Create more voluntary community treatment centers, staffed with professionals trained to help young men at risk, that can stand between troubled boys and locked institutions. Once the centers are established, eliminate juvenile jails except for the minority of boys who are a proven threat to public safety.

I was eventually released from the mental hospital to my father's home. But things did not go well there. For many bad boys, juvenile halls, mental hospitals, and other locked facilities represent the

Fourth Pathway to Prison. With the exception of quality treatment facilities, many are merely prison-prep academies. If we do not turn their trajectory at this point, many boys, if not already involved, will turn toward drugs. In fact, many of us learned all about them in those very institutions. Deep down inside it doesn't feel very good to be labeled as bad or crazy. Some boys take drugs to relieve the pain of being criminalized and pathologized by the world around them.

Drugs and Criminalization

My parents gave me downers to make me less hyper.
Then I started sniffing glue. I don't hardly remember
how I got here. It's like I'm waking up from some
weird dream.
—Doug, 11, after four months in a residential
treatment center

A psychiatrist at the Mayo Clinic recently said, "At times, addiction can seem like a simple, straightforward, obvious condition that one gets into by irresponsible behavior and one should be able to change by willpower and 'just saying no.' On further study, however, it seems increasingly complex."

The problem of substance abuse *is* complex. As such, it eschews simplistic solutions. As I see it, there are roughly six major views defining the use of illegal substances in America today. Each of these perspectives also advocates a different remedy to the problem of drug abuse.

1. It's a private affair: *Drug users are making a personal choice.*

They are exercising their constitutional right to be sovereign over their own mind and body. *Private affair remedy:* End all drug prohibition. Enact similar guidelines for behavior "under the influence" as for alcohol.

2. Law enforcement: *Drug users are lawbreakers.*

Certain substances, for whatever good or bad reasons, are simply against the law. *Law enforcement remedy:* Arrest, incarceration, disenfranchisement (revocation of rights to bear arms, vote, travel freely, enjoy privacy, freely associate, assemble, or access information), and deterrence through the inculcation of fear.

3. Moral: *Drug users are immoral.*

Nonprescribed drugs are "bad." Therefore, people who use or sell them are bad or, in some contexts, sinful, evil, or even demonic. Often used to bolster view number 2. *Moral remedy:* Same as view number 2; however, some advocates additionally promote religious redemption as a cure.

4. Medical and psychological: *Drug users are sick.*

Substance abuse is an illness. Some advocate dispensing drugs and needles to addicts to encourage treatment, decrease fatalities, lower emergency room admissions, and to reduce AIDS, hepatitis, and other public health threats exceeding the harm of addiction. *Medical remedy:* Medical treatment and/or psychotherapy; drug prescription and supervision. Some offer Twelve-Step recovery.

5. Twelve-Step recovery: *Drug users are spiritually depleted.*

Twelve-Step remedy: Connection to a "higher power," accompanied by strong support from a self-help community dedicated to sobriety. Twelve-Step theory views the desire for drugs or alcohol as a misguided quest for a more spiritual life. It has consistently proved highly effective in healing the psychological and emotional pain that drive many into substance abuse.

6. Harm reduction: *Drug users exist.*

Drugs can be harmful to the user and others, as can many of the above "remedies." *Harm reduction remedy:* Follow the course of action that creates the least harm to the user, his or her relationships, and society as a whole.

All these perspectives have some merit. It is the latter ideal of harm reduction, however, that most strongly guides this chapter. Illegal drugs are dangerous and can destroy lives, as can alcohol, automobiles, tobacco, motorcycles, and prescription drugs. It is not my intention to make light of that fact or promote drug use in any way. In fact, my first book was largely a recovery guide for men with substance abuse problems. Today, however, the criminalization of boys appears abundantly more harmful, costly, and generative of violence than drug use itself.

In the years prior to World War II, European Jewry was at first pathologized, then demonized (considered evil), disenfranchised, criminalized, and, ultimately, dehumanized. One consequence of dehumanization is that it becomes easier for some enfranchised citizens to regard outcasts' lives as having lesser worth. When boys who use drugs are deemed lawless, deviant, immoral, or even evil, it further darkens their image in our collective awareness. Authorities use the dehumanization of young, male drug users to justify draconian punishments. Demonization further impedes the capacity of some to perceive bad boys as young people in need. Punishment thus trumps treatment as retribution supplants compassion. As the Red Queen in Alice's Wonderland responded to all offenses: "Off with their heads."

Most young, male drug users, however, are nonviolent, at least before incarceration. Drug offenders represent 60 percent of federal prisoners and over one-third of state and county prisoners. Boys arrested for drugs, however, show nondrug crime rates half that of nondrug arrestees such as burglars or robbers. This suggests that the aim of violent crime control would be better served by focusing more on violent criminals and less on addicts in need of treatment. But the forces of criminal justice keep widening the drug net's scope, thereby swelling youth corrections and prison populations with unprecedented numbers of young men.

Why Zero Tolerance Equals Zero Success

Despite massive campaigns and countless ruined lives, teen substance abuse remains prevalent, though consistently less rampant than adult abuse. Adolescent substance abuse rates rise and fall over the years, with no sustained, long-term trend toward reduction. We have never had a drug-free society. Citizens who do not use antidepressants, tranquilizers and other psychiatric medications, pain medications, diet pills, caffeine, tobacco, alcohol, or some illegal substance, are now a minority of U.S. citizens. The type of drug, level of use, population who uses it, method of distribution, manufacture, regulations, laws, and other features of substance use keep shifting. "Just say no or go to jail," for certain substances, however, does not rise to a stellar psychosocial treatment methodology. We can do better.

One reason so many young people fail to respond to official antidrug campaigns is because those initiatives make no distinction between "soft" drugs like marijuana and "hard" drugs like heroin or cocaine. Any kid getting high, however, knows they are worlds apart. But such "degree of harm" distinctions have been eliminated from the government's "zero tolerance" (all drug use is bad) lexicon. Many young people therefore reject the whole message because they know, at least, part of it is false.

Drug-savvy kids dismiss most antidrug programs as a joke, an insult to critical thinking. But these programs could be extremely valuable to those same children if designed for harm reduction instead of law enforcement's goals. As one advocate writes, "Preventive education for harm reduction seeks to inform and influence individual choices, not only to discourage any use of dangerous drugs, but also to educate those who will nevertheless experiment with them. It thus also teaches them how to minimize the harm they cause themselves and others—just as designated driver programs help reduce the harm of drinking."

The hard line of zero tolerance simply does not deter adolescent male drug use or many other youth problems. According to numerous credible reviews, zero tolerance is a total failure, recapitulating our protracted, failed "war on drugs." The growing intolerance toward bad boys appears more to reflect blind ideology than enlightened leadership offering thoughtful and workable solutions to difficult social problems. Students largely ignore programs that overstate drugs' ill effects or that seem to them to be grounded more in political correctness than science.

DARE (Drug Abuse Resistance Education) is the largest national drug-prevention program. It is widely praised by teachers and law enforcement officials. DARE may, in fact, teach good social and conflict resolution skills and improve student/police relations, all good things. DARE and similar programs, however, show little to no efficacy in reducing teen drug use. I find it sad that many parents actually pin hopes for their children's futures on these weak foundations.

Boys who smoke pot feel especially cynical when adults who drink alcohol tell them not to use marijuana. Boys tend to respect drug information disseminated by "those who have been there" more than from those who they think "don't have a clue." The author of a California Department of Education study notes, "As soon as kids are told that they can make decisions—but there's only one right decision to make, they stop listening." But the director of the federal Safe and Drug-Free Schools program adamantly states that they will not tolerate *any* program "whereby the position is anything less than 'kids are not to use [any] drugs.'" So despite consuming over half a billion dollars a year in funding, these programs simply continue to fail.

In 1995, 16 percent of eighth-graders reported using marijuana. By 1997, eighth-grade marijuana use increased to nearly 25 percent. By 1998, following massive, governmental antidrug campaigns, the 16 percent of eighth graders smoking pot three years earlier had grown to 41 percent of seventeen-year-olds. Additionally, 73 percent of high school seniors reported using alcohol during the previous year.

Bad Boys' Bigger Brother

Boys emulate the adults around them, who purchase and consume the *vast* majority of drugs and alcohol. But like selective gun control today, drug criminalization also falls most heavily on the backs of boys. Without the legal due process afforded adults, students in zero-tolerance high schools are increasingly being subjected to drug-sniffing dogs, warrantless searches, on-campus police, drug testing, and expulsion for possession, even for weekend use off-campus. Some schools do not even allow students to participate in extracurricular activities like chess club or cheerleading unless they are first tested. Other than prisoners, few adults are subjected to this level of official drug resistance and scrutiny.

Chemical patches can now test for "positives" in the sweat of a suspect's skin. Instead of being deeply engaged with their children's lives, parents can now buy cheap drug detection kits at the drugstore. The latest computer-age surveillance tool is the portable Ionscan, an "ion mobility spectrometer detection system." In five seconds it can identify invisible residues of thirty illegal drugs, as small as one-billionth of a gram, on someone's clothing, shoes, body, money, hair, or even in the air around them. In one East Coast prison, 45 percent of visitors stopped visiting their families after an Ionscan was installed.

As a recovering substance abuser I know it is a challenge to maintain lifetime abstinence. As a counselor, I've seen that without treatment, total abstinence is near impossible for many addicts. Over the past few decades, however, inexpensive and quick drug testing has sent huge numbers of parolees to prison instead of treatment. In the late 1980s as many were returned to California prisons from parole as for new felony convictions. In 1998, 30 percent of new prisoners were reincarcerated for parole violation—most for failed drug tests. These latest technologies for continual surveillance assure that even higher numbers of drug suspects, probationers, and parolees will be incarcerated than resulted from the random laboratory drug tests in the past.

Ironically, in an era when the majority of lawmakers advocate increased drug penalties and scrutiny, conservative Republicans quashed a 1998 plan to drug test members of the House of Representatives and their staffs. Representative Joe Barton of Texas reportedly said, "We have a few well placed people who do not want this." Louisiana and other state legislatures have followed suit, preventing the drug testing of their members. Most major employers—87 percent in 1999—do, however, test their job applicants and employees, even where public safety is not a factor. This new cadre of surrogate drug enforcement officers denies people jobs otherwise available to those who use tobacco, alcohol, or prescribed drugs.

The billion dollars this same Congress allocated in 1998 for youth-oriented, antidrug media campaigns did a lot for the prosperity of ad companies and television networks. That money, however, could have sent 80,000 to 150,000 at-risk youth to college or trade school, provided a year of quality outpatient drug treatment for 350,000 young addicts, or provided wages for one million mentors or reading tutors to spend a few hours with an at-risk boy each week. These are the sorts of interventions that create lasting and significant change in self-destructive behaviors like drug abuse. For instance, although there is no positive correlation between incarceration and reduced drug involvement, there is a direct relationship between level of education and drug, alcohol, and tobacco abuse: The less of the prior, the more of the latter.

Treating the underlying social and psychological conditions that provoke youth to seek the temporary pain relief of drugs could be more effective than forcing hundreds of thousands into the criminal justice system. As Reverend Jesse Jackson puts it, the problem isn't that law enforcement has failed to make bad boys *afraid* enough. "The real problem is that our young people are not *hopeful* enough." A campaign for hope, however, calls for different tactics than a war against boys. When I was on the street we used to joke, "Dope will get you through times of no hope more than hope will get you through times of no dope." We believed that because we didn't even know what hope was. Today, however, I do know: Hope trumps dope.

Why Are Drugs So Attractive to Isolated Young Men?

As with prostitution, I never really aspired to become a drug dealer. One day, however, my feet got a painful infection from standing in wet shoes all night washing dishes. I missed a few days of work. They fired me. My roommate Danny and I couldn't raise the next month's rent. We were soon back on the street. I constantly looked for work, but without education or real job training, no one would hire me for a decent job. In the latter half of my seventeenth year, I began a final stretch of homelessness, lasting about two years.

Danny started dealing LSD. As a newly synthesized drug, "acid" was legal. So I joined him. For a short time we could possess and sell it on the street with impunity. A large dealer would give us quantities on consignment. When we sold them, we repaid her and kept the profit. When Danny and I sampled our wares, however, we ended up giving away as much as we sold. Despite keeping us in food and drugs, our drug sales never produced enough money for us to secure new housing.

But even without lodging, life felt rich on Los Angeles streets in the mid-1960s. The vestiges of bohemia yellowed and blew away in winds of social transformation. Beat culture's leavings drifted into cracks of urban culture, becoming compost for the seeds of the hippie movement. I was too young to fit well in bohemia, and the gay scene always felt off for other reasons. But when psychedelic culture's buds opened and spewed forth their paisley and patchouli, the flowering of psychedelic culture enveloped me in a perfumed cloud.

A variety of clubs proliferated at the glittering edge of the "underground" community. Pandora's Box, the Troubadour, the Trip, Whisky-A-Go-Go, Gazzari's, and others wove a web of cabarets for the "scene." Though bohemia was fading, a few coffeehouses remained. The Fifth Estate was in a basement below Sunset Boulevard. Next door a small rotating statue of Rocky and Bullwinkle mimicked a brightly lit, three-story high, rotating statue of a Las Vegas showgirl across the street.

The Fifth Estate showed art films, hosted poetry readings, and had real, live, soon-to-be-famous folk singers. Hashish and acid were as plentiful as the coffee. It seemed strange to me that everyone I met was deemed an outlaw because of drug use. Their universe felt bountiful to me, whereas in the "straight" world little flowed my way but concrete, steel, blood, and dust. Outlaws were often generous and kind in contrast to most of my encounters with upstanding citizens. Some outlaws were just stone crazies, however, and that part got uncomfortable on occasion. But many "heads" (drug users) with "pads" (housing) let me "crash" (sleep), thus periodically giving me a chance to bathe, wash clothes, and otherwise recoup from the street.

Today many boys feel similar dichotomies between gangsters' allure and mainstream invitations. Particularly in our inner cities, boys and young men often feel they must choose between outlaws, who provide acceptance, community, and economic opportunity, and a mainstream culture that often rejects or condemns them.

Today, the glamour of rap music artists, with their excess of drugs, sex, and money, attracts countless young men. Many hang their identity on the profiles of these bad boys who seem to have escaped our decaying inner cities. It will take much more than protests and censorship of rap music's lyrics to break its grip on young men. They need jobs, education, spiritual guidance, and a clear road to a bountiful world before seeds of doubt will be cast on drug culture affiliations that, albeit falsely, promise a better life.

The glitter and romance of my rock'n'roll world hid many features of drug culture's dark side from me. In the same way, the wealth, power, and excitement associated with the "Gangsta" ethos obscures the Cimmerian sinkholes swallowing bad boys today. Crack, coke, smack, or speed—it doesn't matter. If not medically supervised, the use of all these drugs leads to oblivion. The protracted use of street drugs, with their wide variance of purity and potency, is the American version of Russian Roulette. Why then do boys take these risks of suicide on the installment plan? I can personally attest to the fact that isolated, abandoned, or abused boys often feel little reason for living. To many, oblivion may seem like a better place. That gaping void in the soul is the biggest drug lure of all. For a few moments, drugs obscure the demoralizing lacuna in a bad boy's psyche. But like subterranean termites, drugs eat further into psychological foundations already weakened by adverse social circumstances.

As drugs were a central component of my life on the streets, they are an integral part of street life and gang culture today. Every time we exclude a boy from the mainstream, for whatever reason, we create a potential new drug user or gang member. Disenfranchisement is a more powerful generator of drug abuse than any street corner recruitment. Even the risks associated with drug dealing are attractive to boys with few other sources of drama or excitement. Many young men crave risk as an opportunity to display their courage, a traditional means of inclusion in male culture throughout the world.

Drug dealing is very social, intense, engaging, vivid, and dramatic. It promises women, money, power, and a place in the "life." Dealing and drug use are very seductive to young men who lack strong hopes or ties to other sources of social inclusion. Economic opportunity and the attention of older males seduce many lost boys into this dangerous trade.

Some substance users start heavy use in reaction to emotional or physical pain. Traditionally, one of the hallmarks of masculinity has been the demonstrated capacity to repress pain. For many, attempting to live up to that dominant male ethos alone creates oft hidden suffering. Many young men suffer chronic pain from injuries incurred in the wars, physical conflicts, combat sports, high-risk occupations, and dangerous trades still primarily reserved as their sole province. For example, men are killed and seriously injured on the job twenty to one over women.

Many males will not seek help until pain or despair is severe enough to interfere with performance. It never even occurred to me to ask for help as a teenager, nor was I aware of any place where I could receive it without risking reincarceration. Instead of seeking assistance in ameliorating physical or emotional suffering, many men just "self-medicate." One emblem of the traditional male ethos is "I can fix it myself." This is one of many reasons young men are overrepresented among nonprescribed substance users.

Although women have other, equally serious, internalized admonitions that can impede their development, there is no similar "it is unfeminine to ask for help" imperative in most women's psyches. Women are the largest consumers of prescribed tranquilizers, barbiturates, stimulants, and addictive pain relieving drugs. Women visit the doctors, dentists, and psychiatrists who prescribe them in much higher numbers than men do. Men could learn some valuable lessons from women about self-care and safety. Because professionals supervise more of women's substance use, they are less likely to run afoul of drug enforcement or be harmed by impure or incorrect dosages that can accompany street drugs.

The End of Innocence

Although I had some insightful experiences with psychedelics, I also had psychotic episodes. I took them in unsafe settings: at rock concerts, clubs, "human be-ins," the street, and all-night hangouts like Cantor's Delicatessen. What professional literature exists on their appropriate psychiatric use notes all those settings as contraindicated. I was also undernourished and already a little paranoid in reaction to the real dangers of the street. Not surprisingly, any degree of temporary relief gained from drugs was taxed by an equal degree of decompensation. That's the problem with drug-induced insight. Years later, during my clinical training, I realized most of my seventeenth year met the clinical diagnostic criteria for psychosis.

One night in 1967 I caught a ride to San Francisco in the back seat of a lemon-colored Volkswagen bug, the Yellow Submarine. It

belonged to a dear friend we called Wayne Wonderview. Also joining our adventure was a black woman with a shaved head, Doreen,
a flamboyant gay man, Wendy, and a long-haired musician, Jim.

We headed up Highway 101, leaving LA about 11:00 P.M. In
Wayne's duffel bag were three kilos of marijuana, about $360 worth
then. By 3:00 A.M. we were *all* asleep. The car hit a bridge abutment
at 85 miles an hour. The sudden impact ejected me through the rear
window as the car flipped over. I flew several hundred feet, bouncing
down the center of a freeway for the second time in my life. As I
tumbled down the roadway my pants ripped off and I was slathered
with road burns. Half my ribs cracked. I hit my head and went into
shock, unable to move.

Wayne was instantly killed. A four-by-four signpost went through
his chest. Though I lost many friends in those days, Wayne's death
remains the most tragic in my heart. In some ways, efforts I have
made to positively change my life reflect an attempt to make some
meaning out of his needless death. Miraculously, all the others
escaped lasting injury.

Police found the duffel bag in a ditch. We were arrested in the
hospital, transferred to the Visalia County jail, and charged with
"felony possession of marijuana with intent to sell." Given our appearance, the crime, and the era, our "hippie drug invasion" made
headlines for days.

After more than a month in jail, my mother posted bond, bless
her soul. The first round of trials took two years. With four defendants in varying degrees of homelessness and addiction, it was difficult to get all of us to hearings, five hours from Los Angeles, at the
same time. I hitchhiked to court many times, and Gloria also occasionally drove me, putting in a late but welcome appearance in my
life. There were many continuances, pretrial hearings, and motions.
A prosecutor left. The court appointed a new judge. Since we were
passengers, the charge was finally dropped to simple possession for
which we were all found guilty.

Jim and Doreen, both first offenders, got a year. Wendy, however,
had been arrested again, prior to his sentencing, for possession of a

small quantity. As a "repeat offender," the court deemed him a chronic criminal and sent him to state prison. He got into more trouble there. This colorful, nonviolent, cheerful young man spent many years in Vacaville State Penitentiary before he died. Harsh punishment for a homeless gay boy who liked to smoke pot for relief.

Ironically, less than ten years later, possession of under an ounce was decriminalized in California. The state has since saved over a billion dollars in police, court, and prison costs and spared tens of thousands of citizens the trauma of incarceration. If arrested in 1976, Wendy would have suffered a $100 fine instead of a "habitual offender" charge. But then marijuana possession garnered what was essentially a death sentence for some in California. In some states, marijuana possession is still punished more severely than assault.

Today, every year, tens of thousands of boys and young men suffer similar fates for possessing minuscule quantities of crack. Busted one, two, or three times they face mandatory minimum prison sentences of five, ten to fifteen, and twenty-five years to life in prison. The RICO (Racketeer Influenced and Corrupt Organizations) Act was instituted to give the government broad new powers to put away Mafia dons. Now these statutes that allow law enforcement to bend constitutional protections are putting small-time dealers away for life. Crime and punishment are very relative affairs, subject to the changing whims of culture.

Why Young Men of Color Are Favored Targets of the Drug War

Drug abuse is widely distributed among most economic, racial, and cultural groups. Boys from racial minorities, however, suffer the most severe consequences for drug use. Affluent, mostly white, drug users, who represent 80 percent of powder cocaine consumers, are subject to different laws than their street-level, mostly black counterparts, who account for 90 percent of crack cocaine arrests. Powder cocaine users can possess 100 times the amount and value—500 grams as compared to five—before they incur the same penalties as crack smokers. This double-edged law protects the socially advantaged while sending disproportionate numbers of young black males to prison. Even if the intention of this law is not consciously racist or "classist," the outcome is decidedly so.

Affluent addicts avoid drug sweeps and other hazards affecting street dealers. They more easily obtain legal prescriptions and use drugs in more private and secure environments. Socially advantaged addicts receive better legal representation and medical and mental health care. Once arrested, enfranchised whites are more likely to be considered good candidates by the courts for diversion to treatment than low-income or minority addicts. Females are also significantly more likely to be referred to treatment than males.

African Americans are 13 percent of the U.S. population yet 40 percent of drug arrests. They serve longer in prison for the same crimes as whites. One study shows that when white and black teens commit the same crime, black teenagers are seven times more likely to be charged with a felony. They are also arrested six to one over white youth and are surveilled, stopped, and searched by police in greater numbers than white teenagers.

No prohibition has or ever will stop demand for alcohol or drugs. Nor has dumping billions into drug wars diminished supply. In 1999 heroin was available at half its 1980 price. Cocaine and speed are as plentiful as ever. Designer drugs proliferate despite their proven and unknown long-term health consequences. Speed labs are cranking out record quantities of methamphetamine, especially in the Midwest. All this is driven by extraordinary greed.

Alcohol prohibition allowed disenfranchised street hoods to become millionaires. It also generated unprecedented gang violence in competition for profits. Today, drug prohibition generates billions for a handful of drug lords. A United Nations study estimates that as much as 10 percent of the world's annual gross product may flow into their underground coffers.

It is the young men, however, dealing small quantities, in the open, on the streets, who constitute the majority incarcerated for drug sales. They are easy police targets. Few profit greatly from their trade. They are foot solders for the top dogs who make the real money. Boys in minority, inner-city neighborhoods—where the highest national rates of child poverty and young male unemployment exist—are the primary casualties of the drug war. Of 100 small-time dealers, one to two are killed, seven are seriously injured, and over twenty are incarcerated every year. As in most wars of attrition, increasingly younger recruits steadily replace them.

Hundreds of thousands of predominately low-income, young male prisoners of war (on drugs) flood our prisons. There was a 700 percent increase in drug-related, African-American inmates between 1985 and 1995 alone. Latinos are also disproportionate among drug prisoners, even though white adolescents have substance abuse rates similar to both these minority groups.

In Massachusetts, 84 percent of those serving mandatory drug sentences are first-time offenders; 80 percent will spend more time behind bars than the average prisoner convicted of a violent crime. In fact, nationwide today, more citizens are serving time for drug possession than for all violent crime categories combined. In 1998, the majority of California's "three-strikes" prisoners were doing twenty-five years to life for marijuana, not murder.

Filling the Hole in the Soul

In some cases, bad boys stop using drugs simply because they stumble through some open door in a corridor of gateways otherwise bolted shut. Wherever we can pry doors open, new intersections on the road to prison are created that, if taken, can lead a boy back into the community. The closed doors of moral superiority and criminalization merely herd them more speedily down the chute toward slaughter.

After the accident on Highway 101 I started frequenting the Hollywood studio of Vito Polukis. Vito hosted a Felliniesque underground arts scene. In the 1950s my mother lived above the studio where Vito made sculpture for his soul and lamps to pay his bills. His retinue spanned the early bohemian era of my mother to the hippies that now adorned his studio like a flock of brilliant macaws. The Iron Butterfly band rehearsed in the basement, while the rest of us hung out. Underground notables from Lenny Bruce to Jim Morrison, along with poets, filmmakers, record producers, actors, artists, writers, and musicians, came through Vito's door in those days.

I joined his improvisational dance troupe—the Freaks. We regularly showed up at Mothers of Invention concerts. The Mothers were an avant-garde rock band led by Frank Zappa. I could rarely tell whether he enjoyed our interpretive dance of his music or was appalled. But we had a symbiotic relationship. Vito's Freaks had free access to all the clubs and concerts. Our routines were so over the edge that they "made the scene." That was good for business.

Although this group was strange, it was also a community for me. Most young men desperately need to feel connected to some sort of tribe—a church group, the Boy Scouts, an athletic team, or—without a positive option for membership—a gang. Vito's troupe was more dance scene than drug scene. It helped shift my identity from bad boy to performing artist. It kept me off the streets and out of trouble.

Often, it seems, helping professionals try to move angry young men, involved with drugs, gangs, counterculture, violence, irresponsible sexuality, or crime, straight into middle-class models of responsibility. A rap band, guerrilla theater group, street mural art team—any uplifting expression of wild artistic passion—is a good first step away from the soul-grinding, dispassionate wildness of the streets.

I went on the road with the Mothers for a while. Handling equipment by day, I hung out with the band and their bevy of groupies at night. To many, this world seems mad. But for me, it was a breath of sanity and delicious freedom compared to street life and institutions. Any step away from criminality is valuable, even if it looks strange. No big quantum transformation or intervention ever generated rehabilitation in my life. Change happened gradually.

Real madness occurs when a person can't see underlying order in the patterns of their existence. Holocaust survivor and psychiatrist Victor Frankl theorized that it's not so much what happens to us that determines our sanity, but whether we can make meaning out of it or not. Frankl's theory proved true in my own life. Meaning emerged as the bizarre unfolding of my life seemed to point toward a more interesting world than I might otherwise have known.

When meaning is absent, insanity, violence, and criminality rush into the vacuum like thunder chasing lightning. When we avail boys with no other creative opportunity for self-definition, a bad-boy identity can provide a powerful sense of meaning. The graffiti wallpapering our cities is, in part, an outpouring of that quest for expression and recognition. For many, it feels better to be identified as part of gang, even a violent one that puts them at risk, than to suffer the existential anxiety of having no strong definition at all.

I don't use illegal drugs today. And I don't advocate their use. Access to a good education, economic opportunity, and Twelve-Step recovery groups, along with learning how to use relaxation techniques, and the growing possibility of a good life gave me the impetus to stop. When there is more to lose, some people become more protective of themselves.

For example, many Vietnam veterans came home with narcotics addictions. Those young men who came home to intact families and communities, with good access to economic and educational opportunity, were less likely to remain addicted than those who returned to less hopeful circumstances. Addiction often persisted or got worse with those who came home to broken relationships and families, impoverished or disrupted communities, and insufficient support or even obstacles to reintegrating with society. Drug addiction is not simply a physiological dependence; it is deeply tied to a person's social, emotional, familial, economic, physical, mental, and spiritual health.

Opportunities to positively engage life changed me more than any dire predictions in the media, threats, incarceration, bad trips, or even the drug-related arrests, accidents, and deaths of friends. I repeatedly see this to be so in the lives of other recovering addicts. Like posttraumatic stress in combat veterans, the resonance of adolescent incarceration far outweighed any adverse effects I ever suffered from drug abuse.

In the heart of every human being is a deep longing for freedom, something that can only be called the Divine. Connection to something greater than a constrained and unimaginative life, in whatever form it arises, is essential for many otherwise nihilistic young men. Our churches, temples, mosques, and other spiritual centers have an affirmative obligation to reach out to troubled young men in a manner blatantly *relevant* to their lives. For example, Reverend Cecil Williams at Glide Memorial Church in San Francisco doesn't just preach in the church. He goes out on the streets to talk to the drug dealers. He told me,

> You can't just take these young dealers off the streets and expect them to be good boys. They get a certain amount of admiration on the streets for what they do and what they have. If you want them to change they must have an opportunity to receive that glory in some other way. I told one young crack dealer, "You're good with money so why don't you take charge of our meals for the homeless program." We feed 6,000 people. That's a lot of money and goods to keep track of. He did a real good job and, most importantly, he got admired by a lot of good people for doing it. He's not dealing any more. We're going to make him a deacon.

In this way, the dedicated attention of a spiritual teacher and community turned around the life of an otherwise cynical young man. Opportunities for personal enrichment can undercut the psychological and spiritual conditions that lead to substance abuse. And a great deal of harm can be reduced by policy changes and drug treatment.

Decriminalization

Internationally, Germany, Ireland, the United Kingdom, Australia, Switzerland, New Zealand, and other nations are exploring varying degrees of decriminalization. The Frankfurt Resolution, drawn at a conference of international policy experts, states: "A drug policy which treats addiction exclusively as a law enforcement problem, and makes abstinence a precondition for the granting of assistance, is doomed to failure." At the end of 1998, 3,500 international drug policy experts gathered for a conference directed at humanizing drug laws throughout the European union. Most well-informed medical and mental health experts today agree that the collateral trauma, injury, disruption of families and communities, fiscal drain, infliction of mental illness, disease, and death that occurs from drug criminalization exceeds the harm caused by drugs themselves.

It appears that organized crime has the biggest stake in keeping drugs illegal. Decriminalization would cause prices to plummet. If profit were eliminated from the drug business, it is likely that associated turf violence would also disappear, thus making neighborhoods safer. Few addicts would then commit crimes to feed their habits. That proved true in Holland when that nation legalized soft drugs and decriminalized hard drugs.

Fifteen years after inaugurating their decriminalization experiment, the number of addicts in Amsterdam had dropped by 50 percent. Fewer young people became new users. Addicts registered with public health agencies, who offered methadone treatment and clean, AIDS-preventing syringes. In the United States, the use of dirty needles causes about 10,000 otherwise preventable AIDS cases a year. In 1998 the Dutch began providing free heroin for addicts. The first follow-up survey showed that not a single addict committed a crime after enrolling in the program. Although two-thirds of American addicts are employed, they still commit hundreds of thousands of crimes each year to procure money for drugs. On average, each nonaffluent, hard-drug addict commits fifty robberies, eighty-five burglaries, and hundreds of drug transactions each year.

Many experts today believe that drug decriminalization could halve our prison population. Others note that drug-related hospital admissions would also dramatically drop. In 1998 Germany transferred the entire issue of drugs from the realm of criminal justice to the health department. Based on an "addiction as treatable illness" model, the government embraced "Assistance not Punishment" as their emblem. Like the Dutch, they distribute heroin and provide clean needles in safe "injection rooms," where addicts can also receive other health support. The German drug czar's "health and education over law enforcement" approach dramatically contrasts with the sentiments of our former U.S. drug czar, William Bennett, who filled our prisons saying, "a massive wave of [drug] arrests is top priority."

Soft drugs can become a gateway to hard drugs. That's been a rationale for keeping them illegal. However, the incendiary experience of jail blows open a larger gateway to violent criminal culture, victimization, despair, even madness, thus making already alienated young men crave further relief from drugs. Boys incarcerated for drug use are more likely to become filled with hate than scared straight.

In 1998 Nevada, Oregon, Alaska, and Washington joined California and Arizona in decriminalizing medical use of marijuana and, in some states, small-scale cultivation by patients. In the face of this growing, harm-reducing trend in the electorate, some politicians recoiled. The citizens of Washington, D.C., also had a 1998 medical marijuana initiative. But in an unprecedented subversion of the democratic process, the U.S. Congress prevented the ballots from being counted. Just prior to election day, conservative Republicans, represented by Bob Barr, slipped an amendment into the 1999 budget making it illegal to "conduct any ballot initiative" calling for decriminalization of marijuana in the District of Columbia. The conservative mayor of New York also cracked down in 1998. Teams of undercover officers arrested almost 40,000 citizens for marijuana possession that year, eight times that of the previous administration. They went so far as to create a troop of phony street "smoke sellers" to entrap citizens attempting to purchase marijuana.

Over half a million Americans were arrested in 1996 for marijuana, mostly young men; in 1997 they exceeded 600,000. How do we benefit as a society by criminalizing this many citizens each year? If we outlawed alcohol again and added tobacco, few law-abiding citizens would remain. Both those substances are "harder," more addictive, and dramatically more deadly than marijuana. Tobacco and alcohol cause over 500,000 deaths each year. All illegal drugs combined kill about 4,000 per year, while the annual deaths attributed to prescription drugs exceed 100,000. Aspirin alone causes more hospital admissions than illegal drugs. Although there are real hazards associated with it, marijuana use has no known death rate. It is therefore not even counted in mortality statistics. Were marijuana decriminalized, the 24 million citizens now potentially targeted by the war on drugs would decline to about 2.5 million—about 1.9 million cocaine and 600,000 heroin users.

Drug Court and Treatment

A RAND Corporation study calculates that $34 million invested in treatment could reduce cocaine use as much as $380 million spent on interdiction or $250 million on enforcement. One of the most comprehensive drug treatment studies to date found that $209 million spent on treatment for 150,000 addicts saved taxpayers $1.5 billion in one year. Cocaine use in that group dropped 50 percent. Treatment alone, however, did not lead to stable employment. When drug offenders also receive job training to help ameliorate the social components of addiction, recidivism further falls 25 percent, even for those addicted to hard drugs or with long criminal records.

Federal, state, and local governments have spent over $250 billion in the last twenty years to combat drugs. Little of that has gone toward treatment programs that show more promise, better results, and lower harm for the least investment. With the third largest prison system in the world, California has only 1,500 beds for treatment of drug-convicted prisoners. And there is no after-care for addicts who are released, even though continued follow-up treatment is key to the success of most programs. Why is this so?

It certainly is not because law enforcement is more effective. Of all resources available, law enforcement appears to be most costly and least productive as a method to reduce drug use. I can only speculate that decades of demonization, as discussed above, have made many Americans regard drug users as some sort of enemy of the state. And who wants to give our enemies aid and comfort? Some appear to think, "They get what they deserve." This is not entirely unlike sentiments toward union organizers and socialists in the McCarthy era, or antiwar protesters during the Vietnam War. But having been one myself, I do not believe boys with drug habits are dedicated to destroying our nation. Our nation, however, is making war on them. These boys represent the hope or horror of our nation's future, depending on how we treat them.

In recent years, drug courts in our nation have been paralleling the European move away from criminalization toward treatment and assistance. Drug courts represent a bridge between the disparate philosophies of "treatable patient" versus "dangerous criminal." As distinct from criminal courts, drug courts attempt to draw youth away from drugs through treatment, education, community involvement, close supervision, and various non-harm-creating sanctions. Drug court judges lean toward real justice and harm reduction over the deterrence through fear that dominates our national drug enforcement policy.

Drug courts sentence offenders to treatment instead of incarceration. Those who fail to comply with the program, however, still risk jail. Drug courts have one foot in criminal justice and one in my world of the helping professionals. Participation is coerced rehabilitation for the recalcitrant but a welcome opportunity for the majority of addicts who want help. And even those pressured into treatment are generally grateful to have had the option over jail.

Judge Ochoa, the drug court judge in my area, calls it "a no lose situation." The success of drug courts, however, is dependent on cooperation from police and judicial jurisdictions, financial support, collaboration with community agencies, and the quality and efficacy of treatment programs available for referral. Another element that supports success is a consistent judge on the bench. Then he or she can track the progress of defendants, who periodically must appear in court, and personally hold them accountable to their promises.

As of 1998 the average rate of continued use among drug court participants was under 10 percent as compared to 50 to 60 percent for drug offenders going through criminal courts. Some drug courts report recidivism as low as 4 percent. The Office of National Drug Control Policy now believes it could cut prison populations by 250,000 in five years merely by expanding drug courts. But like most prevention and treatment programs, funding for drug courts—at one tenth the cost of imprisonment—remains subservient to the budget allotted to drug law enforcement. Estimates vary, but reliable analysts put the ratio at $7 to $11 saved by taxpayers for every dollar spent on treatment.

A local survey of youth in my area indicated that they were well educated about the dangers of drug abuse. This knowledge, however, did not dissuade use. In response, a private group developed TeenSpeak. This outpatient program focuses on addiction treatment, featuring group and family therapy, drug testing, and education. It costs $300 to start and $10 per session. The program has the best success when parents participate. A six-month program costs about $1,000, within the means of most working families.

For lower-income teens in our area, Project Recovery, funded by Medi-Cal, is based on a similar nonpunitive approach. These treatments focus on addiction recovery as *fundamental* before success can be achieved in other arenas. A drug expert in our police department, a recovered addict himself, says, "Without this program we would see a lot more kids dying out there." Continued funding, however, is not assured. Currently, there are no funds for our drug court. But our county continues packing drug-offending boys into juvenile hall, where I see them now doubled up on the floors of tiny, windowless cells designed for one. I raise these local issues for contrast because the situation in many less affluent communities is worse.

Even with drug courts slowly expanding (one in 1989, 150 in 1995 and 300 in 1999), treatment remains less available for low-income than for middle- and upper-income addicts. That is another reason that the war against drugs is predominately a war against the poor, particularly the boys disproportionately represented in the "criminal class." Those who find the resolve to kick their habits often encounter six-month waiting lists at clinics. When that date rolls around, however, they may have lost their resolve, their freedom, or even their lives. Middle- and upper-income addicts, however, can wake up feeling bad one morning and get "detox on demand" that day.

Dr. Lance Gooberman offers rapid detox on the East Coast for $2,800. He gives patients Naltrexone while they are in a deep, anesthetic sleep. This treatment avoids the chills, pain, vomiting, cramps, irritability, and sleeplessness that discourage addicts even when they genuinely want to kick their habit. The treatment happens in one day. Patients go home, sleep, and by the following day are over the worst of withdrawal. These clients can also get a Naltrexone implant for $475 per month that aids them in staying off drugs. On the West Coast, private doctors set up discreet "clinics" in five-star, Beverly Hills hotel suites to conduct rapid detox for those familiar faces who do not care to be seen, even at posh recovery clinics. Drug addiction carries significant stigma that can easily destroy careers.

Although it is not a cure for the underlying psychology of addiction, ameliorating the intense suffering of physical withdrawal is a major encouragement for addicts to enter programs that can help sustain long-term recovery. Recent research has produced several new chemicals and treatments that show promise in their potential to aid rapid drug detoxification and support sustained recovery. What if rapid detox, followed by treatment and recovery work, were made available to *all* addicts, regardless of their income, legal status, or relapse rate? We do not know what would happen to the incidence of crime, disease, death, and the destruction of lives, families, and communities, as well as the extreme level of prison expansion, now associated with illegal drug use. But we do know that the course of action of recent decades is a spectacular failure.

Some Recommendations to Help Young Men with Drug Problems

- Adopt harm reduction as the guiding principle of national drug policy.

- Support drug courts over criminal courts for low-level offenders.

- Teach natural stress reduction techniques to young men at risk for drug abuse.

- Make immediate on-demand detox and treatment available to all.

- Instigate a national dialogue and scientific study exploring any merit the decriminalization of drug possession may hold.

- Create more therapeutic, collaborative communities that support the reduction of drug use through increasing the educational, social, spiritual, and economic opportunities of boys at risk.

- Provide honest, scientific drug education in schools that makes distinctions among types of drugs, styles of use, and levels of involvement. Reduce harm and win students' faith through good education instead of fundamentalist, zero-tolerance propaganda.

Harm reduction, education, treatment, and decriminalization, however, are merely first steps toward reducing boys' use of pain-relieving drugs. Until our society addresses the social issues and environmental contexts that drive young men into despair, I doubt anything will have much significant effect. But moving away from harm and closer to hope can only further the dream of America as the Land of the Free. Until then, drug use will remain the Fifth Pathway to Prison.

Youth Corrections and Gangs

My father is in prison, my mom works all day. You
want me to give up my gang when I get released?
Whose gonna be my family then . . . you?
—Arturo, 15, in youth authority since age 13
    for car theft

Youth correctional institutions, by any name, are still prisons. Youth prisons occupy a narrow penal territory between lower-level offenders in juvenile facilities (Chapter Five) and men in adult prisons (Chapter Eight). In youth prisons dwell those too young to be sent directly to adult prison. But their crimes are serious enough that officials feel they cannot be safely held in the less secure juvenile halls and camps, hospitals, community-based programs, foster care, or residential treatment centers discussed earlier.

Historically, the philosophy in youth prisons leaned more toward rehabilitation than adult prisons. Officials thought, because of their age, some youth offenders could perhaps still be reached. In most states, however, juvenile penal laws steadily become more stringent each election year. As one astute criminologist puts it, "What began as an attempt to eliminate delinquency ended up as a practical method for getting rid of delinquents."

Ages of youth correction inmates range from twelve to twenty-five. The average age keeps declining. Once a boy makes the leap from juvenile institutions and probation to youth corrections and parole, chances are high he will remain on the prison road for life. In my home state, the California Youth Authority (CYA) administers youth corrections. The average CYA ward spends more than two years behind bars. Over half are back in custody within twenty-four months of release. Most of the rest return in time or matriculate to adult prisons. Within a decade of release, 6 percent of CYA offenders are dead. This gives us ex-youth authority offenders the highest mortality rate for that age group in the nation.

California annually spends about $400 million, and employs over 5,000 people, to keep about 8,000 boys incarcerated in CYA and supervise another 6,000 on parole. I was first committed to CYA when I was fifteen. It remains one of the most utterly terrifying experiences of my life.

Shortly after my stint in the Neuro-Psychiatric Institute at UCLA, I went to Tijuana for a night with some friends. This is a common Saturday night excursion for Southern California teenagers to this day. Early the next morning, San Diego police stopped the car on our way back, ran a check on all the occupants, and somehow discovered I was on probation in Los Angeles. They must have informed my probation officer, because he was waiting for me when I returned. He immediately "violated" me for leaving county jurisdiction without permission and had me returned to locked custody that same day.

After being held in the (county) Sylmar Juvenile Detention Center for about a month, a juvenile judge remanded me to the (state) California Youth Authority—indeterminately. That meant I could remain until the age of eighteen, twenty-one, or, if I really screwed up in the institution, twenty-five. Without ever going through the due process afforded adults, I was sent to a high-security, CYA processing center where I remained for about six months. I turned sixteen there. At this point in my life, even though I had engaged in illegal activities, I had never been convicted of a crime. All my incarcerations, at this point, were for "status" offenses such as runaway, curfew violations, living without adult supervision, and probation violation.

Youth Authority?

The guards were less brutal than those in Chicago. Some hit us, but most did not. Some boys traded sex for favors with them, but I declined those "opportunities." One kind night guard, whom I liked very much because he sat outside my cell door and talked to me when I could not sleep, was severely beaten by some boys during an escape attempt. So the violence went both ways.

CYA significantly upped the ante on my jailhouse survival skills. The boys were bigger, older—up to twenty-one years old—and more vicious and perverse. Older, hardened young men continually extorted candy, personal services, cigarettes, and sex from the more vulnerable inmates. One day, a boy shoved a fork down my throat after attacking me in a walk-in freezer. I naively made some off-hand remark to him and he exploded. I fought him off with a frozen hunk of beef. It seems comical to me now, like a scene from a farcical movie. But at the time I lived in constant fear.

As a slightly built boy, with no jailhouse gang affiliations, I was always at risk for confrontations from older boys. I was constantly vigilant and quick to respond as violently as possible to protect myself. At first, in earlier incarcerations, I struck back only to defend myself. I followed a moral code instilled by my mother during my few years in her home: "Never strike the first blow, son." After being sent to CYA, however, I began striking first if anyone made the slightest gesture of disrespect toward me by comment, deed, or omission. I tried to project a "Don't fuck with me anytime, anywhere" attitude. It prevented most potential assaults from occurring. In this angry young male context, where ultraviolence was the norm and decency was regarded as weakness, acting "bad" created an aura of safety.

I learned that even big, yard-hardened guys didn't like to get smashed in the nose, kicked in the testicles, cut with the honed edge of a plastic comb, or stuck with a sharpened toothbrush. Most of them would leave a boy alone if they thought he was genuinely "a crazy mother fucker."

There were no other Jews in the institution. My Mediterranean complexion, slight build, and familiarity with Los Angeles Latino street culture made many mistake me for Mexican. In time, like a chameleon melding into tawny desert rocks, I started pretending to be one. I mimicked their "walk," wore my pants pulled up to my chest, squatted on my heels with them in the yard, and learned more Chicano slang. The costume most Chicano boys wore on the street was similar to that of a CYA inmate. I came to realize over time that for many, the boundary between street and institutional culture was blurred.

Some second-generation Mexican boys didn't speak Spanish very well. And I kept pretty quiet most of the time, so my language deficit was not a real barrier. One day, using a sewing needle and ink from a pen cartridge, another boy tattooed a "13" on my wrist. The thirteenth letter of the alphabet is M. In those days the number thirteen was a code for marijuana. Although I knew tattoos were an anathema to Jews, many Mexican boys had them. I was never Bar Mitzvahed, however, so I no longer really thought of myself as Jewish.

I later learned that "13" and "M" eventually came to stand more for the Mexican Mafia, the most powerful gang in the California prison system, than it did for marijuana. Jailhouse tattoos are an integral part of prison culture. Once in prison, the only thing a man still owns is his skin. Tattoos, like "flashing" hand signs, showing "colors," or graffiti tags, identify gang affiliations. Tattoos can also designate neighborhoods, the number of times and places previously incarcerated, how many people a man has killed, and more.

After my release, I burned the tattoo off with a cigarette. The smooth round scar left by the deep burn into my hairy forearm never regained sensation or regrew hair. It remains a reminder of a difficult time that I survived. Free tattoo removal for boys trying to reenter society is one way the medical community in some areas is helping bad boys. Jailhouse tattoos are neon signs broadcasting: "I am still an outlaw."

Once the Chicano boys accepted me I had back-up if another inmate tried to start trouble. My affiliation with other outlaws mitigated a seemingly inescapable, abusive situation. One day, for example, a black man tried to bully me into giving him my commissary items. About half a dozen Mexican boys, squatting nearby, slowly and silently stood up. That was it. He looked over at them, looked at me, and just walked away.

I felt a modicum of protection for the first time in my institutional life. In CYA I learned it was difficult to survive without fierce allies. It was better to have violent young men as friends than enemies, no matter what it took to earn their respect. I earned mine through a willingness to fight, regardless of the odds. Paradoxically, I was rewarded for my violent behavior with protection from violence.

The Fraternal Order of Gangsters

Besides ruling the day-to-day lives of most prisoners, prison gangs have enormous influence on street gang activity. Gang members cycle in and out of youth corrections and prison. They must serve the dictates of the prison gang while on the street to assure protection once incarcerated. In many cases, they serve to protect family members already in prison.

Prison gangs perpetuate cycles of violence for generations. Some young men who join gangs are simply aligning with the only family tradition they know, just as I emulated the "hipster" world of my father. When I speak in juvenile facilities today, many of the boys report that they are the sons, nephews, and even grandsons of OGs (original gangsters, the charter members of gang culture). The fact that many of their relatives are dead, disabled by knife and bullet wounds, or imprisoned does little to dissuade their gang involvement. In many ways gangs are extended families, a kinship system in which members regard one another as siblings. But they are generally families with no mature parental guidance. That's the problem. They are siblings without strong fathers, mothers, and elders to direct their energy or temper their wildness.

When gang members refer to someone as "Homeboy," "Homie," or simply "Homes" it means, "This boy is from my home territory; he understands my cultural context. He is my brother. With him, I stand united against all enemies. We are willing to die for one another." These sentiments are not unlike the feelings of men in police or military corps, for whom the nation is the "hood" and combat veterans are the OGs.

As in jail, many young men in the community feel they must curry the protection of a neighborhood gang. For those living in gang territories, there is often little choice. Just as governments draft young men to fight in national conflicts, gang membership looms as forced conscription in an urban war.

To win a gang's protection or simply to avoid abuse, one must follow their dictates. Just as my willingness to fight in CYA demonstrated my worth, new members of gangs must demonstrate their courage. Gang initiation, "jumping in," frequently involves stoically taking a fierce beating by the gang's members. Often it also means committing a daring crime. In a similar, but more socially integrated way, soldiers must often prove their fearlessness in training, hazing, and combat to be included in elite units or to gain rank.

Most adolescent boys search for some form of masculine identity and male community wherever they can find it. They crave affiliation with a group of same-aged boys and a few older males. Despite recent revisions by academics calling for new, improved, more sensitive models of manhood, most young men still seek opportunities to prove their courage, strength, and other "traditional" attributes of masculinity. If the community does not provide them membership in a productive group of men, many will join a gang rather than risk the psychological and physical dangers of remaining unaffiliated.

In common with the majority of all youth at risk, a factor most adolescent gang members and drug addicts share is an absent father. About 80 percent of gang members nationwide suffer father absence, as do the majority of all boys arrested for violent crimes. In fact, one of the chief predictors of crime in a community today is the percentage of father-absent households. Social scientists also correlate fatherlessness with higher rates of youth suicide, teen pregnancy, mental illness, substance abuse, poverty, and school failure, drop out, suspension, and expulsion. The United States leads the world in both fatherlessness and incarceration of young men.

In our economically challenged communities, fathers are discouraged from family involvement by social welfare laws that reduce aid if fathers are at home, bias against fathers in custody and visitation rulings, family agencies that virtually ignore them, and incarcerations that devastate family relations for men in custody. Many fathers feel they simply have nothing of value to offer their children.

In the wake of cultural shifts that have eroded the traditional code of paternal responsibility, children living in single-parent homes have increased from five million to over seventeen million in the last three decades. Coincidentally, the quadrupling of our prison populations, proliferation of gangs, and escalation of youth violence rode tandem with this trend. By contrast, in 1997, I surveyed 100 of my sociology students at UC Berkeley about their family backgrounds. These students were from every imaginable ethnic background—but they had something in common. About 80 percent reported that they came from an intact, solvent, two-parent home in which the father was positively involved with their lives.

Mentor Men

Several "male mentoring" programs across the nation are working to change the social conditions driving so many young men into gangs and violence. These regional and national groups, such as Mad Dads, Boys-to-Men, Los Compadres, Project Return, the Male

Involvement Project, and the Fatherhood Coalition, show promise in this arena.

"Retired" gang members have also formed numerous local and national grassroots groups such as Unity One, No Guns, Focus, Exodus, FACES, BOSS, Islamic Hope, Barrios Unidos, and RISE. They help negotiate gang truces and divert current gang members and young "wannabes" into productive paths. The very best of youth-at-risk intervention programs all create opportunities for stable, successful men to become significantly involved in every level of boys' lives. These grassroots programs, usually operating with shoestring budgets, have been seriously overlooked for their contribution to reducing violent crime in recent years. Government tends to falsely attribute crime reduction solely to increased policing and incarceration.

Mentors in these young-male oriented groups report that socially nurturing behavior emerges from troubled boys when they can connect with a sense of "male honor." Through respectfully appealing to a boy's manhood, by modeling a responsible model of masculinity, older men can reach the unreachable. This is in contradistinction to the juvenile justice system, which often modifies behavior by instilling fear and shame through increasing levels of constraint and degradation.

The failed approach many professionally trained counselors still take today attempts to undercut a bad boy's masculine pride more than build it up. Gender perspectives that see traditional masculinity as the source of boys' violence miss its true character as a misused but otherwise valuable asset. Successful mentors, however, learn to channel and redirect young male pride and toughness. They create meaningful community and relationships that young men thereby naturally want to preserve and protect.

National gang authority Steve Nawojczyk calls gangs "the 5-H Club. They are homeless, helpless, hungry, hugless, and hopeless. They create their own sub-society because they don't fit into ours. Many youth join gangs because they don't have anything else to do. Gangs are the strongest where communities are the weakest."

To facilitate positive change we could offer gang members good education, job skills training, parenting and relationship skills, employment opportunities, drug recovery, and other interventions that restore hope. When we create opportunities for self-determination instead of merely condemning angry young men for being who they are, things change.

Jeff Prieto was "jumped" into a local gang, the Barrio Hoods, when he was a teenager. Drugs, violence, pervasive feelings of anger, and alienation from Anglo culture filled his life. One day a "special education" teacher in a local school where Latinos are the ethnic majority said to him, "If you're going to just sit there, read something." He loved to read, but reading was not "cool." So he read in secret, in the library, and learned a great deal on his own.

When he was a high school senior, not one school counselor ever talked to him about the possibility of college. He never even imagined it himself. But one day the founder of a local chapter of the Brown Berets (Chicano activists), working as a community liaison, saw that Jeff had potential and practically forced him to fill out a college application. He was soon accepted to UCSB, graduated in law from UCLA, and received an additional graduate degree from Princeton.

Today he is an Environmental Protection Agency attorney adviser and director of the Chicano Scholarship Foundation. He was one of only fifteen citizens honored as a White House Fellow for 1998–1999. Among his many credits, he helped organize one of the first End Barrio Warfare Conferences in Southern California. He says,

> I was in the gang for social and economic reasons. But the strongest draw was an overwhelming feeling of power. We used to say, "Somos chicos pero locos" [we are small but we are crazy]. Our wildness made us feel strong.
>
> Even in college the pull back to the street was powerful. I didn't fit in at school. Many middle-class people

acted like I did not belong there. I thought that maybe
I was not intelligent. I felt divided and I dropped out.
I threw away the opportunities people fought hard to
give me.

How did I finally get out of the gang? Familia [Fam-
ily], Amigos [friends], and Carnales [brothers] helped me
take heart. True friends don't grab you as they are going
down so they won't be lonely. True friends lift you up,
they help you find your dreams. So I went back to school.
It was hard. I stayed up late every night and studied. My
sons grew up in married student housing.

Cholos [Chicano gang members] have heart. But they
are fighting for something they do not own. The city
owns the streets, not the gangs. There is something,
however, that does belong to them and is worth fighting
for: their future. It takes a real man to stand up for the
[neighbor]hood. But it takes more to stand up in school.
Education is the key. There is power there, like what I
felt in the gang. How we educate our children today will
determine how our community is in the future. The real
battle in our culture today is not between gangs; it is for
the hearts, minds, and souls of the children in our community.

Another local OG, Mark, from the same era of the Barrio
Hoods, is today the responsible father of seven children in our
community. In addition to working full-time and caring for his
family, he mentors a large group of kids at risk for gang involvement. After Mark and Jeff led a wilderness program called Hoods
in the Woods, many of the young men continued to orbit around
Mark's charismatic pull. One man like Mark or Jeff is worth a 100
college-trained counselors in their potential to reach boys in gangs.
But few ex-gang-bangers ever get the opportunity to give back to
their community. Most community agencies are afraid that they

may lead others astray. Well, that's a risk. Not reaching "wannabe" gang members at all, however, is a greater gamble.

Many bad boys feel they have no chance of ever mainstreaming. Being an outlaw seems like the only recourse for many boys without good education and job skills. That is why Father Gregory Boyle started Homeboy Bakery in Los Angeles. He invited gang members, some from rival gangs, to work there and learn a trade. It had a profound effect in weaning a number of them away from crime and violence.

The film industry, in which I worked for several years, has a program called City Lights that reaches out to at-risk young men. The young men first go through rites of passage designed to evoke responsible "manhood." They also learn about anger management, communication, grooming, and other basic workplace survival skills. Then they learn a good trade. Former OG "Crazy Ace" was a young felon with two strikes on his record. On leaving prison he wanted out of gang life and to dedicate himself to caring for his daughter. After City Light's mentors got a hold of him he said, "I used to dream about a good future. But I couldn't see it. Now I can." At last report he was gainfully employed in the film industry. These are just a few of the approaches to gang prevention that really work.

Reaching Baby Gangsters

In the outcry against gangs it is seldom noted that there are varying levels of involvement: (1) prison leaders, (2) prison members, (3) street leaders, (4) hard-core members, (5) affiliates and spouses, (6) wannabes, (7) young boys at risk, and (8) children of members. Most at-risk boys, fourteen years old and younger, are between levels 5 and 8. This is the time we should be pouring resources into their lives to offer them clearly viable and stable alternatives to gang initiation.

One-shot programs don't work. Just saying no doesn't work. Criminalization and incarceration won't turn the tide. At this age adolescent male identity is in a critical phase. Once boys are "jumped in," it's hard to jump back out. Remember *West Side Story?* "When you're a Jet you're a Jet all the way; from your first cigarette to your last dying day." That's still the code.

Gangs offer cultural pride and self-rule. They challenge a dominant culture, often perceived by disenfranchised youth more as an oppressor than a source of opportunity. Gangs are attractive because they fill an essential need in adolescent male psychology for membership, acceptance, display, recognition, pride, a sense of mission, and a feeling of power.

Gangs provide community for lonely boys, economic opportunity for poor boys, adventure for bored boys, action for restless boys, protection from violent males outside the gang, and connection with powerful (in their social context) older men. So for all the despair they can bring, gangs are as attractive to disenfranchised boys—from inner cities to suburban high schools—as the underground scene was in my day.

A question that often arises in my seminars is "How can we reach troubled boys who do not respond to the techniques we learned in training?" One of my good friends, a colleague in the Fatherhood Coalition, answers that question well.

Hector Sanchez Flores is a research associate for the Institute of Health Policy. He has shown remarkable success in working with the angry young men of our community and designing effective male-involvement programs throughout our state. He is particularly skillful in engaging marginalized young men in family planning, responsible fatherhood, education and job-skills acquisition, and fostering positive relations with their female partners. Hector says,

> Before there is rapport built with these boys, I address them as Mister _____. I treat them as colleagues. They are in the process of becoming men. So I treat them like men. This throws them off balance, in a good way.
>
> Many people [in the helping professions] think that

giving respect and genuine caring is too simplistic to be
effective. Every young man I come in contact with is a
genuine human that is deserving of respect. Within their
roughness is a positive purpose and a human goodness.
Then it is incumbent on us to polish the stone.

Instead of changing the young man, you change your
tack. You try to find the most effective strategy to smooth
the rough edges. Recognize that every adolescent boy is
capable of doing some good. I've worked with many
young prisoners. What they did was bad, but I don't know
if that made them bad people.

Instead of just condemning their behavior or trying to
control them, I try to reinforce *any* level of success they
have. For example: the fact that he isn't high *today*; he
went to school three days this week instead of one; he
has a book with him even though he hasn't read it—yet;
he had a fight but did not pull a weapon. So, I accentuate the positive. Because of that I can work effectively
with anyone.

I build my male involvement programs with staff who
can be *completely* respectful to young men with problems.
I tell them, "If you don't have the stomach to work with
what these young men bring, then perhaps you should
find an another place to cut your teeth." If you burn them,
it will be more challenging for the next helper.

Just one trustworthy, committed, honest, caring, consistent, and
capable adult like Hector, who will hang in with bad boys through
all their ups and downs, can make the critical difference between a
boy positively moving toward community or trying to destroy it.

Boys Behind Bars

In the wake of the passage of the most expensive crime bill in history, the 1994 Violent Crime Control and Law Enforcement Act,
Senator Paul Simon convened a Subcommittee on the Constitution.

He noted, "For all the new prisons we've built and filled over the last two decades, we feel less safe today than we did before." The committee surveyed the nation's prison wardens to find out what those closest to criminalized men thought could help reduce crime.

- 92 percent believe greater use should be made of alternatives to incarceration.

- 85 percent say elected officials are not offering effective solutions to America's crime problem.

- 71 percent believe improving the educational quality of public schools would make a difference in fighting crime.

On the average, the wardens feel half their inmates would pose little danger to public safety if released. They call for a more *balanced approach that mixes punishment, prevention, and treatment.* They want to see the development of more prevention programs, the repeal of mandatory minimum sentences, judges granted greater discretion, and an expansion of alternatives to incarceration.

Ironically, as a former prisoner, I find myself in close accord with today's prison wardens. So do the majority of the nation's judges and police chiefs, according to similar recent surveys of those professions. But the politically driven 1994 crime bill, and most that followed, allocated only token amounts to prevention, treatment, and rehabilitation. Higher education grants for prisoners were virtually wiped out over the last five years. The majority of crime prevention funds continue to pour into law enforcement, punishment, and prisons.

In 1998, for example, Texas allocated $49 million to reduce gangs that reportedly claim over 150,000 young men in that state. More than $41 million was allocated to expand juvenile lockups. The rest was mostly for policing, identification, and tracking. Little to nothing went toward the approaches above that actually have the power to create lasting change. It is little wonder that Texas is starting to be called the prison capital of the world.

It is impossible, within the context of this book, to detail every juvenile justice proposal in legislative process at press time. Some clear trends, however, are evident. The climate toward adolescent boys has steadily become more punitive over the last few decades. Recent state and federal bills now aim to

- Significantly expand the processes by which boys can be tried and convicted as adults. (In 1998 over 5,000 boys were already in adult prisons.)

- Abolish federally funded juvenile rehabilitation while increasing juvenile prison construction.

- Eliminate the confidentiality of youthful offenders' records and thus the possibly of their ever participating in mainstream culture.

- Reinstate "status offense" incarcerations, thus allowing states to put runaways and truants behind bars even if they're not arrested for any crime.

- Increase sentence lengths for many crimes. (Juveniles already serve longer sentences than adults for some crimes.)

There is no clinical or forensic evidence, however, that adult-level prosecution or incarceration reduces juvenile violence in any way. Young men who become tangled up in youth corrections *enter lockup like uranium:* They have a potential for destructiveness, but most have not fully realized it. The systematic isolation, abuse, neglect, assault, and degradation of young male prisoners breeds ever-increasing levels of societal violence in an endless feedback loop. *Young men leave prison like plutonium:* The constant bombardment by concentrated streams of violence in prison dangerously enriches a boy's latent potential for harm.

If we want to break the cycle of violence, however, we could provide protection from subjugation to assault, torture, and rape in locked facilities. We could implement programs designed to heal young lawbreakers' lives, rather than merely punish them or break their spirits. As well said by many others before me, youth prison, as it stands today, only prepares young men for admission to adult prison. Ultimately, as police states of other cultures have demonstrated, no amount of law enforcement can permanently contain the social upheavals that occur in reaction to injustice.

Bad Boys Need Friends in High Places

A caring older man liberated me from my deepening despair in the CYA. He was a parole officer named Vincent Price. He showed up one day, disturbed that the system had warehoused me in limbo for so long. He was the first professional to come along, in my two plus years of incarceration between the ages of eleven and sixteen, who genuinely cared and was willing to help.

Other than my doctor at the mental hospital, Mr. Price was the first adult who showed compassion or expressed any outrage about how I slipped through the cracks in the juvenile justice system. He lobbied to get me released to a new program—the first CYA halfway house—located a few blocks from the Ambassador Hotel in Los Angeles, where Sirhan Sirhan assassinated Robert Kennedy a few years later. In the latter half of my sixteenth year, the CYA released me, on parole, to share a rambling old house with eight other boys and a pair of house parents.

It was full of other discarded boys hoping for a better life. The state provided funds to buy me some basic clothing. I was fed home-cooked meals and, most important, was not subjected to abuse by the house parents or other boys. Though programs like these can save the life of a prison-bound boy, funds for alternatives to incarceration remain meager. This is a social tragedy and a bad investment in our future human capital. But I was lucky. The grace of God and the dedication of a concerned public servant gave me a chance.

I wanted to attend high school. But the ninth grade was the last I had completed. My records were a mess; I had attended over a dozen different junior high schools as I bounced from place to place. And I received no education in the juvenile halls or the CYA. They made us go to "school." But it was just make-work and remedial reading with *Reader's Digests* as primary texts. I read well, so I was pretty underwhelmed by what they offered. Today, the CYA requires wards to complete high school before release. Parolees with a high school diploma are two and half times less likely to reoffend. CYA is to be commended for instituting this program. I only hope the boys also get full support to overcome their learning disabilities and are therefore not unfairly punished for school failure with longer imprisonment.

Even though I was motivated and capable, school officials said I was inadmissible because I lacked sufficient credits from earlier grades. Many boys gravitate to crime at this point in their lives as their options for a good future narrow. But I was determined to remain free. With Mr. Price's help I secured a full-time job working as a clerk for the same school system that would not accept me as a student. Every weekday I rode the bus to downtown LA and stamped numbers on teachers' paychecks all day. In the evening I returned to my bleak but clean dormitory, had a late supper, watched TV, and slept.

It looked as though I would have to stay there until I was eighteen. But as I approached my seventeenth birthday Mr. Price felt I demonstrated the capacity to live and work as an adult, so there was no good reason for me to remain a ward of the state. With his help, I successfully petitioned the court to designate me as an emancipated minor. That meant I was no longer subject to arrest for living on my own or being out after curfew.

I left the halfway house and was delighted to be free. But like many boys in my circumstances today, I was unable to secure stable economic independence. This failure precipitated the final round of homelessness I previously discussed. But I greatly preferred homelessness to incarceration. Some economic help at that time would have aided a transition from criminal class to working class. And surely I would have benefited by counseling, job training, and education.

The halfway house and emancipation was really the best that the CYA could do with the resources they had. I remain grateful for the opportunity they gave me. And I eventually succeeded anyway. So all is well. Sometimes, however, it has felt like I was persevering just to spite everyone who believed I would never amount to anything.

PTSD Makes It Hard to Stay Free

My incarceration experiences were so unsettling that I became quite phobic about returning to jail. I did not trust police because of my negative encounters with them over the years. Even though adverse traumatization doesn't work to keep the vast majority of criminals from returning to jail, it had the desired effect in my case. But paradoxically, the fear authorities instilled in me also made me subject to irrational behavior. It returned me to jail one last time and brought me within a clear line of sight to state prison.

At a meditation retreat I attended when I was nineteen, my teacher suggested that, along with my spiritual studies, I should also pursue a formal education. I followed his advice and worked hard to complete my Associate of Arts degree at LA Community College. Wherever possible, I also began trying to clean up my past so that I could eventually get decent employment. At age twenty-one, I went to get my first driver's license. The DMV declined, however, because I had an outstanding ticket for hitchhiking on the freeway several years earlier. I went to court to clear it up.

The judge was a conservative fellow who, I later learned, had a reputation for being extremely hard on counterculture members and ethnic minorities. I came before him and apologized for neglecting to pay the $15 ticket. He gave me an angry lecture about my generation's wanton disregard for the law and ordered me to pay a $600 fine.

Six hundred dollars probably doesn't seem like much to the average reader, but in 1971, as a City College student living in a $50 a month apartment, it exceeded my entire net worth. I told the judge I didn't have that much money on me and would need a few days to raise it. He replied, "Then you can just do thirty days in jail."

The judge ordered the bailiff to take me into custody. I was stunned, then outraged. I came in voluntarily and was willing to pay my dues given half a chance. I had two part-time jobs and a full-time academic load, all of which would be wiped out by a thirty-day absence. I couldn't bear the thought of the tiny bit of progress I made being cavalierly smashed by a biased public official. And I was terrified of returning to jail. In a fit of blind rebellion, I lit out of the court room as fast as I could run.

Deputies followed me down the hall and tackled me on the stairway. They beat me with nightsticks and hauled me to jail. I could not stop screaming in outrage. They continued to beat me in the holding cell until I did. I was very lucky that no one shot me that day. In fact, one of the cops later told me that had I made it outside the building, they would have gunned me down.

The police charged me with felony escape. The same judge found me guilty. A good lawyer probably would have had him recuse himself, but my young public defender—the overworked legal protectors of the indigent—clearly felt intimidated. The probation department recommended I be sent to state prison.

Friends of good repute, employers, and my teachers at LACC all sent strong letters of recommendation for me. The probation department reversed its recommendation, the public defender somehow got me a different judge for my sentencing, and the court released me on probation. During those demoralizing days in the Riverside County Jail I imagined walking onto the yard at the state penitentiary and being asked,

"What are you in for man?"

"Hitchhiking."

I'd be the laughing stock of the prison, like Arlo Guthrie, in *Alice's Restaurant*, doing time with "mother-rapers and father-stabbers" for the crime of littering.

The American Crime of Poverty

Justice in America was built upon a foundation of English Common Law. This body of law was primarily organized to protect the rights of persons with established property, most notably the king and his peers. As a young nation, we embraced liberty for a wider spectrum of people than did European monarchies. However, we still retained a double standard with a large underclass dominated by a small upper class.

Today, after our two-century long quest for democracy and equality in America, that class division persists. A significant segment of our population remains disenfranchised. That poverty breeds crime is a truism so blatant as to appear trite. Even so, we have done little to deal effectively with this precursor to crime, focusing instead more on its effects. We will still spend four times as much to incarcerate a boy as to educate him.

With over ten million impoverished males in America, young men represent the fastest growing segment of the economically disenfranchised. As blue-collar jobs evaporate and entry-level jobs require greater technical skills and education, these fading bastions of work, traditionally filled by lesser trained young men, are leaving increasing numbers of them out in the cold.

Even a cursory analysis of the distribution of wealth in America demonstrates the connection between lack of economic opportunity and the crimes that precipitate the majority of incarcerations. Moreover, besides breeding crime, poverty is often a crime itself, as it was for me in Riverside. Most property crime, the highest arrest category for juvenile males, is fueled by poverty. Dr. Bob Roberts, director of the nation's most successful prisoner after-care program, notes that his parolees can be returned to prison for failing to pay as little as $40 to the state for "supervision fees."

In the Great Depression, America created public work programs to restore our nation's workforce to hope and productivity. But the publicly funded work programs that once restored unemployed men to dignity are meager today. "Jobs not jails" would be a good slogan for a political candidate who really cared about reducing violence. Or as Reverend Jesse Jackson says about our young men, "We need to lift them up instead of lock them up."

In 1998 those in the lower economic 20 percent earned less than 4 percent of the nation's wealth; the top 20 percent took home about 50 percent. This is the largest economic gap in the Western world. A steady widening of the gap between these upper and lower income groups has directly paralleled our rising incarceration rates. The larger the economic gap, the higher the level of violence in most nations. In most European nations, for example, child poverty rates are about a quarter that of the United States, mirroring their similarly lower violence and incarceration rates.

Perhaps it is easier for those with the power to buy their way out of various troubles to see crimes of poverty as moral defects, to which they themselves are not subject. But any poor person who has ever gone to jail while those with bail, private attorneys, connections, influence, and other socioeconomic advantages go free for the same offense, may see it otherwise. A two-tiered system of justice that protects one class above the other could also be analyzed as a moral defect. Wealthy men commit murder, but they do not wind up on death row. That domain, like the prisons that surround it, is the exclusive territory of poor, young men. If there is an American crime of poverty, it is this.

Last Offense

A few months after my Riverside visit to "debtors' prison," I lost my final appeal for the marijuana trial in Visalia. The court returned me to the county jail to await sentencing. The accident was four years past. I was a steadily employed, 4.0 college student, about to complete my first degree. The probation office was set to recommend probation. Unfortunately, however, a Riverside officer had written that my behavior there indicated I must have been on drugs.

No one conducted a test to verify his cavalier analysis. In fact, I'd been clean and sober for over three years. I was just crazy. I was willing to risk death before jail. But when the Visalia probation officer read the drug inference, she advocated state prison. For the tens of millions of us with arrest sheets, the slope toward reincarceration is slippery and steep. The system is sticky; it's hard to jump out. A great deal of new violence happens in response to the PTSD men suffer from incarceration. Though bad boys rarely admit it outside our councils, some would rather get shot or shoot someone else than risk rearrest.

In my early twenties it seemed that no matter how I tried to turn myself into a productive young adult I was irredeemably doomed by my adolescent past and my own personal failings. But I finally had connections of my own. Vincent Price was now an executive on the state board of the CYA. Because I was still on CYA parole he insisted the court was obliged to return me to them. He still believed in me and rescued me from adult prison. Instead, he arranged my immediate release on parole. Some would call this action "coddling." Ironically, though I thought of CYA as my nemesis for years, it became my savior in the end.

Mr. Price warned that this was the last chance. He personally stuck his neck out. He told me that if I failed it was going to be harder for other boys to get similar breaks. These admonitions went deep. Other than a one-night arrest for "stealing a ride" from the Canadian Pacific Railroad, it was my last incarceration. Partially to repay his faith in me, I went on to become a counselor for other bad boys. Like myself, once tangled up in the system, many need more than just one chance to get their lives on track. Because one man had mercy and was willing to take a risk, I now pay taxes instead of consuming them.

Some Ways to Help Boys at Risk for Gangs and Incarceration

- Open mentoring programs to stable, ex-gang members, recovered addicts, and former prisoners. Incorporate them into program planning and implementation.

- Respect gang leaders' power to influence their con-
  stituencies for good or ill. Host community councils
  where gang conflicts can regularly be addressed.

- Build secure, small-scale, community-based juvenile
  facilities instead of expanding state institutions far
  from family and local resources or sending boys to adult
  prisons.

- Make free job training, like high school, available to all
  young men who seek it.

- Favor collaboration between agencies over competition
  for funds and clients, integrated services for youth over
  one-shot programs, community-based leadership over
  top-down management, and local program designs over
  standardized approaches.

As the leader of an Outward Bound program notes, there are
three ways of trying to the win the young: persuasion, coercion, and
attraction. "You can preach at them, that is a hook without a worm.
You can say 'you must volunteer,' that is of the devil. And you can
tell them, 'you are needed,' that appeal hardly ever fails."

By my early twenties, I was well primed for a life of criminality.
I had been referred to state prison twice and then diverted. I didn't
want to find out what would happen the third time. In the next
chapter I'll discuss what does happen to those less fortunate boys
who take that next step in their criminal careers.

The youth corrections system and the gangs that generate the
bulk of their inmates merge to create the Sixth Pathway to Prison.
If we do not catch bad boys here and help them change course, as
I was helped, the majority will career along this path till they slam
against the iron gates. Since the early 1970s, when I began to turn
my life around, *California's prison population has increased seven-fold*.
One could infer that the chances I had for diversion away from
prison have become increasingly rare for other angry young men.

8

The American Gulag

When I got here a guard told me, "Boy, if you want to survive here you better get your self a big tough boyfriend right away."
—Malcolm, 17, starting 15 years in adult prison
   for small quantity drug sales

Once a bad boy arrives at adult prison, our hope for his future dims. Imprisonment signals that we failed to forge crossroads along the prison highway that could have turned him toward community. I was blessed to stumble onto such a fork in the road, so my personal narrative pauses here, allowing the facts and other voices from adult prisons to speak for themselves. For some boys, there was little any of us could have done to divert them from prison. But most young men who pass those gates embody our collective failures in parenting, education, counseling, community support, legislation, economic policy, and juvenile justice.

Federal Judge James Doyle wrote in 1971: "I am persuaded that the institution of prison probably must end. In many respects it is as intolerable within the United States as was the institution of slavery, equally brutalizing to all involved, equally toxic to the social system, equally subversive of the brotherhood of man, even more costly by some standards, and probably less rational." When Judge Doyle wrote this, the U.S. rate of incarceration was about 100 per

100,000. The following year, the National Council on Crime and Delinquency declared, "no new penal institutions should be built before alternatives to incarceration are fully achieved." In 1973, the National Advisory Commission's Task Force on Corrections called our penal system a "shocking failure." They advised a ten-year moratorium on prison building and the closing of juvenile institutions. Since then, justice experts have repeatedly called for moratoriums to no avail.

Today's national incarceration rate is up over 500 percent since those alarms started sounding in the early 1970s.

- Two million Americans are behind bars.

- Four million more are on probation or parole.

- Eight to ten million pass through jails each year.

- One in thirty-three Americans are in prison, jail, probation, or parole, a statistic that includes one in 400 women, one in twenty men, and one in four black men.

All these citizens have been affected by the culture of our bizarre nation behind bars. Some remain a few days, others a lifetime. In a nation that prizes openness, prisons remain a largely obscured world with closed borders. In California, reporters are no longer even allowed to interview prisoners. If we care at all about bad boys, however, it is important to know what awaits them where the six roads (on which we can still reach them) all terminate. And since there is a widespread push to sentence more boys to adult prisons, I believe we should all be aware of exactly in what sort of situation they are being placed.

Interviews I've conducted with former inmates reveal that most experience worse conditions and significantly more violence than did I during my few years of youth incarceration. At first, I was reluctant to even tell my own tale in this book. My own experiences feel inconsequential compared with those of many others. But as one African-American colleague, a program director and ex-prisoner, once told me, "When you've got the podium, Aaron, you tell our story too." OK, brother, I will.

Cruel and Usual Punishments

The rate at which we are imprisoning our citizens—645 of 100,000—exceeds that of every other nation but Russia (at 685). By comparison, the pre-apartheid rate for South Africa was 368 per 100,000; China's is 342; Singapore, 229; and Turkey, 55. The incarceration rates of other Western democracies are all fractions of our own: England and Wales, 120 per 100,000; Spain, 115; Italy, 85; Netherlands, 75; and Scandinavia, 60. Japan's rate (36) is merely 6 percent of ours. The rates of most former USSR satellite countries even pale against our own: Romania, 200; Poland, 160; Czech Republic, 165; and Hungary, 135.

As our rates skyrocketed, most European rates rose only slightly or even fell during the last few decades. Sentence length for most nonviolent crime is considerably longer here. Criminologist Eliot Currie, whose excellent work helps guide this chapter, notes that the severity of Texas's "punitive scale" ranks it between United Arab Emirates and Nigeria.

When Alexander Solzhenitzyn wrote the *Gulag Archipelago*, he inflamed the passions of many and brought the plight of injustice against the Soviet people to the world stage. He said, "If only it were so simple! If only there were evil people somewhere insidiously committing evil deeds, and it were necessary only to separate them from the rest of us and destroy them. But the line dividing good and evil cuts through the heart of every human being." Today, I believe an American Gulag is proliferating, filled with angry young men from our urban wastelands. The world will also judge the true measure of our humanity by how we now deal with this similar crisis.

In late 1998, Amnesty International shocked the world by announcing a year-long campaign against prisoner abuse in the United

States, the first such action against a Western nation. They issued a detailed report documenting the many ways that "people incarcerated in [U.S.] prisons are very often the victims of very serious human rights violations."

Many state prisons are filled to 150 percent of capacity. California, with the largest system in the nation, is operating at 185 percent, with some facilities at 220. Double celling is routine, thus reducing the fifty-four square feet allotted a prisoner in a nine by six foot cell to twenty-seven square feet. I invite the reader to mark out this much space on the floor with tape and read this chapter within it. Not surprisingly, tensions are mounting in many prisons. They are unsafe for guards and inmates, both of whom suffer high assault rates. The pressured atmosphere seriously affects prisoners' mental health and undermines the few rehabilitative programs that still exist.

In response to prison violence, California created a new, ultra-secure, "super maximum" prison at Pelican Bay, set in the woods, far from human habitations. Here are sent male "problem prisoners" who use drugs, drink "pruno" (prison-made alcohol), possess other contraband, fight, join gangs, make weapons, threaten, assault or disobey guards, destroy property, or break other rules.

Some criminal justice circles dub this trend toward increasing severity "Marionization," after the "supermax" prison in Marion, Pennsylvania, where Mafia boss Don Gotti is incarcerated. But most prisoners are not Mafia Dons, convicted of multiple murders, who must be totally isolated to inhibit their capacity to instigate new crimes from or in prison.

Pelican Bay represents a new breed of Orwellian, mechanized, computerized, highly isolative, stark, behavior modification institutions where most of the facility is beneath the ground and direct sunlight never shines. Various investigative reports document torture, beatings, and scalding, resulting in serious injury further aggravated by denial of basic medical care. Supermax sensory deprivation, similar to other nations' brainwashing of prisoners of war and political prisoners, has driven some inmates into severe mental illness. Amnesty International finds this factor alone a blatant violation of international prisoners' human rights.

In 1995 a U.S. federal court found "a pattern of needless and officially sanctioned brutality" at Pelican Bay. Guards were rarely disciplined for excessive force and covered up abuses with false or inadequate reports. In 1996 a United Nations torture expert reported "cruel, inhuman, and degrading treatment" there and at other U.S. supermaximum sites.

According to a series of 1998–1999 investigative reports, guards at Corcoran state penitentiary staged "gladiator competitions" between rival gang members. They then shot them to break up the fights—fifty inmates between 1989 and 1995 alone. Some were merely bystanders, hit by bullets that missed intended targets. State oversight investigators claimed that the prison guards, their union, and state officials covered up allegations of brutality with a correction officer's "code of silence." A subsequent investigation found the majority of shootings "unjustified."

Why Is Prison Growth Exploding Only in America?

One reason we imprison more men than the rest of the world is that we can afford to. A tremendous amount of money is at stake in our national commitment to large-scale incarceration. America spends over $40 billion a year managing current prisoners. We annually pour billions more into prison construction, county jail administration, judicial systems, law enforcement, and the probation, parole, and social service agencies needed to deal with released prisoners. Some analysts aggregate these costs at $100 billion. As spending on prisons steadily rose over recent decades, job-training funds plummeted, and the rate of higher education spending was also stunted.

California built twenty-one prisons and one university from 1984 to 1994. According to various studies by the Sentencing Project and the National Justice Institute, in that same period the state added over 25,000 corrections employees and eliminated 8,000 from higher education. In 1984 the higher education budget was two and one-half times that of corrections; by 1994 both budgets were equal. One result of this shift from education to incarceration is that five times as many African-American young men are now in California prisons as are in public higher education. Similar reports are emerging from various states as they pause to conduct an analysis of their prison-education trade-offs.

The Sentencing Project notes that from 1991 to 1998, Maryland spent $147 million more on incarceration and $29 million less on higher education. Funding for Washington, D.C.'s, corrections system increased 312 percent from 1977 to 1993, compared with 82 percent for its university. Our nation's capital now has more residents in jail than enrolled in its public university.

Nationally, in 1995, more was spent building prisons than universities for the first time in U.S. history. Prison construction increased by $926 million (to $2.6 billion) while university construction dropped $945 million (to $2.5 billion). In 1999 nothing indicates any reversals in this classrooms-to-cellblocks exchange.

Given the degree of the problem, there is little definitive research on the social politics driving our dramatic prison expansion. Criminologist Franklin Zimring, whose research makes valuable contributions to this chapter, observes that the "scale" of our prison system "has long been ignored both by political scientists and by criminologists specializing in corrections." He observes that no one has really established guidelines for an upper limit to the size of a prison system for a free society.

From the end of World War II through the 1950s the U.S. rate of imprisonment showed little change. In the 1960s, it actually decreased. In the early 1970s, however, subsequent to the antiwar movement and other baby-boomer challenges to the established order, new legislation significantly increased the strength of the criminal justice net, and a war against a generation of young men began in earnest. Our prison population began its relentless ascent to today's previously unimaginable level.

Contrary to conventional wisdom, studies by the Department of Justice indicate no definitive relationship between crime rates and incarceration rates. Incarceration rates are, however, somewhat linked to fluctuations in the total numbers of young men. The larger the ratio young men represent in our population at any given time, the more appear in prison. Various studies also indicate some parallel links between crime and the ebb and flow of young male employment rates.

Changing governmental policies that correlate with prison expansion include

- The criminalization of broader classes of behavior

- Mandatory minimum sentencing and the curtailment of judicial discretion

- The lengthening of sentences and reduction of parole

- Greater scrutiny of parolees, particularly through drug-testing

- Increased allocation of funds for prisons over prevention, treatment, and diversion

- The war on drugs

A number of social forces also drive prison expansion:

- A growing public thirst for vengeance, which alternatives to incarceration fail to emotionally satisfy

- A belief that only prisons can appropriately deal with lawbreakers

- Eroding faith in the viability of rehabilitation and treatment

- The voting public's growing fear of violent crime independent of its actual rise and fall

- Racism and poverty

- The widening gap between the rich and the poor

- A growing cultural bias against boys and young men, particularly those of color

In 1995 U.S. Attorney General Janet Reno said, "If we keep sending people to prison at the rate we're sending them, we're going to have a tremendous shortfall with moneys necessary to open the prisons and then operate them." What is more important, our failure to respond adequately to this crisis is undermining our status as a civilized culture: It is a stain on our national soul.

California supports one of the largest prison systems in the world, now one of the state's largest industries. California's $4 billion annual correction's budget exceeds that of the entire federal prison system. In an era when legislators slashed funding for education and social welfare—from the late 1980s to late 1990s—spending on prisons became the fastest growing part of the budget.

Despite these facts, lawmakers continue proposing ever-longer prison terms for offenders. As the number of prisoners tripled over the last decade alone, rehabilitation incentives such as sentence reductions for good behavior, education, and drug and alcohol recovery programs were systematically dismantled. Some say, "As goes California so goes the nation." At least half the states have emulated this trend of reduced vocational training and education for prisoners. Higher education programs for prisoners fell from 350 nationwide in 1990 to only eight in 1997.

According to studies by the Prison Activist Resource Center, the top ten reasons for Californians entering prison today are

1. Possession of a controlled substance

2. Possession of a controlled substance for sale

3. Robbery

4. Sale of a controlled substance

5. Second-degree burglary

6. Assault with a deadly weapon

7. Driving under the influence

8. First-degree burglary

9. Petty theft with a prior conviction

10. Vehicle theft

The crimes heralded by officials peddling prisons to a fearful citizenry—murder, rape, child sexual abuse, armed robbery, and kidnapping—are absent from the top ten. In a reverse parallel of trends, as crime rates dropped during the mid- to late 1990s, the rate of crime stories in the media steadily increased, outstripping all other news categories by far. "If it bleeds it leads" is the ratings-competition banner of today's news media. The media are thus highly complicit in generating the disproportional degree of fear that is driving prison expansions.

Of course, crime is still high in America. We have a legitimate right to be afraid. In a curious reversal of crime indexes, however, those who fear crime the most—older white women—live in the safest areas, on average, and are the least likely to become victims. Those who complain about crime the least—young, low-income males—live in the most dangerous neighborhoods and represent the majority of crime victims.

Politicians know that it is safer to court the first group. They vote. The voter registration of young ethnic minority males, however, is so low that some jury pools lack any young minority men, even where their "peers" represent the majority being judged. In the 1998 elections, one out of seven adult African-American males (1.4 million) were denied the right to vote or sit on juries, due to prior felony convictions. In some communities and several states, 25 to 33 percent of African-American men are now disenfranchised by this covert repeal of the Thirteenth Amendment.

We are the only industrial democracy to disenfranchise massive numbers of citizens from the electorate. This fundamental right is only denied by other industrial democracies in cases of treason or other direct threats against the democratic process. In South Africa, for example, all prisoners have the right to vote. Disenfranchisement practices, like sentencing guidelines, vary widely from state to state. So some citizens regain their right to vote in time; many, however, lose that unique herald of democracy for life. All together, four million Americans—one out of forty-eight eligible voters, or one in thirty registered voters—have lost their right to vote. Some elections are lost or won by these margins. When one of three men in some communities are subjected to this invisible gerrymandering, their constituency is even more severely undercut. This is not the vision of American democracy I learned in school. Nor does this practice encourage the marginalized to ever embrace or work within the system.

Buying and Selling Bad Boys on Wall Street

Despite a steady decline in violent crime during the increased employment of the mid-to-late 1990s, "build 'em and fill 'em" prison policies continued unabated. In fact, for some, prisons enhanced that prosperity. The privatization of the American prison system grew in response to an incarceration crisis, not a crime crisis. As prison building sapped more fiscal resources from the states, some corporations sensed opportunities. Several mounted vigorous campaigns to take this problem off government's hands—at a price.

As the incarceration juggernaut gained speed, savvy businessmen promised the government to save money while building cleaner, safer, more efficient prisons for inmates rapidly outgrowing existing facilities. Investors gathered capital. They created networks of construction companies, materials and product suppliers, and other private subcontractors. These new collaboratives were then able to provide every aspect of prison construction and management from guard uniforms and food services to razor wire and stun guns.

One of the first and largest conglomerates of this kind is Wackenhut Corporation, founded by a former FBI employee who was subsequently joined by others formerly employed by justice, law enforcement, corrections, and intelligence agencies. They entered the prison business in 1987. By 1992, Wackenhut, traded on the New York Stock Exchange as WAK, had annual revenues of $630 million. By 1999 they grossed over $1 billion, operating forty-seven facilities with 32,000 beds. Transportation contracts, health care services, and prison construction create additional earnings.

Wackenhut describes itself as "A Proven Company at the Dawn of a New Era" and a company with "A Big Heart." One of the ways they display their generosity is by offering to fully finance the facilities they build. Instead of governments floating revenue bonds to a public wary of exploding prison costs, this approach keeps prison building expenses off the public books. Government then contracts with the companies that own the prisons to send them prisoners and pay for them per capita.

Any way one looks at the "New Era" being heralded, it is also about profits. Its raw material resource is primarily poor young men. Bad boys are big business. With state-guaranteed payments, young three-strikes inmates—40,000 in California alone since three-strikes began in 1994—are worth as much as $1 million apiece in gross revenue.

Corrections Corporation of America is another major player in the lucrative, private-prison industry with seventy-seven facilities and 63,000 beds. Share values soared from $50 million to $3.5 billion between 1987 and 1997 when *Fortune* magazine listed CCA as one of "America's 100 fastest-growing companies." *The Cabot Market Letter* advises potential investors that a private prison is like "a hotel that's always at 100 percent occupancy."

Prison Realty Trust, traded as PZN, took over CCA in 1997. They offer investors significant tax advantages for investing in prisons. With approximately $4 billion in total market capitalization, they became the world's largest private owners of prisons and jails, the fifth largest prison system in America. Their literature states: "Prison Realty Trust was formed to capitalize on the opportunities created by the growing trend toward privatization in the corrections industry, including the increased demand for private correctional and detention facilities."

Various states are also privatizing prisoner health care systems and charging fees to prisoners. Idaho Department of Corrections defends the practice, believing inmate's "frivolous" doctor visits will drop 20 to 40 percent. Some managed care providers, which receive annual lump sums per prisoner, can keep any balance at year's end. This could create a climate that encourages cost-cutting medical neglect.

Numerous specialty businesses are also reaping record profits from prison privatization and expansion. For just one example, the earnings of some companies making electronic devices to monitor prisoners and parolees quadrupled in the later half of the 1990s. Computerized remote monitoring devices have been around a few years now. The latest wrinkle in electronic monitoring is a global positioning system that determines the exact coordinates of a subject anywhere on the planet. A monitoring computer raises an alarm if the person strays from a designated area. These new technologies could someday become viable *alternatives* to incarceration. When they are instead used *in addition* to prison expansion, however, the implications evoke visions of an Orwellian society.

With private prisons growing at four times the rate of government prisons, experts estimate they will double again in five years. One private prison lobbyist states, "There is no insurmountable legal obstacle to *total privatization of prison operation.* Government should set punishments for felons and let the private sector supply prisons." Should penal policy, however, be mandated by private stockholders with a vested interest in prison expansion?

Private prisons match the government's failures. Private prisons do not rehabilitate. If anything, their profit-motivated, cost-cutting measures—ranging from larger prisons with less staff to reduced programs, services, and quality of care—contribute more to criminal behavior than they cure. They are as violent, with similar rates of escape and prisoner abuse, as state facilities.

In 1998 Missouri officials sought to relieve overcrowding by sending prisoners to recently privatized Texas jails. As caught on videotape, guards welcomed the new inmates, mostly young minority men, by forcing them to crawl on their stomachs as they prodded the unresisting, prone men with stun guns. They released an attack dog, allowing it to repeatedly tear at one man's leg as he lay writhing in pain, but otherwise unresisting, on the floor. The shrill screaming of the terrified prisoners literally made my hair stand on end.

Corporations cannot save us from the incarceration crisis. Ironically, most analysts concur that these companies, with annual raises in their management contracts, do not even save the public money in the long run. In any case, tying justice policies to private, economic self-interests is a slippery slope for a democratic society to tread.

A Plantation by Any Other Name

Jumping on the capital-driven bandwagon, a spokesman for the National Center for Policy Analysis spoke to the House Judiciary Committee's Subcommittee on Crime in 1998. He said, "It's time to make wardens marketers of prison labor rather than the uncompetitive producers of shoddy prison-made goods." A 1995 report from the same center states, "Today, prison inmates are a huge drain on taxpayers, despite the millions of available hours of healthy, *prime-age* [my emphasis] labor they represent."

Fruitful work reduces recidivism. We know that. Therefore, any legitimate job-training skills offered prisoners are to be prized. Employment is a major crime deterrent. Cash flow to prisoners aids them in accumulating savings prior to release, supporting their families, and paying restitution to victims and government—all good things. Good jobs with good training, fair wages, and safe working conditions create opportunities for young men to gain the skills needed to get off the prison road.

Although prison work initiatives are potentially beneficial, we must also examine possible motives of self-interest behind the utilization of "prime-aged" prison labor. After all, regardless of any benefits gained by society, prisons, or prisoners, prison work is essentially slave labor.

Work not in accord with free labor practices is unfair and exploitive. It undercuts businesses that must conform to free workers' rights. Unions thus oppose most private enterprise use of prison labor. But if prison enterprises began competing fairly with the free market, the employment opportunities afforded prisoners could be welcomed by all concerned.

To my sensibilities, turning prisoners' labor into a commodity that can be bought and sold to private industries is morally repugnant. It smacks of slavery, when human beings were once bought and sold in the public square. In fact, today's prisoners share a number of elements in common with the slaves of America's history.

- They are disproportionately young minority males.

- They are not free to choose their work or improve work conditions.

- They are frequently abused and have few of the workplace hazard protections afforded free workers.

- They are coerced to labor.

- They are rarely compensated fairly for their labor, nor do they accrue benefits such as unemployment insurance, Social Security, health insurance, or retirement.

- Their "owners" (the state, corporation, or private contractor) profit from their labor.

- They are denied most rights afforded free men, including free speech, free association, and the right to vote.

- Most are kept undereducated and undertrained, thus diminishing their potential to succeed when freed.

- They are often demeaned and degraded as inferior to free men, even subhuman.

- They are not counted in justice statistics as victims of rape and violence or most census categories such as unemployment.

On this last point, criminologist Franklin Zimring notes that if our two million prisoners were counted among the unemployed, official jobless rates would jump significantly, thereby skewing our analysis of the real state of the nation's economic health.

The last time America suffered any similar sudden rise in incarceration was just after the Civil War. Prisons were not an integral part of the American landscape until the abolition of slavery doubled the free population of nineteenth-century America. The Thirteenth Amendment, however, created a deliberate loophole. It abolished slavery and involuntary servitude "except as a punishment for crime."

Subsequent to Emancipation, alarmed whites subjected former slaves to a host of new laws that returned them to the unpaid labor force. Slave Codes were rewritten as the so-called "Black Codes" that criminalized activities otherwise legal for whites. These prohibitions for African Americans, North and South, included loitering, curfew, association with other former slaves or Indians, and rights of assembly, even in church. My wife's African-Methodist Episcopal Church was secretly founded in a barn then to avoid such sanctions.

Former slaves were not allowed to carry a stick, much less a weapon, unless they could prove necessity for a cane. "Pig laws" in Mississippi made the theft of a chicken or pig, or anything else worth $10, a felony punishable by five years of hard labor. Today, $10 of crack buys the same sentence, seemingly making the economics of racism inflation-proof.

A huge prison system soon replaced the plantation system. Thousands of freed slaves were promptly sent to prison. As the new pool of "prime-age" male labor increased, the prison farm replaced the slave plantation. And in many ways, it was the same old thing. Prison farms had segregation, forced labor, neglect, abuse, torture, and the casual murder of prisoners. White overseers controlled black prisoners. Convicts were "leased" to private contractors to build railroads, mine rock, iron, and coal, cut down trees, and hew timbers. Plantation owners kept right on using them to clear land, drain swamps, and grow cotton.

Contractors paid fees to the state and agreed to house the prisoners at their own expense. Like private prisons today, the degree of such care directly affected their profits. In essence, slavery was nationalized. The government made it illegal, took it away from private industry, and then, particularly in the former slave states, reinstated it in prisons. In Mississippi, Parchman prison farm was established for the sole purpose of growing cotton with convict labor on 20,000 acres of undeveloped land. The largest state prison farm still operating today was built on 18,000 acres of a former slave plantation in Louisiana—Angola Prison.

Although African Americans are only about one-eighth of the general population, they represent almost half of our prisoners. Franklin Zimring notes this is four times the incarceration rate for Black Africans during apartheid South Africa and eight times the rate for European Americans in the U.S. today. In 1997, for every 100,000 U.S. residents there were 3,098 black males, 1,278 Hispanic males, and 370 white males in prison.

Angola Prison's 5,000 inmates serve the longest sentences in the nation. Louisiana has the nation's toughest sentencing laws and third highest incarceration rate (672). Eighty percent of Angola's prisoners will die there. Like the slave plantation that preceded it, most of the men are African Americans. Burl Cain, the warden, admits that today, "It's like a plantation of days gone by . . . when the slaves were brought here from Angola, Africa."

In many rural areas, prisons are a major economic force in communities where good jobs are hard to find. A female guard at Angola says, "We're all guaranteed a job here, we have good job security." So do the prisoners. Awakened at 5:00 A.M., they are sent to the farm. Everyone works. Angola is a multimillion-dollar enterprise. It is the only "community" in America where young African-American men have full employment. They earn four cents an hour for their labor in the fields. The best jobs pay twenty cents an hour.

For every three prisoners, one free prison worker earns more per hour than a prisoner does per week. Two hundred prison worker families raise their kids inside the main gates of Angola Prison. They call it the "safest town in America." But for the men behind the walls it's been known as the most dangerous and bloody U.S. prison over its 100-year history.

In 1998, settlement was reached in a 1971 lawsuit brought by inmates to force changes at Angola. The suit claimed that guards regularly beat prisoners, ignored rapes and stabbings, allowed food to be infested, and let serious medical problems go untreated. In 1973, the annual rate of murdered prisoners was one in 125. That's roughly 100 times the national homicide rate. As a result of the twenty-seven-year-old lawsuit finally being addressed, the murder rate dropped about 90 percent when the prison came under U.S. District Court oversight.

Prisons' Impact on Public Health

Historically, prisons did little to protect the physical or mental health of their wards. One hundred years ago the death rate among convicts in Mississippi exceeded 10 percent each year. According to race relations historian David M. Oshinsky, who wrote about Parchman farm in *Worse Than Slavery*, "Not a single leased convict [of that era] ever lived long enough to serve a sentence of ten years or more." Warden Bradberry, former head of the Missouri State Penitentiary, reportedly claimed: "I guess I have whipped more men than any man alive."

Mortality rates have improved over the years, due to advocates for humane prison conditions in whose footsteps I now try to follow. But many inhumane conditions persist that do nothing to aid rehabilitation or protect the public. For example, in 1995, more than 600 Arizona State prisoners were handcuffed outdoors for four days. They were left to defecate in their clothes. Many suffered serious sunburn, heat exhaustion, and dehydration. Dehumanizing abuse endangers us all. Prisons release understandably angry young men daily from depraved environments directly onto the streets where we all go about our daily lives.

Animal rights protesters are highly vocal in their repudiation of product testing on live animals. Curiously, however, no similar widespread protests were lodged on behalf of the tens of thousands of American inmates used for decades as live human test subjects for perfume, soap, and cosmetics. Medical ethicists finally curtailed most such prison experiments in the last decade.

But skin testing of cosmetics was the least of the travesty. According to Allen M. Hornblum in his 1998 book, *Acres of Skin*, various chemical warfare agents were tested on numerous prisoners for the U.S. Army. One such "incapacitating agent," identified only as "EA 3167," reportedly left prisoners with hallucinations and disorientation for weeks. LSD was also widely tested in American and Canadian prisons, according to official reports that surfaced in 1998. Canada also conducted clinical trials of numerous pharmaceuticals, kept prisoners in darkened solitary cells for sensory deprivation research, and subjected them to powerful electric shocks in other experiments.

In the decades between the 1950s and the 1980s, *massive* doses of dioxin (of Agent Orange fame) were tested on American prisoners for Dow Chemical. Today many health professionals believe prior dioxin exposure is creating health problems, even birth defects, in Vietnam era combatants from both sides of the war. Experiments with radioactive isotopes were also conducted on prisoners. During the 1960s, 85 percent of all new pharmaceuticals were first tested on inmates before release to the public.

The American prison system created a human subject experimental lab unparalleled since medical experiments were conducted on the inmates of Nazi death camps. Feminist activists rightly protested in the 1970s that a disproportionate number of medical studies were based upon males. There was no similar outcry in the culture, however, that most of those male subjects were impoverished, coerced young prisoners.

The lasting effects of these practices go untreated today. No one has followed up with these prisoners, who are no longer young. Subsequent to Hornblum's publication, many former prisoners came forth to report severe, lasting disabilities from these experiments. What will surface in a few decades about today's practices? It is difficult, except in retrospect, for researchers to get an accurate picture of what goes on inside prison. The situation begs for professional, independent oversight.

What we do know is that a variety of diseases are being cultured in the virulent crucible of today's overcrowded prisons. Decades of dedicated efforts by public health officials nearly wiped out tuberculosis in our country by 1985. Now, its rate is steadily increasing in prisons as the overall health of the average prisoner declines. This decline is largely due to deplorable health services for prisoners, aggravated by their higher incidence of poverty, drug addiction, homelessness, malnutrition, and AIDS before incarceration. The rate of tuberculosis infection in California prisoners is about one in 1,000—over 100 times that of the general population.

No one really knows how many men are being infected with AIDS through the rampant frequency of forcible anal rape, coerced prostitution, and "consensual" homosexual sex. Throughout the nation, little is being done to prevent the spread of AIDS to prisoners. Prison officials refuse to provide condoms. Needle sharing goes on among numerous inmate addicts, but officials provide no access to disinfecting chemicals like bleach. By various independent studies and estimates, HIV-positive men represent from 3 to 7 percent of 1999 prison populations. Even official reports, which often understate the true picture behind bars, document a prison AIDS rate fifteen times that of the general population.

Since most prisoners return to society, their undertreated illnesses also diminish public health. In 1998, epidemiologists noticed AIDS rates for black women were rising significantly faster than for other groups. One etiological theory emerging is that many black men with undiagnosed, untreated, or improperly treated AIDS in prison, are passing it along to women when released.

San Francisco Supervisor Mark Leno charges, "The California Department of Corrections routinely administers incomplete and inconsistent HIV drug treatment to its HIV-infected inmates. Furthermore, released inmates are given inadequate medication and almost no follow-up treatment . . . [Therefore] the City is left to deal with a heightened AIDS crisis featuring a more resilient virus." Hepatitis C is also epidemic in our prisons, infecting the majority of inmates, in many institutions, with an incurable and potentially fatal disease.

Sentenced to Rape

Of all the indignities I encountered in the criminal justice system, none was greater than the constant threat of rape. Although my sentence to state prison was miraculously circumvented, I have counseled those who were not so fortunate. Perhaps some survivor guilt keeps me attending to this topic today. Rape in prison is the most hideous and psychologically damaging experience most young men ever endure.

Incarcerated boys and young men are often repeatedly raped, over a period of years, by multiple perpetrators. Many are then subjected to deeper humiliation when their rapists force them to serve as "wives," personal slaves, or prostitutes. After all, a lot of rapists wind up in prison. Once behind bars, some do not care which sex they rape next. Many men feel disempowered, even emasculated, by incarceration. From a psychological perspective, sexually dominating another man can be seen as a perverse attempt to restore some sense of power and control to their lives.

Millions of dollars today are earmarked to help female rape victims—as it should be. And much more is needed. We have no rape crisis centers and few trained counselors, however, to deal with the posttraumatic stress disorders of males sexually victimized in the penal system. Just like battle-shocked war veterans of decades past, we turn these traumatized young men on to the streets with no opportunity to heal the after-effects of protracted sexual torture—if such insults to the male psyche can ever even be completely healed.

Now that male rape is coming out of the closet, Veterans Administration hospitals note that increasing numbers of men are seeking services at sexual trauma clinics. Many, raped on the battlefields of Vietnam, are just now coming forward. V.A. sexual trauma counselor Karyl Drake notes that many spent decades feeling ashamed and afraid to talk about their experiences, yet they are just as traumatized as the women she counsels.

Few studies have been conducted on this class of victims. Criminal justice officials are not motivated to conduct studies that might put them in a bad light. Most of my colleagues in psychology and sociology also show little concern, as evidenced by the paucity of research on this issue. Anecdotal accounts by former prisoners, however, indicate that prison rape is not incidental or anomalous. Rather, former prisoners report that it is rampant and frequently ignored or even sanctioned by authorities.

What published research exists indicates that roughly one in five male prisoners is forced to submit to sexual assault at some time during his incarceration. One survey of a New York youth prison found 71 percent of the white male inmates there had been sexually assaulted.

A Philadelphia district attorney found that even short-term male prisoners are frequently raped. Of the 2,000 sexual assaults documented during his two-year study of the Philadelphia jail, only twenty-six were reported to police. A Chicago official also reports gang rapes to be "routine occurrences at Cook County jail." They certainly were in Cook County Juvenile Hall when I lived there.

Just as the statutory rape of boys is underenforced, most justice arenas do not even regard male-on-male sexual assault as rape. The FBI's *Crime Classification Manual* does not even mention male prisoner rape among its dozen plus rape categories. Nor is it included in "hate crime" categories, even though many of these assaults are motivated by racial and gender issues that clearly fit the criteria.

The study with the lowest published estimate of prisoner rape puts the victimization rate at 10 percent of male inmates. Another prison sex survey puts it at 14 percent, though its authors note, "Our study is likely underreporting certain types of sexual behavior such as sexual coercion and assault." The highest published study reports a rate of male prisoner rape of 28 percent. These surveys imply that 190,000 to over 500,000 of current male prisoners have been sexually assaulted. This does not include the inestimable percentages of the eight to ten million males that annually pass through jails or the cumulative number of rape survivors released from prisons in past years.

Like others of the few deeply concerned about this issue, Steven Donaldson was gang-raped in jail. His assault occurred after he was arrested for participating at a Quaker "pray-in" at the White House. He subsequently founded *Stop Prisoner Rape*. Based upon this organization's compilation of reports and studies over the last two decades, and accounting for the fact that many victims are *frequently and repeatedly assaulted*, their analysis indicates that as many as 50,000 male prisoners are raped each day.

Regardless of the exact numbers, even the most conservative estimates indicate that the aggregate number of male sexual assault survivors in our culture today is staggering. At the very least, these reports beg for an independent, nationwide survey on prisoner sexual assault. Besides the blatant dearth of public concern and professional research on the issue, male prisoner rape has other characteristics that make it distinct from most female rape:

- Gang rape is much more common.

- Victims are also more likely to be subjected to multiple rapes by multiple perpetrators over time.

- Weapons are more likely to be used.

- Both the rate and degree of injury are higher.

- There are few protections or recourses to escape rape, prevent future rapes, or hold perpetrators accountable.

- There are systematic attempts to convert the gender status of young heterosexual males into ersatz women.

- Other prisoners force some victims into prostitution.

- Rape is far more likely to be interracial.

- Men who are young, low-level offenders, nonviolent, first timers, physically smaller, middle-class, white, mentally ill, without gang membership, or known homosexuals dominate victim profiles.

- The demand for sex always exceeds the supply.

In his chilling book about life inside Angola Prison, Wilbert Rideau writes, "A searing raced through his [the victim's] body as the hardness of one of his attackers tore roughly into his rectum. 'Shake back, bitch!' a voice urged. 'Give him a wiggle!' His rapist expressed delight as his body flinched and quivered from the burning cigarettes being applied to his side by other inmates gleefully watching. . . . Even after the last penis was pulled out of his abused and bleeding body, he still cried, overwhelmed by the knowledge that it was not over, that this was only the beginning of a nightmare that would only end with violence, death, or release from prison."

In another account, former legislator William Laite reports that when he was held in a Texas jail, five men taunted him with threats of rape. But when a seventeen-year-old boy was admitted that day they instead "knocked the boy out and were on him like jackals, ripping the coveralls off his limp body. Then as I watched in frozen fascination and horror, they sexually assaulted him, brutally and savagely like starving animals after a raw piece of meat. Then I knew what they meant about giving me 'six or eight inches.'" To his lasting astonishment, guards showed little concern.

Prisons do have protective lockups for prisoners at risk. But as Chapter Five discussed, the psychological torture of solitary confinement is, to many prisoners, worse than the "freedom" of life in the general population. It's not a great choice. Rape victims in jail are no longer considered "men." As sexual commodities they command no respect. In many prisons prostitution is an integral part of the sexual culture and the underground economy. Prostitutes' services are bought, sold, and traded by their "pimps" for a variety of goods and services, including illegal drugs.

Many adult prisoners previously spent most of their adolescence behind bars. Incarcerated at the peak of their sexual development, they have never known intimate relations outside jail's rape-submission sexual culture. This issue needs professional attention when they are released, but it is seldom addressed by helping professionals.

Administrative Rape

An investigation into a New Mexico prison riot found that guards regularly threatened to put new inmates in cells with known rapists unless they agreed to become "snitches" (informants). At Corcoran Prison, guards reportedly directed a known rapist called the "Booty Bandit" to rape specific prisoners as punishment for defying them. One would hope that if officials were aware of prison rape they would use their law enforcement powers to protect victims. Instead, the threat of rape is used as an attempt to deter youth crime, coerce confessions from suspects, and control inmates' behavior. Perhaps this is why most officials do little to prevent it.

Feminism has taught us that the threat of rape or sexual coercion should not be used to force behavioral change in anyone. Rape is what young men fear most about prison; some men fear it more than being shot by police, life imprisonment, or the death penalty. Sexual assault can destroy a person's identity, humanity, and feeling of self-worth. When I asked the director of our local rape crisis center whether they offered any programs for the boys and men returning to our community from locked institutions, she was incredulous. Although by law, gender discrimination is not allowed by their federal, state, and local grant sources, she said, "We have no intention of ever offering services to men."

Out of a traumatized psyche, victimized men are more likely to use alcohol and drugs to assuage their emotional pain. Forensic psychology indicates some may also be at risk for becoming rapists themselves. Some posttrauma victims unconsciously regard their perpetrator as a model of power. They may mimic him in a pathological attempt to somehow reclaim their own lost personal power, a psychological complex known as the Stockholm Syndrome. The destruction of humanity and self-esteem that happens in the wake of sexual assault can taunt victims to symbolically regain their stolen "manhood" by sexually overpowering someone else.

Therefore, if for no other reason, rape assault protection in prison and rape survivor treatment for male victims should be implemented to protect women. None of this entire discussion, however, is meant to excuse the sexual assault of women in any way, minimize the severity of trauma they suffer from rape, or mitigate the penalties their rapists should incur.

The sexual assault of young men in prison is one of many arenas in which cultural expectations for men to be emotionally tougher than women are inimical to their recovery when victimization occurs. Male sexual violence survivors are more likely to be seen as having failed as men because they did not protect themselves. For prison rape survivors, the shape of their wound remains invisible to the world.

One survey of male prisoners who reported being "pressured or forced to have sexual contact" with other inmates noted serious, lasting bad effects, including depression, flashbacks, nightmares, and suicidal thoughts. These symptoms are classic heralds of PTSD as often seen in combat veterans. Few victims told prison staff about the incidents, saying they feared retaliation, ridicule, and "protective custody" (solitary confinement).

Male prison rape victims are not counted by U.S. Department of Justice statistics or even by most victim advocacy centers. So no funds or programs are earmarked for their care. I do not know of a clinical training program in America that offers a seminar on this topic, much less a program on treating this class of victims. Those of us who care about reducing violence and, in particular, want to reduce sexual assaults, would do well to conduct research on how to better serve this population.

Any clinician should suspect a history of sexual assault when working with previously incarcerated male clients, especially if they meet the victim profiles noted in the preceding list. If we do not ask, they will not tell. And even if asked, it will often be a slow and painful process for most men to open up and heal these wounds. Peer groups, similar to those successful with combat veterans, are also effective in treating this population. The rape trauma guidelines for treating females largely apply to males. However, with men there are several distinct differences in treatment.

Men are often more resistant to discussing victimization of any kind than women. In my experience this is most true concerning sexual assault. Not only has their humanity, like that of women, been assaulted, but for many their gender identity has also been attacked. Being of the same sex as the victimizer can make the victim feel confusion or shame about his own sexuality. Whether the survivor is straight or gay, exploring issues of manhood, masculinity, return to previous sexual norms, and validation that it is normal for men to feel deeply disturbed about their rape experiences can all help.

A Real New Era

Any way we view them, prisons, as we know them, cry out for a new vision. For the most part they do little to deter crime, rehabilitate criminals, increase community health, or enhance the economy (except for a few). They do, however, frequently harden "soft" criminals, victimize nonviolent offenders, increase inmates' violent tendencies, reduce the quality of public health, drain the economy, destroy families, and even dismember some entire communities. And yet we are compelled to keep confined the minority of men in prison today who represent a genuine threat to public safety. Perhaps by diverting the majority of incarcerated men who do not belong there, an unburdened penal system could use its resources more effectively to help the violent men who provoked our cultural imagination to create prisons in the first place.

I hope that the penal system of a new era will emphasize ways to reduce criminal behavior instead of contributing to its proliferation. Just as many factors combine to create an ecological crisis, the conditions fueling prison expansion are complex. Prisons, next to poverty, which Mahatma Gandhi called "the deadliest form of violence," are the most virulent pollutants of our social ecology today.

No one leader can solve the problem alone. It is going to take a major effort on many fronts to save our culture from the social time bomb our violence-, mental illness-, and disease-breeding prisons represent. To return our society to a true democracy that upholds international standards of human rights will require real changes in the justice system. We will also have to rethink our approaches to young men at risk in general.

As anyone who has experienced it knows, loss of freedom alone is dramatic punishment enough for most crimes. This is especially true in America, where we hold freedom as sacred. Few but the most institutionalized or sociopathic do not grieve the loss of freedom of movement; choice of information, entertainment, food, and clothing; friends and loved ones; making love; driving a car; watching a sunset; having a glass of wine; or any of the myriad experiences we free people often take for granted. The loss of freedom is horrific. For those undeterred by that specter alone, it is likely no other threat will do more.

Torture, rape, degradation, unjustified shootings, sensory deprivation, electric shock, chemical sprays, injurious and deadly physical restraints, beatings, medical experiments, medical neglect, forced prostitution, slave labor, and the abuse of psychiatric medications do nothing to rehabilitate prisoners or ensure public safety. Even men who have perpetrated horrible crimes should have the opportunity to make productive use of their time. With over one million fathers now in prison their children needlessly suffer from reduced contact and support. At least prisoners should be enabled to make whatever restitution they can to their victims and their families. If not for humanity's sake, we should change the system simply to protect the rest of us when prisoners are released. In addition to the following, many of the suggestions made for incarcerated youth in previous chapters are equally applicable for adults in prison.

Some Ways to Reduce Penal Harm and Support Rehabilitation

- Enact a national moratorium on new prison building and expansion. Once stabilized, begin strategic planning to start "safe and smart" reductions of prison populations.

- When drug use is the primary reason for reincarceration of a parolee, offer treatment as an alternative.

- Build smaller, secure, community-based prisons where inmates can get rehabilitative support from family, local volunteers, educational institutions, and community agencies. Use these facilities to educate, job-train, treat addiction, and enhance the mental health of prisoners.

- Create independent oversight teams that include Occupational Safety and Health inspectors, physicians, and mental health professionals to monitor prison conditions. Empower them to force compliance with humane international standards of safety, sanitation, human rights, and decency.

- Hold guards personally accountable for actions, in excess of their duties, that would otherwise be crimes against free persons.

- Eliminate the standard of lesser care for prisoners. Create instead zero-tolerance standards for psychological and physical torture, medical and mental health neglect, deliberate degradation, and sexual assault.

- Do not allow adolescents to be imprisoned with adults, and separate predatory prisoners from those more vulnerable to predation.

- Graduate the staged reentry of prisoners to the community with lowered security levels, restoration of privileges, furloughs to the outside, increased contact with family and helping professionals, and transfer to halfway houses. Following full release, provide intensive after-care for at least six months.

The costs for the above are secondary to the human and fiscal cost of recidivism. Most prisoners were already marginalized prior to incarceration. Upon release from prison few are better equipped to succeed; most are worse off. Freedom can be startling, disorienting, and overwhelming. Ex-prisoners need these supports to make the transition to productive citizenry.

Since most prisoners re-offend and return, prison and parole themselves create the Seventh Road to Prison. Or perhaps we should just think of it more as a circular driveway. In prison, bad boys grow up to become bad men. There are limits to what the average reader can do to help angry young men behind bars. A lot of fierce politicking lies ahead. But there is a great deal that any one of us can do to help bad boys become good men once they are released, as the next chapter will reveal.

9

From Bad Boys to Good Men

*Today, my little boy is the most important person in
the world. Everything I do to keep my life straight is
for him.*
—Richard, 18, ex-gang member,
   at a training class for young fathers

Although I was diverted from prison, at eighteen I was still
semihomeless, impoverished, uneducated, and without significant job skills or familial support. That year I joined the Student's
International Meditation Society (SIMS) at UCLA, a few blocks
from where I had been hospitalized three years earlier. There, I became acquainted with people who mirrored a new set of ideals for
my life.

Due, in part, to my new associations, my identity again shifted
from the underground drug culture to a drug-free, health-oriented
community. I learned relaxation techniques that helped me deal
with stress in new ways. The meditation groups also lent direction
for an awakening curiosity about higher states of consciousness.
Before meditating, I suffered migraines. After a one-month meditation retreat, however, I never had another. I also lost the craving
for drugs. Slowly, through meditation and yoga practice, a more
even capacity of mind developed that allowed me to sustain long
periods of academic study and productive work. I read a range of

religious literature from the Bible to the Upanishads, earned a simple living making candles, and tried to live a moral life.

One day, after waking from a dream about Mt. Shasta, I hitchhiked up to Northern California on impulse and headed up the mountain. Two days later I reached the summit. As I gazed 360 degrees around me, all the other mountains were far below. I was soaring. Free, finally free. Some dark despair, collected from jail's stagnant chasms, eased its grip on my psyche. Glaciers in frozen cascades glistened below with diamonds in the sun. I suddenly realized that beauty was both freeing and free. In later years, while leading other angry young men on wilderness rites of passage, I witnessed some similar epiphanies.

I spent that night in a rock shelter under a blizzard of stars. Wisps of mist drifted through the glacial moraine, creating a wonderland of incomparable splendor. The next day I slid half the way down on a glacier and hiked back to Panther Meadows. A sparkling, clear, elf-sized stream winds through that meadow. The spring is sacred to the local Native Americans who, today, still regularly perform ceremonies there. I drank the water and felt utterly renewed. In later years, I was fortunate to attend a number of sacred rituals conducted by Native American elders. Those experiences continued to deepen the healing I felt that day.

Spiritual Renewal

For many former bad boys who are good men today, some sort of spiritual experience turned the direction of their lives. So in paying full homage to the power of good parenting, education, counseling, real justice, community support, and economic opportunity, it would be remiss not to acknowledge the power of a spiritual community or teacher to restore a boy's moral compass to working order.

Intrinsic to bad-boy psychology is a deep emotional constraint. Sociopathy is the extreme of this complex, in which a boy's "emotional body" has been buried alive, extinguishing whatever spark of moral conscience he may have once had. Most bad boys find themselves in hostile territory. Homes on fire, mean streets, pathologizing schools, undertrained counselors, indifferent communities, police scrutiny, gang violence, punitive institutions, jails, and prisons are all bars of their emotional prisons. Their thirst for freedom, release, and transcendence is deep.

One way the hunger for relief can actualize itself is through an unconscious but profound longing for death. Not unlike a powerful sex drive, there also exists a death drive that can take over someone's life. Hard drugs, shoot-outs, suicide attempts, criminal activity, poverty, poor medical care, self-abuse, and incarceration all contribute to giving bad boys premature death rates comparable to soldiers in combat. Suicide by police confrontation—in which desperate men intentionally force officers to shoot them—is now so frequent that forensic psychologists identify it as a syndrome.

There are many routes out of the ghettos that leak into our hearts and take residence in our souls. An impoverished interior life recapitulates the landscape of a bankrupt environment inside a bad boy's heart and mind. When our inner life is deadened, we project deadness into the world. Coming alive in our emotional and spiritual life, however, is one antidote to despair.

Mixing public policy with spirituality is a tightrope walk. But we might want to walk it anyway. In my case, meditation and yoga created a deeply expanded experience during my late teens and early twenties. I previously only felt similar relief with drugs. In retrospect, I realized that meditation was naturally providing the stress reduction, feeling of peace, and expansion of consciousness I had sought through drugs. So I stuck with it. For several years I voluntarily reentered a cell of sorts. For every day in jail as a child, I spent another licking my wounds in various monasteries as a young adult.

For me, study with yoga masters, rituals with Native American elders, and intensive work with my psychology professors all helped me come alive. For others, Jesus, Allah, Buddha, Krishna, Jehovah, Kuan Yin, or simply the Great Spirit aids them on their road to recovery. By the time they get to prison, however, many young men have rejected the conventional religions that failed to reach them earlier.

For many years, Bo Lozoff, author of *We're All Doing Time*, has directed the Prison Ashram Project. He observes that prisons are quite similar to monasteries and thus has taught meditation and other spiritual practices to prisoners all over the nation to help them make better use of their "penitent" time. Twelve-Step recovery groups also provide a cost-free, supportive, spiritually oriented community to help young men live without substance abuse. Paths to wholeness abound.

For some bad boys, what finally grabs them is their specific culture's pride and spirit. For example, urban "hip-hop" music is finding its way into church gospel music, much to the chagrin of conservative congregations. But when their generation's culture is honored, more young people feel drawn into the church because they feel more accepted than rejected for their unique expression of spirit.

The specter of racism cannot be excluded as a causal influence in minority boys becoming the majority of citizens in our penal system. Spiritual leaders, like the Muslims who have helped thousands of African-American men in jail, are often highly effective. As a cultural Jew who directs programs, I could protest by saying, "They are anti-Semitic, we won't fund them." But if someone can move a bad boy into life, they deserve support and respect. Even if we don't agree with all their politics or practices, we still can't quantify the value of simply moving in *any* positive direction. In a war, one takes the most expedient action and sorts out the collateral damage later. We can't afford to get lost in methodological or theological debates while so many boys are still getting chewed up in the crossfire.

If it's away from illiteracy, poverty, guns, crime, hard drugs, hopelessness, and violence, and closer to spirit, in whatever form it is understood, it's most likely right. Even if we don't fully understand the method, let's look at the results. If the method turns out imperfect, a boy and his guides can always change course. Any move toward hope, however, undercuts the entropic pull of the past and increases developmental momentum toward life.

Is the Mark of Cain Indelible?

At age nineteen, a successful jazz musician, Emil Richards, who was active in SIMS, took me in to live with his family. We meditated together every day. Emil introduced me to avant-garde composer Harry Partch, who employed me as a dancer, singer, and recording artist in his performing troupe. Again, a caring older man renewed my life by regarding me as artist and seeker instead of freak and outlaw. I thought if good people were willing to help me, perhaps I was also good. For the first time in my adolescence, I identified more with productive citizens than outlaws and dope fiends.

I lived with Emil and his family for several months until I saved enough money to rent a $50-a-month studio apartment. I frequently attended meditation retreats and enrolled in LA City College full time. But the ongoing marijuana trials in Visalia and the threat of a state prison sentence cast a shadow of futility across every attempt to improve my life. I graduated, at age twenty-one, with an Associated Arts degree and my first stable relationship, with Satri. Even so, it remained difficult to get decent employment. I was still a felon. I couldn't work for the federal government, state, or city, hold positions requiring licensure, be bonded, or get security clearance. Most employers, even small business owners, refused to hire me when I told the truth.

For many young men a felony conviction is tantamount to a lifetime sentence to poverty. In this computer age, it stays on record, forever. Every time police officers run a record check for a traffic stop they learn they have a felon. They are thus likely to more extensively investigate him. This makes felons subject to more scrutiny, search, and arrest than the average citizen who may also be in violation of some law. This is particularly true for young minority males for whom merely committing DWB (driving while black-brown) assures dramatically higher stop and search rates than Caucasian drivers in many communities. For many, "once at risk, always at risk" becomes their emblem.

Even if a man goes through the exhaustive procedure to get his youth offender records sealed, as I did, a permanent record of the order remains. This can look worse to others speculating about it than the original record does. In addition, state license applications, job applications, and security investigations often ask: "Have you *ever* been arrested for *anything* other than a traffic ticket?" This burden remains, regardless of records being sealed or expunged, completion of probation or parole, or any other sentence reversal, including being found innocent. Our legal system does not appear to display a strong belief that people can redeem lives once in error. Debunking this myth of Cain has been a primary hope in writing this book.

Anyone with a criminal record, from a teenage joy ride to a simple drug possession, faces a lifelong paradox: (1) Lie and risk being subsequently fired, losing a hard-won professional license, being charged with false representation, or having parole violated if found out; or (2) tell the truth and risk never being hired. Today tens of millions of American men bear such identifying pockmarks from bouts with our incarceration epidemic.

As a young man, after dozens of employers turned me away, I finally started lying on job applications. This violated my parole and my own emerging moral code against lying—a code I believed supported my recovery and restoration to citizenry. Ironically, by lying, I got work as a security guard. Without any background check or training, the company issued me a uniform and a loaded .38 revolver. They put me on twelve-hour, weekend-night shifts at a munitions plant that made amphibious landing vehicles for the Navy. In the afternoons and evenings I worked in a downtown liquor store. Satri taught me how to drive an old Dodge we bought for $100, the first time anyone let me near a car. This allowed me to get a third job delivering packages during the day. Satri waitressed and managed the home front. In this way, we eventually saved enough money to leave LA.

We sold all our stuff, bought a battered VW bus with a wooden bumper, and headed north to attend Sonoma State University. We never returned to LA. That year, I was honorably discharged from CYA when my parole period ended. For the first time in twelve years I was no longer a "ward of the state." The only time I've been behind bars since is as a counselor who, at the end of the day, goes home to a place where he is loved and safe.

Work as a boat builder and house carpenter largely financed our early years at the university. Those professions didn't care about the past. Some group home employers actually thought my history was more an asset than a liability. But unfortunately, much as I enjoyed that work, it paid little. I always needed other jobs on the side. During my junior year I secured a half-time position as assistant to the public defender.

After a year of service to the county, however, the sheriff one day ran a check on everyone who entered the jail. I was fired the next day from a job I did well and had come to love. The chief public defender was mentoring me toward a career in law. But he said the sheriff had tied his hands and that no former inmate could interact with prisoners, my primary duty. He expressed genuine regret, wrote a letter of reference, and wished me good luck.

I had burnt the jailhouse tattoo off my forearm long ago but could not erase the indelible stigma of my record. Losing my job because of an arrest five years past made me feel immutably tainted. It defeated my burgeoning aspirations to become a juvenile rights attorney. Eventually, my marijuana possession conviction was expunged under the Youth Offender's Act. This "fresh start" opportunity for juvenile offenders is now under attack from incarceration advocates nationwide.

I was then able to acquire a state license to sell real estate. A real estate broker, Paul Schafer, mentored me in the business. He was on the board of the treatment center, where I was a counselor for several years, and saw me working hard to get my life together. Paul let me work under his wing throughout my undergraduate years. That opportunity made it possible for Satri and I to lift ourselves out of poverty.

Paul's integrity in business impressed me. He set a standard that I previously did not know existed in commerce. I learned that trustworthiness was the greatest asset in anyone's portfolio. As my business mentor, he taught principles quite different from those "get it any way you can" ones I learned on the street. Many times I saw him walk away from short-term gains that required some unethical behavior. But many other brokers we did business with thought nothing of a little misrepresentation to make a sale. They came and went, however, while Paul's business flourished. The ethical principles I learned there guided me well in adult life.

Satri and I used the housing portions of our student loans to make a down payment on a funky cabin. With materials recycled from flood-damaged houses, we fixed it up. This allowed us to rent rooms to students, refinance the cabin, and buy another "fixer" to rehabilitate. In this way, we parlayed our small loans into enough money to finance our master's degrees.

I am disturbed by the current move to deny loans to students with drug convictions. Had that been true in my era, I'd probably be dead. Without education there is little hope for those of us who've gotten off to rough starts. What are legislators thinking when they further isolate, undercut, and marginalize the already disenfranchised? Do they hope they will just disappear? That isn't what happens. Without work and education we become the nightmares that fill the nation's headlines. Retribution is trumping rehabilitation at almost every turn.

Gradual Transformation Creates Lasting Change

During my university years, through social osmosis I gradually acquired a new identity. Though some make miraculous turns on a dime, most personal growth happens incrementally. An acorn becomes a sapling. It adds annual rings of growth. Then, bang, there's an oak with acorns of its own to give back to the earth.

I cut my hair, dropped my street-imbued speech, and lost the jailhouse walk. The diffident mask that dominated my emotional display began to soften. I worked hard, consistently making the dean's list. Beyond my own efforts, I was also fortunate to be white. This made class migration easier than it is for many men of color with similar backgrounds.

I tried to blend with these educated people from a world quite foreign to me. They had different behavioral protocols than those of my previous life. After a time, I gradually changed into a new person with new values, eventually gaining acceptance in my profession, academia, corporate arenas, and even some upper-class social circles.

Having sort of faked it till I made it, I no longer embraced the outlaw persona of my past. Instead, I identified with the goodness of the present and the promise of the future. Thanks, in part, to a string of student loans and the lower fees of the California University system in my era, I acquired a good education. Ultimately, I earned enough through real estate to finance more expensive doctoral and postdoctoral studies, and to repay all student loans on time.

It's taken years of education, meditation, therapy, spiritual inquiry, recovery work, and self-reflection to work through the trauma of adolescent immersion in the American Gulag. Due perhaps to my familiarity with that world, I now catch the peculiar scent in our cultural wind of boys being hurled into its fiery, Baal-like chasm. I cannot seem to just simply enjoy my good fortune now without reaching back to boys still burning in chains.

Even with the many blessings I've received, my history touches me at times, as though that mark of Cain might still be visible in certain lights. I retain an irrational insecurity that my past precludes my right to belong to the good world I now inhabit. By the same token, however, few middle-class professionals gain cultural literacy with the "underclass" sufficient to engage angry young men positively and gain the respect needed to provoke positive change. To some degree, our collective failures with bad boys reflect a precipitous cultural gap in both directions.

Helping "marked" men become good men generally requires a thoughtful, well-developed, committed plan of action; leaders who work well with challenging clients; wide access to resources;

and vigorous support from community institutions. One such program, for prisoners returning to community from the Louisiana state prison system, embodies the best of these elements. Project Return is currently the most successful prison after-care program in the nation.

The Road to Return

My friend and colleague Dr. Robert E. Roberts (Bob) directed a literacy and leadership program for male inmates in a Louisiana state prison for several years. Not a trained literacy teacher, however, he approached the program by first building a mutually supportive, respectful, and cooperative learning community. One prison feature rarely depicted in film is the constant, chaotic din of inmates yelling, metal clanging, and other ambient noise. It is not an atmosphere conducive to study. Bob had the men play drums in synchrony, talk about their lives, and engage in other "community-building" activities that had nothing to do with reading. One effect of this approach was that violence and conflict between the inmates decreased. A better atmosphere for learning emerged.

Inmate literacy then leaped. Their reading ability rose, on average, a whole grade level every seven weeks. This far exceeds literacy experts' predictions, who view this population as somewhat intractable. Bob was so effective in supporting cooperation between inmates, however, that some staff started to regard him as a threat to status quo, an "inmate advocate."

Guards found various ways to punish inmates who chose educational and vocational training over labor in the fields and factories. The brutal slave labor system in Louisiana pays for half that state's corrections budget. Prisoners were therefore offered no incentives to learn new skills. Eventually, prison staff sabotaged the project. Grateful inmates warned Bob that his safety and even his freedom were at risk. He decided to continue his work, but outside the hostile atmosphere of prison. In response to what he learned and the horrors he witnessed behind bars, he established Project Return at Tulane University in 1993.

Today, Bob, a European-American, and his team of mostly African-American men concentrate their efforts on those *most* at risk for returning to prison. They admit released prisoners regardless of the number or nature of their past crimes. Many other programs "load" their studies with select subjects likely to produce superior results and thus keep grant money flowing. Project Return tries instead to rescue those most likely to fail, even admitting those with active substance abuse and other problems that would prevent admission to most other programs.

Roughly two-thirds of Project Return graduates are employed today, most at decent jobs with living wages and good benefits. Their success rate far outstrips the Department of Labor's projected outcomes for this population. Project Return's recidivism rate is under 10 percent, the lowest in the nation. This compares to about 75 percent for the rest of the state and 65 percent nationwide.

How does Project Return maximize the employability and rehabilitation of serious felons? Through a pragmatic, holistic approach to rebuilding lives in a respectful manner, including self-development in an intensive, supervised community; communication, conflict resolution, interpersonal, and financial skills development; job placement assistance; literacy and GED courses; substance abuse treatment; stress and anger management; family preservation activities; and more.

Working together as a self-help community offers ex-offenders opportunities to address the serious emotional challenges often common to bad boys and angry young men. For most, this is the first forum in which they have been able to critically examine their lives while receiving the appropriate support needed to change course.

The project leaders focus on developing the *whole* person. Over 90 percent of their clients initially lack even a high school diploma. Most are functionally illiterate. A key to their success is in treating the men with respect and honoring their human dignity—like a doctor with a patient—regardless of their past. Enhancing an ex-prisoner's ability to read, write, communicate, and solve problems gives most a good shot at self-sufficiency for the first time in their lives. Few blow a *real* second chance once given. With realistic, visible hope for a good life, few men will risk actions that could return them to prison.

A few years back I spent a week with Bob and several men from Project Return. One of them was Nelson Marks, an African-American man central to the project's success. Nelson, a recovering drug addict, spent twelve years in Angola Prison for robbery. After going through Bob's prison program he then assisted for three years. After receiving a pardon from the governor he was released and became cofounder and associate director of Project Return. Bob says, "A lot of these men look at me, see this educated white boy, and think 'What can I learn from him, what does he know about me?' But when Nelson speaks, they listen with respect. And then they are also willing to learn from me. But I could not reach them without him."

Of his prison experience Nelson Marks says,

> I never saw people getting stabbed or hung outside of prison. Prison is where I witnessed my first murder. And to this day, I have never witnessed that outside of prison. One of the most horrible experiences of prison for me was witnessing another man get raped, crying out. And that is a horrible, horrible sound to hear. And that sound is like hearing a man scream who has been set afire. I have heard that too. The smell of burning flesh is engraved on my soul. So, there was a lot of fear with being in there, and just by the grace of God I made it. I will always be scarred by that experience, but I don't think I was as scarred as many people I know.

Since his release from prison Nelson has dedicated his life to helping others heal those wounds and prepare for success in their lives.

Part of Project Return's strength, like most effective approaches to reaching bad boys, is its capacity to first rehabilitate and then integrate ex-offenders into leadership roles in the treatment program. Technically skilled, well-meaning, but otherwise culturally illiterate professionals can be impotent in this setting. Sometimes it is more expedient to train culturally astute bad boys as counselors than it is to teach professionals how to build therapeutic alliances with this population. Two-thirds of Project Return's staff are former offenders who have been through the program.

As for practicality, Project Return is a bargain. It saves the state millions every year. Additionally, it averts the incalculable costs of new crimes by the hundreds of men they have turned around. To send one person through Project Return costs $3,800 plus $1,200 in stipends paid to participants. This compares to a conservative Justice Department estimate of $100,000 for pursuit, arrest, arraignment, trial, and detainment for re-offenders.

Yet for every fifty men who enter the ninety-day program, 350 on the waiting list are turned away for lack of funds and facilities. But no one is turned away from prison. We just build more. There they deepen associations with the criminal class, only to be released into the general population in most cases. Instead of funding more "crime schools" we could create more Project Returns, reduce crime, save money, and restore hope. With law enforcement, criminal justice, and prison spending reaching the $100 billion mark, we clearly have sufficient resources to reduce the need for prisons.

If this were the only program spotlighted here, it alone would be a sufficient model to offer real hope for reducing violence and deescalating the incarceration onslaught. Fortunately, Dr. Roberts will publish a book in the foreseeable future. Till then, the 1997 documentary Road To Return is a must-see for anyone curious about this approach. During its screening at the Simon Wiesenthal Center for Tolerance, a standing ovation from the sold-out audience filled the room with electric hope.

Community Coalitions

Integrated after-care, with a spectrum of services implemented by bad boy–sensitive providers, is essential to break the chain of criminality and despair in the previously incarcerated. Confinement in our penal institutions is so traumatic that without help, few of us stay harm-free or secure productive independence from the system. Integrated precare for those at risk for incarceration is equally imperative to divert young men from the prison road. Ultimately, we need Project Return at one end of the prison road and Project Never Went Away In the First Place at the other.

Our aforementioned Fatherhood Coalition collaborates with the Pro-Youth Coalition—formed to reduce local gang violence—and with many other local agencies. Our community was one of eleven in the nation to receive a multimillion dollar grant from the National Violence Prevention Funding Collaborative.

Why was Santa Barbara County so lucky? Largely because of our ability for diverse agencies, organizations, and concerned citizens to work in collaboration to develop local, effective, long-term solutions to intractable social problems. The approach of this public-private funding group is to support multidisciplinary services that respectfully include *all* voices at the table.

One of our local tactics is to focus on strengthening the families of bad boys. The Fatherhood Coalition's contribution to this effort is in supporting positive father involvement at every level of family life. Regardless of any program the community can offer, the family remains the fundamental institution for supporting and directing the lives of children. If a family is not strong, it is difficult for their children to be so.

Babatunde Folayemi, a friend, neighbor, and member of my wife's church, is executive director of the Pro-Youth Coalition. He's presided over several gang summits and has incorporated ex-gang members into the Coalition's outreach and mentoring programs. Babatunde says, "Every young man has potential beyond belief. But unless people get beyond their prejudices, their comfort zones, and their fears, all that energy is going to be wasted. As a community, the most important gift we can give our youth is security, faith, and the confidence to dream."

Babatunde successfully lobbies our judges to sentence bad boys to his programs instead of jail. One summer he gathered all the local boys caught for graffiti "tagging" and raised a grant to pay them to paint our bus benches instead of going to jail. For troubled young men, one of the most important conduits through which to receive that "gift" is a caring and capable adult. Many need just one to guide their journey toward responsible manhood and let them know they have a unique gift to give the world.

At one of many conferences we've organized, we gathered about 100, mostly Latino, men into a circle. Starting with the youngest, an eleven-year-old inmate, the circle graduated by age around the room to the oldest, a seventy-seven-year-old community leader. The thirty or so young men present were mostly inmates, under guard, as in our Boys to Men conference described in Chapter Five.

Next came teachers, mentors, fathers, social workers, probation officers, a policeman, and a judge. The remainder were community leaders and elders, grandfathers, and retired men with time to give. We opened a dialogue between these three generational groups. Each shared what it was they wanted of the other or just did not understand about them. For a long time, however, the young men remained silent.

Finally, the judge said, "Look, I sent a lot of these young men to jail. Maybe I should just leave the room. My presence is probably inhibiting them." But we urged him to stay. I asked all the older men to just sit silent and give the younger ones a clear space. Several minutes passed. Then the youngest one, Ricardo, stood saying, "I just feel so angry all the time I can hardly think straight."

After Ricardo broke the ice and the boys saw the adults paying rapt attention to him, most started talking about their own lives. The older men listened carefully, occasionally asking questions or offering advice. Some offered assistance to the boys once they got out of lockup. Though informal and supported only by our friends in the community and a small state grant, the first threads of a mentoring community were born. At the end of the day the judge was visibly moved by the emotional, honest, and seemingly fruitful dialogue between the groups. He said that in the future, whenever possible, he would sentence young men to our program instead of jail.

Boys to Men Programs

In Wisconsin, I periodically consult to another collaborative of men administrating Boys to Men programs statewide. Dr. Roger Williams, at the University of Wisconsin, conceived and founded this network. He is a friend and colleague who has brought me in to teach several male psychology seminars over the years. In 1997, a Johnson Foundation grant allowed program leaders and agency directors to meet for several days. The racially, culturally, and economically diverse group came from inner-city, rural, institutional, grass roots, governmental, and academic settings.

These leaders ran the spectrum of the state's organizations: 100 Black Men, Project Pride, La Causa, the Red Cliff Tribe, and Wisconsin Public Health, to name just a few. To our mutual surprise, we shared many observations that cut across our cultural, racial, regional, or theoretical differences. The obstacles we all face in gaining support for Boys to Men programs and the common elements that create success inform the central themes of this book.

Previous to our gathering, most of these men were working in isolation. They had little knowledge of the others' approaches to helping young men at risk. That feeling of isolation, of working alone in the trenches wondering whether the calvary will ever arrive, was shared by all. The creation of a statewide network provided new support for these warriors fighting for the young male souls of their communities.

We created a collaborative potentially more able to seek funds, document success, share information, and collaborate on projects. As distinct from many conferences I've attended, the emphasis here was more on leadership than case management. Someone has to tend the nuts and bolts of programs: that's essential. But someone must also have the courage, confidence, and commitment to *lead* young men for real and lasting change to take place. Training programs for helping professionals emphasize the former but often lack either the initiative or ability to develop the latter.

One of the most profound moments in our summit was a shared observation from the men that they felt less racial tension and more fellowship than in any other previous mixed race gathering. For many, it was also the only time they had ever been in a professional all-male meeting. Most were a male minority in their agencies; one was the only man working with twenty-nine female social workers. Many expressed feeling less defensive discussing their work in our context.

Turf battles for funds, program recognition, and personal agendas, common to gatherings of diverse agencies, were largely absent. Instead, our common concern about the war against young men transcended our differences. If program leaders cannot create community among themselves, how will bad boys learn to live well in a diverse world? Professional gatherings such as this, however, remain largely self-initiated, unfunded, and even perceived, in some professional circles, as politically incorrect.

"Rights" of Passage

In our culture today various events mark adolescent boys' passage into adulthood. For some it is high school graduation. For others, it's the independence and responsibility that comes with a car. Some feel that their first sexual experience or parenthood marks that transition. Joining the army, going off to college, getting a full time job, leaving home, all, for some, make them feel they have crossed over into an adult world. Among bad boys it is often "making their bones": committing their first crime on behalf of the gang. But none of these events properly conveys a transition from boyhood into a mature and responsible adult role.

The boy-to-man transition isn't clearly marked in our culture. A close approximation is the image of a Boy Scout collecting enough merit badges to become an Eagle Scout. It is something hard won and highly admired by the adults of that particular community. It gives boys an opportunity to demonstrate their talent, courage, strength, discipline, integrity, and usefulness to that community— albeit, in this case, only heterosexual and god-fearing ones.

In a Jewish boy's Bar Mitzvah, his rite of passage is witnessed in front of his entire family and community. The Rabbi declares, "Today you are a man." Thousands of years ago, that was probably true for a thirteen-year-old boy. Confirmation for Christian boys has a similar function in that community. Today, however, the day after a boy's Bar Mitzvah, his mother still tells him to wash behind his ears and take out the trash. The confirmed boy still has to go to school the next day. The Boy Scout only gets admired at Scout gatherings. Moreover, most bad boys are excluded from all of the above. I was behind bars on Bar Mitzvah day.

If a boy cannot win the respect of his elders he will turn toward other means to attempt commanding the attention he craves. Gang initiation has more in common with the traditional rites of passage than most institutional approaches today. When a boy is initiated into a gang he gets a new family. He becomes part of a powerful tribe. His "jumping in" ceremony confirms his courage. He is thus regarded, by the other homies, as a man. The fact that gangs expose him to danger feels inconsequential compared to the emotional power membership conveys.

For thousands of boys today, incarceration marks their transition to adulthood. Prison tattoos mark, to all "initiates" who can read them, their induction into the American Gulag fraternity. So we are left with a challenge. On one hand, most contemporary attempts to draw angry young men across the bridge to responsible manhood are too irrelevant to our time and their culture to be effective. The powerful initiation approaches of gangs, on the other hand, suck boys into a vortex of belonging. Whether in South Chicago or Littleton,

Colorado, they create affiliation inside the group by setting boys against the world.

According to anthropologists such as David Gilmore, author of *The Making of Manhood*, most young males do not experience manhood as an intrinsic birthright. It must be won. Most important, young men need to know they are seen, valued, needed, and that they have an important role to play that is essential to society. Boys to Men programs try to develop ways to create meaningful male-affiliation groups, with mature male leadership, dedicated to the common good of the community.

Most bad boys have highly developed bullshit detectors. They instinctively know if we are "jiving" them or if we are for real. If powerful and successful men steadily admire, support, and praise them as they try to become better men, many claim that role instead of looting their environment for survival or simply as the outward expression of anger, frustration, and despair. Successful leaders of Boys to Men programs have learned a few things from their experiences. To be effective with angry young men we could

- Meet them as they are instead of how we think they should be.

- Accentuate the positive in anything they do.

- Treat them with respect, knowing the sum of a young man's worth is greater than his worst act.

- Talk directly, simply, openly, and honestly. Be authentic about ourselves. Never make promises that cannot be kept or guarantee outcomes that cannot be assured.

- Create diverse collaboratives to provide services integrated with *all* local organizations and concerned citizens. Meet frequently, share information, settle agency turf disputes, and join forces to weave a strong net of support for boys at risk.

- Use recovered, even recovering, bad boys in visible

positions of leadership wherever possible. Learn their
language and incorporate their input into every aspect
of program design and implementation.

- Assure that the specific culture being served is well
  represented among the program leaders.

- Assume that attempts to change boys from a stance of
  victim advocacy or moral superiority are likely to fail.

- Provide real, *sustainable* opportunities for economic
  advancement and social inclusion. When boys fail,
  help them learn. Give them another chance. They
  want to win.

- Ask *them* to teach *us* about bad-boy life and what they
  really want. Then strategize together about how to
  effectively claim their dreams. In our work we call
  this "coming up alongside" instead of "coming down"
  on them.

Finding a boy's real passion and then building a custom boy-to-
man plan with him, on that foundation, is a golden key to success.
For example, some years ago I worked with a twelve-year-old,
Matthew, who often drew horrific pictures during class. His teachers were upset. The school psychologist thought the highly detailed
images of monsters, vampires, bizarre weapons, and bloody wounds
were indicative of a deeply disturbed mind. Yes, Matthew was disturbed, that's why he was in a residential treatment center. But
instead of trying to change his mode of expression, we arranged for
him to get art lessons from a teacher not offended or frightened by
his imagery. That is, we encouraged him to go more deeply into his
peculiar passion rather than suppress it.

Today, Matt makes a much better living than I do, illustrating
science fiction book covers, posters, and comic books. And he's
stayed out of the criminal justice system all these years. Matt had a
gift to give; a drive to create that was weird but, for him, it was the
ticket out of the American Gulag.

Voices of the Ancestors

In many indigenous cultures a boy takes a "vision quest" as his rite of passage. Native American teachers taught me that on this quest a boy's physical stamina, emotional strength, and spiritual comprehension are all put to the test. Through accomplishing the tasks set before him, he has an opportunity to demonstrate his capability to assume both the rights and responsibilities of adulthood.

In the African-American community, men like my close friend and colleague Akani Fletcher are dedicated to aiding the boys-to-men passage. Akani and I are in a men's group where teachers, community leaders, and program directors periodically meet to share their hopes, fears, and insights. Activists need such regular councils to avoid burnout and build capacity for greater endeavors. Collaboratives are not merely important for sharing resources; they are essential to the well-being of those who put their assets on the line for the community. The lone male hero approach is a sure recipe for exhaustion and failure.

Akani is the director of Project BEGIN and the "Rite Way." He introduces inner-city, at-risk boys to a "council" process in which they learn how to speak about what they feel, what they fear, who they are, and who they long to be. His process draws, in part, on the work of another of our group's members, Jack Zimmerman, director of the Ojai Foundation and coauthor of *The Way of Council*. For many years, Jack researched the best of indigenous cultures' and humanistic psychology's community-building, deep-listening, and conflict-resolution techniques. He put them into practice and trained facilitators for various institutions, most notably a number of urban public schools.

Akani incorporates the traditional spirit of council process with his own perspectives as a minister, twice-decorated Marine, combat veteran, father, athlete, and committed community activist from the "hood." Beyond the power of any programmatic approach, he possesses extremely high cultural literacy congruent with the population he serves. Cultural literacy, like Zen, is difficult to quantify, document, or teach. But most who lack it get eaten alive when they try to work with angry young men.

In addition to hosting regular councils, Akani also arranges physical challenges to strengthen the boys' community, courage, and commitment. For example, one day he took a group of his boys to a beachside cliff face. Although these boys grew up in South Central Los Angeles, twenty miles from the ocean, many had never been to the beach. Furthermore, not one had ever been rock climbing or engaged in any remotely similar outdoor activity.

With the help of professionals who volunteered their time and equipment, the young men learned to scale the cliffs. Their feelings of triumph were so profound that unrelated beach-goers gathered at the base of the cliff to cheer them on. They could feel the power and the passion of the moment for these boys. One pair of climbers was a boy whose brother had killed the other boy's brother. Akani said to them, "This is it man, are you going to go with the code that says, 'retaliate as soon as the opportunity comes' or are you going to help each other move along?" They chose the latter, belaying one another on the line as they took turns inching up the cliff.

Just a day on the beach, but for some of those young men the seeds of a gang truce were planted, self-esteem was born, a feeling of community emerged, and a sense that life held greater opportunity than they previously imagined. One boy said, "This is the first time in my life I did something right." Another, who had been completely mute for weeks in council meetings, spoke for the first time near the summit. "I'm scared," he cried out. But with encouragement from the group, he got up there to raise his arms in triumph above his head. Thereafter, he had a lot more to say.

Outward-bound type experiences like these, though potentially cathartic, are usually insufficient to produce lasting change alone. That takes time, follow-up, integration, and reinforcement with more success in different arenas. So Akani always follows activities with more meetings. The next time that group of boys met in council, there was a very different feeling in the room.

The shuck and jive, rebelliousness, embarrassment, withholding, and disrespect, all evident in their earlier sessions, evaporated. Now they were quiet, focused, paying rapt attention to Akani whenever he spoke. They were straight talking, even eloquent when their turn came to speak and more respectfully listened to their "brothers" as they spoke in turn.

They had shared an intense challenge together. Most boys crave intensity. Now they had a brief, but vivid, common history that contrasted with their chaotic world. Not unlike a gang, but completely unlike a gang because Akani is a man of peace leading them toward a better life. Physically, he is an imposing figure. But he wins bad boys' respect with quiet strength, visible caring, and by providing opportunities, not through force or intimidation.

The Male Involvement Project

There are many other grassroots programs and leaders across the nation doing similar work. Most operate with meager funds and facilities. They are largely staffed with volunteers and underpaid professionals. Many therefore have difficulty sustaining programs over time.

The government does not collect, evaluate, or disseminate information on the efficacy of most individually tailored, community-based programs. Nor can most programs afford the costs of scientifically rigorous self-study. I've provided statistical information wherever it exists. But many cutting-edge groups are not in the institutional funding and evaluation loop. So word of those who are catching boys falling through the cracks of our failed institutions is often anecdotal. Enthusiastic reports from community leaders, teachers, parents, probation, parole, my own observations, and the positive response from boys who go through these boys-to-men-type programs indicate that more attention is needed, at the very least.

The state of California took a chance by funding our local Male Involvement Program (MIP) for teen pregnancy prevention. Though we fully serve the state in that capacity, we also tend to other aspects of young men's lives. Our approach to the state is this: Instead of just handing out condoms, shaking a finger at sexually active young men, and saying "bad boy," threatening, or even jailing them, let us work on creating a male-mentoring community. If men whom they respect talk about responsible manhood and fatherhood while also offering visible support for their lives, boys listen. Fatherless boys in particular (the majority of those contributing to teen pregnancy) are reluctant to behave in ways that might risk severing their connection with men holding a nurturing, father-like role.

After years of mixed results in solely focusing on girls, state leaders thought they had little to lose by trying to reach young men as well. The state also now supports us in training helping professionals how to work effectively with young men. From one of the highest in the state, our local teen pregnancy rate dropped every year following the implementation of the MIP. Of course, other factors and programs may have contributed. But the state is convinced that MIP is viable and is expanding the statewide program. Each county or region is empowered to design its own program in a manner they determine most attractive to their local young men and likely to sustain their involvement. In effective treatment and human services, unlike condoms, one size does not fit all. To reach the unreachable we need the power to be creative and experimental.

Programs that meet the needs of the whole person work. Programs that just focus on one symptom or one desired outcome generally fail. Approaches that try to change angry young males through coercion, denigration, moral judgment, pathologizing, or criminalization do worse than fail; they create more harm. Supporting bad boys' transformations into good men is complex, hard, and even occasionally dangerous work. But it can be done, is being done, and will continue to be done. Funding sources, however, could put a lot more wind under the wings of those dedicated men and women who are using collaborative community approaches and get a good return on the investment.

A good place to start would be to document the success rate of various grassroots groups in turning young men away from violence and incarceration. Bad boys often respond to unconventional approaches. It is a travesty that tough-on-crime politicians claim full responsibility for the recent downturn in crime. There is *no* empirical evidence that longer prison sentences have any positive effect on crime rates. Yet advocates of these unproven, even failed tactics give no credit to the thousands of concerned citizens, repulsed by violence and poverty in their communities, who dedicate themselves to improving the quality of life where they live.

Some Ways to Help Bad Boys Become Good Men

In summary, some of the influences I've discussed in this book that helped me transform my own life were

- Access to affordable education and working hard thereafter.

- Job and financial skills acquisition that led to employment above the minimum wage.

- Introduction to meditation and other healthy practices that helped mitigate the traumatic impact of drugs and abuse on my nervous system.

- Association with "normal" people at work and school. This changed my core identity from a survival-driven affiliation with the criminal class to one defined by learning, caring, creativity, and productivity.

- The attention of older men—teachers, mentors, healers, and social servants—who believed in me and treated me with respect.

- Spiritual experiences, alone and in community, that raised hope and buoyed me against the downward pull of the past.

- Psychological work that lent insight into reasons behind my behavior, helped me become accountable for my actions, and directed me toward alternative ways of being.

- Alcohol and drug recovery through Twelve-Step programs.

- The sealing of my juvenile records, thus giving me a fresh start and allowing me to mainstream.

- The compassion and support of friends, lovers, spouses, teachers, and the miraculous kindness of strangers.

I believe these are also integral elements needed for most programs to achieve lasting results in drawing forth good men out of bad boys. This work is simple and it is complex. Many young men who lose their way need sustained services from multiple arenas before they can get on the good-man track. They also need room to fail without the specter of unredeemability looming as a consequence.

One-shot programs rarely work. Brash get-tough laws with sound-bite slogans do not breed justice. Half-hearted interventions foster more disappointment and cynicism than they cure. Every time a mentor, teacher, parent, or social servant walks away from a young man in trouble, for whatever reason, they drive another nail in his coffin. Real change usually takes time and a dedicated team.

Not all of us, however, are professionals with a mandate to help these boys. Many nonprofessionals who care also do not have the time or resources to be fully engaged activists. But there are numerous things we can all do to stop the proliferation of angry young men in our communities without being heavily involved in organizations or programs. Simply being well informed, the intent of this book, is a huge first step.

10

Honoring the Spirit of Young Men

The sum of a boy's worth is far greater than his
worst act.
—Dr. Aaron Kipnis, 1999

While a psychology undergraduate, I participated in an experiment that made me realize that, for many people, criminal behavior is just a circumstance or two away. One of my professors, Dr. Grunwald, was very interested in how the environment affected human behavior. I took several classes from him in "psycho-ecology": the relationship between environment and psychology.

After a few years, I became his graduate assistant. He conducted a number of experiments in which he put students into various survival situations. He then observed how the new circumstances changed both their individual behavior and the psychodynamics of their group. The first few years Dr. Grunwald's work focused primarily on taking entire classrooms of students into the wilderness for one to two weeks. There, after teaching them survival and group living skills, he would put them through a variety of experiences. Native Americans, who came as guest teachers, taught us how to identify, prepare, and eat native plants for food, medicine, and even mind-altering experiences. They also taught us how to build shelters and ritual sweat lodges from natural materials, and how to make fire with a wooden bow.

Many of the psychological techniques we used were the sorts of group processes popular with humanistic psychologists in the 1970s. Most of these "encounter" strategies are designed to break down the psychological barriers that can obscure the deeper truth of a person's experience and to raise their self-awareness. The trips were very intense, interesting, informative about human nature, and, for me, a great deal of fun. It was hard to believe that I was getting college credit for camping and playing psychology games. But to my surprise I learned many things of more lasting value than most professors ever taught me in a classroom.

One semester, Dr. Grunwald decided to shift environments. We took a group of thirty students into a different kind of wilderness for a week—downtown San Francisco. The guidelines for the experiment were

1. Each student could bring fifty cents and the clothes on his or her back.

2. Everyone agreed not to contact anyone they knew during the week-long trip.

3. Everyone agreed not to tell anyone they met in the city that they were part of an experiment.

The goal was simple: survive.

The Underworld Is Just a Step Away

I had often felt unsure of myself during the first few wilderness trips. Many of the other students had backpacked for years. In the city, however, I was the master of survival. This was my turf. Just as none of our wilderness guides would ever starve or freeze to death in the woods, I felt completely at home on the city streets. Finally, the lessons learned in my youth were of some practical use to my adult life. This, in accord with Frankl's "meaning" theory, took away some of the crazy-making sting of my past.

I taught the students urban survival tricks that helped us stay in food and shelter. We scrounged the fast-food diners' dumpsters at shift changes when, by law, workers have to toss out all the uneaten burgers from the previous shift. When the weather suddenly turned colder, we dove into Salvation Army depositories for warmer clothing or as a place to sleep. One night, we had an eight-course vegetarian dinner at the Hari Krishna temple. Another night we dined en masse at the rescue mission relief center. We performed street theater, sold hastily written poetry to tourists, and panhandled for money and food.

One night we sang and chanted in front of the De Young Museum, where poets Gary Snyder, Allen Ginsberg, and Phillip Whalen were giving a reading. Between the thirty of us we had enough money to buy one ticket. Similar to my experience with Vito's troop, they let us all in for free, at the poets' request, to sit on the floor in front of the sold-out seats. At the end of the reading I got up and said, "There are thirty folks here who need a place to sleep tonight. Can anyone help?" Five people came forward to offer their homes.

Even though we were never terribly hungry, I noticed a decided behavior shift in some of the students after only a few days on the street. A number of them began to steal. Even the professor stole food out of the back of a restaurant kitchen. A cook almost caught him in the act. He returned to us, triumphant—his pockets stuffed with food—after losing his pursuer in a mad dash though the subway station.

One girl, Deborah, performed oral sex for $30 in the car of a man she met on the street. She proudly shared her story with us as though she had earned some sort of merit badge. Deborah gave the money to another student, who bought some pot from a street dealer. He then rolled the pot into individual joints and sold them on the street for a profit. Another student stole boxes of empty pop bottles from behind a restaurant and took them to a market for deposit returns. Another rifled cars for change. I didn't teach them any of these things. They figured it out all on their own.

Most of my offerings were about legal ways to find food, clothing, and shelter. It's easy to live off the surplus largess lurking in almost any environment if one is trained to find it. In those days, I was vigilant to not violate even the smallest of laws, taking pride in my newfound ability to merge into the privileged ranks of the educated.

During the entire week of urban survival, not one student in that class sought legitimate work of any kind. To a person they relied on scrounging, begging, hustling, and stealing to get by. And these were mostly privileged, middle- and upper-middle-class white kids with good educations and families. Whenever someone brings a troubled young man to me these days, I try to keep the "Grunwald" experiments in mind.

Desperate situations often make people desperate in their behavior. We all want to survive. For some, that imperative feels more immediate than for others. Many of us will violate our cherished ideals or risk punishment once hungry, cold, or in danger.

Reaching Out

The crimes committed by the underclass of bad boys are frequently more situational and circumstantial than positive indicators of their inveterate criminality. This book has discussed many things parents, educators, helping professionals, concerned citizens, community leaders, and policymakers could do to help. And it has examined a number of things we could stop doing that hinder the often uneven progress of at-risk boys toward productive citizenry.

Each of the chapters spotlighted perspectives and programs I believe helpful in creating crossroads that can divert young men away from crime, violence, and prison. Underlying these arguments is a specific point of view, a paradigmatic approach to helping bad boys become good men. More than any technique, program design, or policy change, I believe the most important aspect of success with bad boys is attitude. And those in the trenches who are experiencing success on the front-line battles for the hearts and minds of young men at risk generally agree that a culturally responsive attitude is key. From a bad boy's perspective you are either cool or you are not. And if you are not cool, it is hard for them to respect anything you say.

What is cool? Being direct, courageous, at ease, authentic, egalitarian and, most of all, being unimpeachably "down" for the "homies." That means that your words come from your heart, and the actions you take demonstrate that no matter how challenging or novel your intervention may look, a bad boy can trust that every move is designed for his welfare, not his subversion. For angry young men "tude" (attitude) means a lot. Lives are lost over bad attitudes.

One principle of bad-boy culture is "Diss [disrespect] me and suffer the consequences." This bottom note in bad-boy psychology is the herald of a self-esteem so damaged that what may seem slight to many of us can be devastating to scant reserves of self-worth. Respect is magical. It is self-propagating. If we want bad boys to respect our communities we could try modeling the same respect we desire. If we want them to respect the mainstream culture we could try showing respect for at least some aspects of their subculture.

In review, some major tenets of this male-positive, humane-justice, harm-reduction ideal are

- The worth of a boy is greater than his worst act.

- Bad boys are elements of a *system*. The majority of their unsanctioned behavior is linked to preventable economic, social, familial, educational, institutional, medical, and legal issues.

- Pathologizing, criminalizing, dehumanizing, demonizing, and disenfranchising bad boys has proved ineffective as a strategy for provoking lasting positive change.

- A male-positive attitude toward bad boys utilizes compassion, responsibility, fierce challenge, cultural literacy, and social inclusion to create therapeutic alliances that can effectively provoke positive change.

- Interventions that create the least degree of harm to all are of most benefit to all.

- The powers of government are more effective and less costly when allied to attempts to restore and rehabilitate citizens instead of to punish and destroy them.

- Adults are responsible for the majority of social ills now ascribed to young men. Ignorance, not boys, is our common enemy.

- Anyone can change.

- Every bad boy has a hidden gift to bring into the world.

Grassroot Interventions

One need not be a parent, educator, therapist, law enforcer, or policymaker to significantly help boys in trouble. There are many things a concerned citizen can do to change the apocalyptic trend the incarceration juggernaut represents for our young men. Here are a few:

- Half of all legal gun sales eventually end up in the hands of outlaws. Citizens can help reduce violent crime in their neighborhoods by zoning gun shops out of the area and supporting handgun "buy back" programs. At the least, banning sales of "Saturday night specials" could keep many guns out of boys' hands. At best, responsible gun control laws could reduce access.

- The majority of domestic violence and other violent crime happen under the influence of alcohol. Community planning can eliminate liquor sales near residential neighborhoods and support wide access to recovery programs.

- Poor lighting in urban settings can encourage criminal activity. Lobby local governments to support adequate street lighting and subsidize home security lighting in troubled neighborhoods.

- Poorly maintained property, broken windows, graffiti, abandoned vehicles and buildings, trash, and vacant lots are all cuts in the social membrane that can become infected by crime. Neighborhood improvement is not just an esthetic concern. Environment has a powerful effect on bad boys' psychology. Community gardens, public art, parks, and playgrounds can help transform collections of buildings into communities.

- After-school activities hosted on and off campus give boys alternatives to gang involvement and the high degree of criminal activity generated simply out of boredom.

- Mentoring, befriending, god-parenting, or otherwise committing time and resources to just one fatherless or otherwise socially handicapped boy in your community has more power to save lives than any other social program.

- Community policing works. Work closely with cops on the beat to make their presence welcome. Incorporate them into the social and community life of the neighborhood.

- Create ongoing local forums for citizen-police dialogues on mutual aid in crime prevention and for resolution of conflicts.

- Neighborhood watch groups and regular town meetings, where *all* elements of the community are welcome, can help reweave the broken threads of the social fabric.

- When feeling safe to do so, say hello to the bad boys in your area when you pass by them. Let them know by acknowledgment of their presence that you see them as part of the community. Let them see that you are a real human being, not some anonymous, potential target.

There Are No Bad Boys

As I hope the reader has determined, I do not believe there really is such a thing as a bad boy. I am simply not wise enough to divide the world neatly into goodness and badness. The third Zen Patriarch advised that the "Great Way" belongs to those who do not make distinctions between these poles, but rather, try to hold both within a compassionate heart. Evil, if such a force truly exists, could not merely be deposited in the hearts of the poor, the young, the disadvantaged, and the disenfranchised—those easiest to confine and punish. An ancient Zen story, which I have contemplated for many years, ironically observes that the White Crane callously swallows alive the fish he catches and yet is revered as the symbol of purity. The Vulture, who does not kill, cleanses the earth of disease, stink, and rot and is regarded as the symbol of evil.

When I began writing this book, I was aware, as is any educated person today, that racism has shadowed our democracy from the early American colonies up to today. In 1999, however, Rosa Parks was invited by the president of the United States to attend the State of the Union Address in Congress instead of taking a ride in the back of a bus. We have made some progress toward actualizing the vision of America as the Land of the Free with its high ideal of equality for all. Even so, what has shocked me most during my research and continues to trouble me deeply today are the apparent racist outcomes of our educational, social, economic, legal, and justice polices. To a large degree these institutions and the people who control them create huge disparities in who is poor or rich, who receives the least or most educational opportunity, who can vote and who cannot, and who is free or whose freedom is taken away. Since democracy is more of a process than a product, my hope is that this book, and others like it, will increase the national dialogue on these issues.

Epilogue

During the course of writing this book a lot of maintenance got deferred around my home. As it mounted up I started feeling overwhelmed. One day, I called one of the program administrators in our Fatherhood Coalition and asked whether any of their young men could use a few days of work. He called that afternoon and said one of his guys was trying to earn some Christmas money and could start the following day. At 8:00 A.M. a sixteen-year-old boy showed up at my door ready to work. He introduced himself as Carlos. He looked familiar. As we talked a bit, I realized that he was the boy with the old car and the loud CD player. I immediately felt a little apprehensive, knowing that he and his friends lived only a few blocks away and now he was going to get a good look at everything in my home. But I was already committed. So we went to work.

He was a great help. He worked hard and thoughtfully. We accomplished a great deal in a few days—more than I could have done alone in a week or more. And we talked a lot along the way about his school, the neighborhood, and other elements of his life.

I referred him to some other friends for more steady part-time work. One thing I learned from poverty is that offering good employment is often the most sincere demonstration of respect. I paid Carlos and he left, apparently pleased by our brief collaboration. He was grateful for the work; I was extremely grateful for the help.

Afterwards, I never felt safer in my neighborhood. I knew that next time he was on the corner that we could talk, easily. Although I could not count on it, I felt I had a better chance of being protected by Carlos than exploited.

During the course of our exchange we came to know one another a little. Now my experience of him as part of my neighborhood is not merely some cerebral exercise, but a genuine experience of being in community with him. It was a small event in both our lives, but within it was the core of what I have attempted to voice in this book. The building of bridges begins with a single, slender cable stretched between two distant poles. One need not have a Ph.D. in psychology to help many of these boys. A compassionate heart and courage to risk a little goes a long way. I hope this book will encourage us all to try, in whatever way we can, to at least look out for the life of one young man, beyond our commitments to our own children.

Notes

Abbreviations for U.S. Statistical Sources Frequently Cited in This Book

AP, Associated Press

BJS, Bureau of Justice Statistics/Sourcebook

CDC, Centers for Disease Control and Prevention

CJCJ, Center for Juvenile and Criminal Justice

CYA, California Youth Authority

DHHS, Department of Health and Human Services

DoE, Department of Education

DoJ, Department of Justice

ERIC, Educational Resources Information Center

GPO, Government Printing Office

JPI, Justice Policy Institute

NCANDS, National Child Abuse and Neglect Data System

NCCAN, National Center on Child Abuse and Neglect

NCES, National Center for Educational Statistics

NCFY, National Clearinghouse on Families and Youth

NCH, National Coalition for the Homeless

NCHS, National Center for Health Statistics

NCIPC, National Center for Injury Prevention and Control

NCPA, National Center for Policy Analysis

NHSDA, National Household Survey on Drug Abuse

NIJ, National Institute of Justice

NIMH, National Institute of Mental Health

OJJDP, Office of Juvenile Justice and Delinquency Prevention

OJP, Office of Justice Programs

ONDCP, Office of National Drug Control Policy

SA, Statistical Abstract of the United States

UPI, United Press International

Sources Other than U.S.

AI, Amnesty International

WHO, World Health Organization

Unless otherwise noted below, U.S. data for this book came from the following sources:

Maguire, K., & Pastore, A. L. (Eds.) (1998). *Sourcebook of criminal justice statistics 1997* (NCH-1711147). Washington, DC: GPO.

DHHS, National Center on Child Abuse and Neglect. (1997). *Child Maltreatment 1995: Reports from the states to the National Child Abuse and Neglect Data System.* Washington, DC: GPO. Available: http://www.acf.dhhs.gov/programs/cb/stats/ncands/index.htm

Office of Juvenile Justice and Delinquency Prevention. (1996, Feb.). *Juvenile Offenders and Victims: Update on Violence, 24.* Washington, DC: DoJ.

Snyder, T. D., Hoffman, C., & Geddes, C. (1997). *Digest of Education Statistics, 1997* (NCES 98–015). Washington, DC: GPO.

Statistical abstract of the United States: The national data book. (1997). Washington, DC: GPO.

Current population reports: Money income and poverty status in the United States. (1997). (Series P-60-193). Washington, DC: GPO.

Chapter One

P. 9. Wiesel, E. (1995). *All rivers run to the sea.* New York: Knopf.
P. 9. Barks, C., et al. (trans.) (1995). *The essential Rumi.* New York: Harper San Francisco.

Chapter Two

P. 14. Braun, E., & Lustgarten, K. (1994). *Breaking the cycle of child abuse.* Woodland, CA: Childhelp USA.
P. 14. Roman, N. P., & Wolfe, P. B. (1995). *Web of failure: The relationship between foster care and homelessness.* Washington, DC: National Alliance to End Homelessness.
P. 15. Teen rage linked to exposure to anger. (1998, June 5). *Science News* [On-line]. Available: http://www.medserv.dk/health/0698/16/news5.htm
P. 15. Edmonds, P. (1994, Apr. 7). Maltreatment, neglect cases overwhelming. *USA Today,* pp. A-1–2, 8.
P. 15. DHHS. (1993). *Survey on child health.* Washington, DC: NCHS.
P. 15. Smith, S. M., Hanson, R., & Nobel, S. (1980). Social aspects of the battered baby syndrome. In J. V. Cook & R. T. Bowles (Eds.), *Child abuse: Commission and omission* (pp. 217–220). Toronto: Butterworths.
P. 15. Malkin, C. M., & Lamb, M. E. (1994). Child maltreatment: A test of sociobiological theory. *Journal of Comparative Family Studies, 25,* 121–130.
P. 15. Wisdom, C. S. (1992, Oct.). *The cycle of violence.* Washington, DC: DoJ, pp. 1, 2.
P. 15. Dodge, K. A., Bates, J. E., & Pettit, G. S. (1992, Dec. 20). Mechanisms in the cycle of violence. *Science, 250,* pp. 1678, 1683.
P. 15. Schwartz, D., Dodge, K., Pettit, G. S., & Bates, J. E. (1997, Aug.). The early socialization of aggressive victims of bullying. *Child Development, 68*(4), 665–675.
P. 15. Straus, M. A., & Mather, A. K. (1995, Apr. 7). *Corporal punishment of adolescents and academic attainment.* Paper presented at the annual meeting of the Pacific Sociological Association, San Francisco.

P. 15. Straus, M. A., & Kaufman, K. G. (1994). Corporal punishment by parents: A risk factor in the epidemiology of depression, suicide, alcohol abuse, child abuse, and wife beating. *Adolescence, 29,* 114.

P. 15. Turner, H., & Finkelhor, D. (1994). Corporal punishment and the stress process. In M. Donnelly & M. A. Straus (Eds.), *Corporal punishment of children in theoretical perspectives.* New Brunswick, NJ: Transaction.

P. 15. Gimpel, H. S., with Straus, M. A. (1994). Alienation and reduced income. In M.A. Straus (Ed.), *Beating the devil out of them: Corporal punishment in American families* (pp. 137–146). San Francisco: Jossey-Bass.

P. 15. Kandell, E. (1991). Physical punishment and the development of aggressive and violent behavior: A review. *Family Research Laboratory.* Durham, NH: University of New Hampshire.

P. 15. Dodge, Bates, & Pettit, Mechanisms in the cycle of violence, pp. 1678, 1683.

P. 15. Larzeler, R. E. (1986, Mar.). Moderate spanking: Model or deterrent of children's aggression in the family? *Journal of Family Violence, 1,* 27–36.

P. 15. Sickmund, M., Snyder, H. N., & Poe-Yamagata, E. (1996–7). *Juvenile offenders and victims: 1997 & 1996 updates on violence.* Washington, DC: OJJDP.

P. 16. Sobsey, D., Randall, W., & Parrila, R. K. (1997, Aug.). Gender differences in abused children with and without disabilities. *Child Abuse & Neglect: The International Journal, 21*(8), 707–720.

P. 16. Louis Harris and Associates poll for the Commonwealth Fund. (1998, Mar. 31). *Washington Post,* Health, p. 5.

P. 16. U.S. Advisory Board on Child Abuse and Neglect. (1995, Apr.). *A nation's shame: Fatal child abuse and neglect in the United States.* Washington, DC: U.S. Congress.

P. 16. Dawson, J. M., & Langan, P. A. (1994, July). *Murder and families* (Special report). Washington, DC: BJS, Table 2.

P. 16. *OJJ Bulletin* (1997, Aug.). Washington, DC: DoJ, Office of Justice Programs.

P. 16. Federal Interagency Forum on Child and Family Statistics. (1997). *America's children: Key national indicators of well-being.* Washington, DC: GPO.

P. 17. Smith, C., & Thornberry, T. P. (1995). The relationship between childhood maltreatment and adolescent involvement in delinquency. *Criminology, 33,* 451–479.

P. 17. Mott, F. L., Kowaleski-Jones, L., & Nenagehen, E. G. (1997, Feb.). Paternal absence and child behavior: Does a child's gender make a difference? *Journal of Marriage and Family, 59,* 103–118.

P. 17. Margolin, L. (1992, July/Aug.). Child abuse by mothers' boyfriends: Why the overrepresentation? *Child Abuse and Neglect, 16*(4), 545–546.

P. 17. Sedlak, A. J., & Broadhurst, D. D. (1996, Sept.) *The third national incidence study of child abuse and neglect: Final report* (DHHS). Washington, DC: NCCAN.

P. 17. Fagan, P. (1995, Mar. 17). The real cause of violent crime: The break-down of marriage, family, and community. The Heritage Foundation, *Back-grounder*, 1026.

P. 17. Burton, D. F., Bwanausi, C., Johnson, J., & Moore, L. (1994). The relationship between traumatic exposure, family dysfunction, and post-traumatic stress symptoms in male juvenile offenders. *Journal of Trauma Stress, 7*, 83–93.

P. 17. Cooley-Quille, M., Turner, S., & Beidel, D. (1995). The emotional impact of children's exposure to community violence: A preliminary study. *Journal of the American Academy of Child and Adolescent Psychiatry, 34*, 1362–1368.

P. 20. Craig, C., & Herbert, D. (1997). The state of the children: An examination of government-run foster care (NCPA Report, No. 210). Dallas, TX: NCPA. Available: http://www. forchildren.org/soc/tsotc.html

P. 20. Weber, T. (1998, May 17). Caretakers routinely drug foster children. *Los Angeles Times*, pp. 1, 30–32.

P. 20. A shameful child system. (1998, May 24). *Los Angeles Times*, p. M4.

P. 20. Pasco, J. O. (1998, Sept. 3). Orange County unveils children services plan. *Los Angeles Times*, pp. A1, 24.

P. 23. Craig & Herbert, The state of the children.

P. 25. Kipnis, A. (1991/1992). *Knights without armor: A practical guide for men in quest of masculine soul.* Los Angeles: Jeremy P. Tarcher, Inc., New York: Putnam and Sons, p. 24.

P. 32. Sonkin, D. S., & Durphy, M. (1985). *Learning to live without violence: A book for men.* San Francisco: Volcano Press.

P. 33. World Health Organization (1995). *World health statistics annual 1993: Causes of death by sex and age.* Geneva: WHO, Table D–1.

P. 33. Greene, J., & Ringwalt, C., et al. (1995). *Youth with runaway, throwaway, and homeless experiences: Prevalence, drug use, and other at-risk behaviors.* Washington, DC: NCFY. Available: http://www.ncfy.com/chapt2_youth_run.htm

Chapter Three

P. 38. Straus, M., with Donnelly, D. A. (1994). In M. A. Straus (Ed.), *Beating the devil out of them: Corporal punishment in American families* (p. 117). San Francisco: Jossey-Bass.

P. 39. Hyman, I. A. (1997). *The case against spanking: How to discipline your child without hitting.* San Francisco: Jossey-Bass.

P. 40. Ibid., pp. 112–113.

P. 40. Grossman, H. (1998). *Ending discrimination in special education.* Springfield, IL: Thomas.

P. 40. Artiles, A., & Zamora-Duran, G. (1997). *Reducing the disproportionate representation of culturally diverse students in special and gifted education.* Reston, VA: The Council for Exceptional Children.

P. 40. Markowitz, J., Garcia, S. B., & Eichelberger, J. (1997, Mar.). *Addressing the disproportionate representation of students from racial and ethnic minority groups in special education: A resource document.* Alexandria, VA: National Association of State Directors of Special Education. (ERIC No. ED 406810)

P. 40. Robertson, P., & Kushner, M., with Starks, J., & Drescher, C. (1994). An update of participation of culturally and linguistically diverse students in special education: The need for a research and policy agenda. *The Bilingual Special Education Perspective, 14*(1), 3–9.

P. 41. Summers, C. H. (1994). *Who stole feminism: How women have betrayed women.* New York: Touchstone, p. 165.

P. 41. Summers, C. H. (1995, July 17). Equity act. *Washington Post.*

P. 41. *The condition of education.* (1992). Washington, DC: NCES.

P. 41. Gurian, M. (1998). *A fine young man: What parents, mentors, and educators can do to shape adolescent boys into exceptional men.* New York: Jeremy P. Tarcher/Putnam, p. 15.

P. 41. Pollack, W. (1998). *Real boys: Rescuing our sons from the myths of boyhood.* New York: Random House, pp. 233–239.

P. 41. *The condition of education.* (1997). Washington, DC: NCES.

P. 41. Harper, K. L., & Purkey, W. W. (1993). Research in middle-level education. *National Middle School Association, 17*(1), 79–89.

P. 41. Snyder, T. D., Hoffman, C., & Geddes, C. (1997). *Digest of Education Statistics, 1997* (NCES 98–015). Washington, DC: GPO, tables 175, 178, pp. 185, 188.

P. 41. A parent's guide to prevention of sports injuries. (1998, Aug. 28). *Mayo Clinic Health Oasis* [On-line]. Available: www.mayohealth.org/mayo/9808/htm/safesport.htm

P. 41. Kipnis, A. (1991/1992). *Knights without armor: A practical guide for men in quest of masculine soul.* Los Angeles: Jeremy P. Tarcher, Inc., New York: Putnam and Sons, pp. 25–28.

P. 41. Robinson, M. (1998, May 5). Survey finds 10-year-olds may be using steroids to pump up muscles. *Santa Barbara News Press,* p. A6.

P. 42. Weisman, L. (1998, Oct. 25). Criminals abound in NFL. Trouble: One in five players has committed serious crime, authors report. [Book review of Don Yaeger & Jeff Benedict, *Pros and cons: The criminals who play in the NFL.* New York: Warner Books, 1998]. *San Jose Mercury News.*

P. 42. Yi, D. (1998, May 4). A closer look at campus fights. *Los Angeles Times*, p. B1.

P. 42. Steinmetz, S. (1985). Battered husbands: A historical and cross cultural study. In F. Baumli (Ed.), *Men freeing men: Exploding the myth of the traditional male* (pp. 203–207). Jersey City, NJ: New Atlantis Press.

P. 42. Straus, M. A., Gelles, R. J., & Steinmetz, S. K. (1988). *Behind closed doors: Violence in the American family*. London: Sage.

P. 42. Gelles, R. J., & Loseke, D. (Eds.) (1993). *Current controversies on family violence*. Beverly Hills, CA: Sage.

P. 43. Hobbs, D. (1998, May 31). Could Oregon happen here? [Sidebar: Warning signs of potential for exploding violence]. *Santa Barbara News Press*, p. A-1.

P. 43. Marquis, J., (1998, May 8). Study finds alarming rate of risky behaviors by boys. [National survey of adolescent males. Bethesda, MD: National Institute of Child Health and Human Development, Demographic and Behavioral Sciences Branch.] *Los Angeles Times*, p. A1.

P. 43. Turner, C. F., Ku, L., Rodgers, S. M., Lindberg, L. D., Pleck, J. H., & Sonenstein, F. L. (1998, May 8). Adolescent sexual behavior, drug use, and violence: Increased reporting with computer survey technology. *Science, 280*, 867–873.

P. 43. *Violence and discipline problems in U.S. public schools: Executive summary*. (1996–1997). Washington, DC: NCES.

P. 43. Yi, A closer look at campus fights, p. B1.

P. 45. Whittemore, H. (1992, Sept. 27). Dads who shaped up a school. *Parade Magazine*, pp. 20–22.

P. 45. Healy, M. (Oct. 3, 1997). Fathers at school give children an edge, study finds. *Los Angeles Times*, p. A27.

P. 45. Nord, C. W., et al. (1997). *Fathers' involvement in their children's schools* (NCES 98-091). Washington, DC: GPO.

P. 45. Shulman, S., & Seiffge-Krenke, I. (1997). *Fathers and adolescents: Developmental and clinical perspectives*. Florence, KY: Routledge.

P. 45. Haeseler, M. (1996). The absent father: Gender identity considerations for art therapists working with adolescent boys. *Art Therapy: Journal of the American Art Therapy Association, 13*(4), 275–281.

P. 45. Cooksey, E. C., & Fondell, M. M. (1996, Aug.). Spending time with his kids: Effects of family structure on fathers' and children's lives. *Journal of Marriage and the Family, 58*, 693–707.

P. 46. Addison, L. (1998, June 21). Fathers joining ranks of school volunteers. *Los Angeles Times*, p. A3.

P. 47. Woo, E., & Colvin, R. L. (1998, May 17). Why our schools are failing. *Los Angeles Times*, pp. S1–8.

P. 47. Burkholder, B. (1998, Winter). Study shows men twice as likely to fail in college. *North West Educational Consortium for Men's Issues Journal*, 1(1), 1–2.

P. 47. Cahill, B., & Adams, E. (1997, Apr.). An exploratory study of early childhood teachers' attitudes toward gender roles. *Sex Roles: A Journal of Research*, 36(7–8), 517–529.

P. 47. Phillips, A. (1994). *The trouble with boys*. New York: Basic Books.

P. 47. AAUW outlines programs that foster girls success. (1996, Sept. 18). *Education Daily*, pp. 1–4.

P. 47. Robertson, A. S. (1996, Nov.). Fostering school success in adolescents: Girls' issues/boys' issues. *Parent News*.

P. 47. Tannen, D. (1990). *You just don't understand*. New York: Morrow, pp. 246, 268–269.

P. 48. Pacifica Graduate Institute. (1998–1999). Diversity committee discussions and policy implementation. Carpenteria, CA.

P. 48. Sadker, M., & Sadker, D. (1994). *Failing at fairness*. New York: Macmillan.

P. 48. Snyder, Hoffman, & Geddes, pp. 185,188.

P. 48. *Students voice their opinions on: Violence, social tension and equality among teens*. (1998, Mar. 2). [The Metropolitan Life Survey of The American Teacher, (1984–1995). Pt. I. Metropolitan Life/Louis Harris Associates, Inc.] *Business Week*, p. 32.

P. 48. Hoffman, D. L., & Novak, T. P. (1998, Apr. 17). Bridging the racial divide on the Internet. *Science*, 280, 390–391.

P. 48. *U.S. national education longitudinal study of 1988, second follow-up survey*. (1992). Washington, DC: NCES.

P. 49. Ibid.

P. 49. Wehlage, G., Rutter, R., Smith, G., Lesko, N., & Fernandez, R. (1989). *Reducing the risk: Schools as communities of support*. Mukilteo, WA: Alpin Books/The Falmer Press.

P. 49. Newmann, F. (1992). *Student engagement and achievement in American secondary schools*. New York: Teachers College Press.

P. 49. A first-grade kiss gets boys suspended. (1996, Sept. 25). *San Francisco Chronicle*, p. A1.

P. 50. *Schools and staffing survey*, (1993–1994). Washington, DC: NCES.

P. 50. Majors, R. (1986). Cool pose: The proud signature of Black survival. *Changing Men: Issues in Gender and Politics*, 17, 56.

P. 50. Pasteur, A. B., & Toldson, I. L. (1982). *Roots of soul: The psychology of Black expressiveness*. Garden City, NY: Doubleday.

P. 50. Lee, C. C. (1991, 31 Dec.). Empowering young black males. *ERIC Digest* (ED341887).

P. 50. Gibbs, J. T. (Ed.) (1988). *Young, Black and male in America: An endangered species.* Dover, MA: Auburn House.

P. 50. Levine, B. (1993, July 4). Skipping school. *Los Angeles Times*, p. E5.

P. 51. Kipnis, A., & Herron, E. (1995). *What women and men really want: Creating deeper understanding and love in our relationships.* Novato, CA: Nataraj.

P. 52. Wallace, M. (1995). Why a boys' school? *Certified Male* [On-line]. Available: http://www.pnc.com.au/~pvogel/cm/spring96/whya.htm

P. 54. Kipnis, *Knights without armor*, p. 24.

P. 54. Miles, T. (1983). *Dyslexia: The pattern of difficulties.* London: Granada, p. 160.

P. 55. *The condition of education.* (1997). Indicators 15, 16, 17, 21. Washington, DC: NCES.

P. 55. Esposito, J. (Sept., 1995). Incarcerated youth task force report of the advisory commission of special education. *The Learning Disabilities Association Gram, 29*(3), 3, 9, 15.

P. 55. Bailin, A., Mann, M., & Springer, F. (1990). *Representations of children suffering from dyslexia and other learning disabilities in the family court.* The Appellate Division, First Judicial District, Supreme Court of the State of New York.

P. 55. Sikorski, J. B. (1991, Dec.). Learning disorders and the juvenile justice system. *Psychiatric Annals, 21*(12), 742–747.

P. 55. Ross, J. M. (1987). Learning disabled adults: Who are they and what do we do with them? *Lifelong Learning, 11*(3), 4–7, 11. (ERIC no. EJ 361 993)

P. 56. Fletcher, R. (1995). A night out with the boys. *Certified Male* [On-line]. Available: http://www.pnc.com.au/~pvogel/cm/sum95/niteout.htm

P. 56. Riley says Clinton agenda will help schools fight crime. (1998, June 9). (AP) CNN [On-line]. http://www.cnn.com

P. 57. Colvin, R. L. (1998, Mar. 19). Study backs phonics "whole language mix." *Los Angeles Times*, pp. A1, 20.

P. 57. Nguyen, T. (1998, Oct. 4). Remedial reading efforts in California not on same page. *Los Angeles Times*, p. A1.

P. 57. Cohee, C. (1998, June 7). Great expectations: An impoverished Inglewood school has earned a wealth of success from its reading program. Will it work here? *Santa Barbara News Press*, pp. A1, 18.

P. 58. Biddulph, S. (1995, Winter). The Cotswold experiment. *Certified Male* [On-line]. Available: http://www.pnc.com.au/pvogel/cm

P. 58.   Biddulph, S. (1998). *Raising boys: Why boys are different and how to help them become happy and well-balanced men*. Berkeley, CA: Celestial Arts.

P. 59.   Rothstein, R. (1996, Jan. 21). Single-sex schools: Why ruin good experiments with politics? *Los Angeles Times*, p. M6.

P. 59.   Guthrie, J. (1998, Mar. 13). Study: Single-sex education not necessarily a benefit for girls. *Santa Barbara News Press*, p. A5.

P. 59.   Tamara, H. (1996, Sept. 18). A new push for girls-only public schools: N.Y. experiment in leadership. *USA Today*, pp. D1–2.

P. 61.   Piaget, J. (1967). *Six psychological studies*. New York: Vintage Books.

P. 61.   Pollack, *Real boys*, pp. 254–255.

P. 62.   Breggin, P. R. (1994). *Toxic psychiatry: Why therapy, empathy, and love must replace the drugs, electroshock, and biochemical theories of the new psychiatry*. New York: St. Martin's Press.

P. 62.   Breggin, P. R. (1998). *Talking back to Ritalin: What doctors aren't telling you about stimulants for children*. Monroe, ME: Common Courage Press.

P. 62.   Breggin, P. R., & Breggin, G. R. (1998). *The war against children of color: Psychiatry targets inner-city youth*. Monroe, ME: Common Courage Press.

P. 62.   Barkley, R.A. (1995). *Taking charge of ADHD*. New York: Guilford Press.

P. 62.   Divoky, D. (1989, Apr.). Ritalin: Education's fix-it drug? *Phi Delta Kappan*.

P. 63.   Hurt, C. (1998, Mar. 8). Michigan ranks third in nation in prescribing the drug Ritalin. Some say schools turn to medication to control students. *Detroit News* [On-line]. Available: http://www.detroitnews.com/1998/metrox/ritalin/1lead/1lead.htm

P. 63.   Plasker, E. H. (1997, Mar./Apr.). What if Albert Einstein was on Ritalin? *Today's Chiropractic*.

P. 63.   *Physicians' desk reference* (51st ed.) (1997). Montvale, NJ: Medical Economics, pp. 866, 937, 2052.

P. 63.   American Psychiatric Association. (1994). *Diagnostic and statistical manual of mental disorders* (4th ed.). Washington, DC: American Psychiatric Association.

P. 63.   Breggin, *Toxic psychiatry*.

P. 63.   Breggin, *Talking back to Ritalin*.

P. 64.   NIMH: www.nimh.nih.gov

P. 64.   Whalen, C. D., & Henker, B. (1980). The social ecology of psychostimulant treatment: A model for conceptual and empirical analysis. In C. D. Whalen & B. Henker (Eds.), *Hyperactive children: The social ecology of identification and treatment* (p. 38). New York: Academic Press.

P. 64.   Heinrich, J. (1998, Jan., 22). Students popping Ritalin to stay alert. *Montreal Gazette*, p. A1.

P. 64.   Chacón, R. (1998, Feb. 12). On campus, Ritalin getting attention as a 'good buzz.' *Boston Globe*, p. A1.

P. 64.   Motluck, S. (1998, Apr. 18). Calm before the storm. *New Scientist*.

P. 65.   Burkstrand, B. (1997, May 14). Teens are found to be abusing Ritalin. *New York Times*.

P. 65.   Schachar, R. J., Tannock, R., Cunningham, C., & Corkum, P. V. (1997, June). Behavioral, situational, and temporal effects of treatment of ADHD with methlphenidate. *Journal of the American Academy of Child and Adolescent Psychiatry, 36*(6), 754–763.

P. 66.   Cantelon, S., & LeBoeuf, D. (1997, June). *Keeping young people in school: Community programs that work.* Washington, DC: OJJDP.

P. 66.   Manzano, R. (1997, Dec. 27). Building for the future. *Los Angeles Times,* p. B1.

P. 66.   Fritz, M. (1998, May 23). Student's home yields cache of weapons. Violence: Schools adopt different tacks. *Los Angeles Times,* pp. A1, 19–20.

P. 66.   Garner, S. (1998, Apr. 20). Group helps at-risk students to excel. *Santa Barbara News Press,* p. B1.

P. 66.   Smith, H. (1998, Jan. 4). Why these schools work. *Parade Magazine,* p. 12.

P. 66.   Chira, S. (1993, July 14). Is smaller better? Educators now say yes for high school. *New York Times,* p. A1.

P. 66.   Curtis, M. E., & Longo, A. M. (1996, Apr.). *Reversing reading failure in adolescents with behavioral disorders.* Paper presented at the 74th Annual Council for Exceptional Children International Convention, Orlando, FL, pp. 1–5.

P. 66.   Cronin, E. M. (1994). *Helping your dyslexic child: A guide to improving your child's reading, writing, spelling, comprehension, and self-esteem.* Rocklin, CA: Prima Publishing.

P. 66.   Schweinhart, L., Barns, H. V., & Weikart, D. (1993). *Significant benefits: The High/Scope Perry Preschool study though age 27.* Ipsilanti, MI: High/Scope Press.

Chapter Four

P. 70.   Somé, M. (1994). *Of water and the spirit.* New York: Tarcher/Putnam.

P. 70.   Folayemi, B. (1999, Jan. 24). Personal communication.

P. 76.   Hunter, M. (1990). *The sexually abused male* (2 vols.). San Francisco: Jossey-Bass.

P. 77.   Marin, P. (1991, July 8). Why are the homeless mainly single men? *The Nation,* pp. 46–51.

P. 77.   Larson, R. (1998, July 30). Health linked to wealthy, wise. *Washington Post,* p. A6.

P. 77. Greenblatt, M., & Robertson, M. (1993). Lifestyles, adaptive strategies, and sexual behaviors of homeless adolescents. *Hospital and Community Psychiatry, 44,* 1177–1180.

P. 77. Steinbeck, J. (1939). *The grapes of wrath.* New York: Viking.

P. 78. Myers, D. G. (1993). *Social psychology* (4th ed.). New York: McGraw-Hill.

P. 78. Waxman, L., & Trupin, R. (1997). *A status report on hunger and homelessness in America's cities.* Washington, DC: U.S. Conference of Mayors.

P. 78. Greene, J., & Ringwalt, C., et al. (1995). *Youth with runaway, throwaway, and homeless experiences: Prevalence, drug use, and other at-risk behaviors.* Washington, DC: NCFY. Available: http://www.ncfy.com/chapt2_youth_run.htm

P. 78. Federal Task Force on Homelessness and Severe Mental Illness. (1992). *Outcasts on main street: A report of the federal task force on homelessness and severe mental illness.* Delmar, NY: National Resource Center on Homelessness and Mental Illness.

P. 78. Cwayna, K. (1993). *Knowing where the fountains are: Stories and stark realities of homeless youth.* Minneapolis: Fairview/Deaconess Press.

P. 78. NCH Fact Sheets # 3, 6, & 11. (May 1997–Jan. 1998). Washington, DC: NCH. Available: http://nch.ari.net. See also: http://www.ncfy.com/bi-resch.htm

P. 78. Larkin Street Youth Center (1984). Client Statistics. San Francisco.

P. 78. Gibson, P. (1989). *Gay male and lesbian youth suicide, report of the secretary's task force on youth suicide.* Washington, DC: DHHS.

P. 78. Report to the Congress on the runaway and homeless youth program of the Family and Youth Services Bureau for fiscal year 1995, 1996. Washington, DC: DHHS.

P. 78. Suicide Death and Rates per 100,000, United States, 1989–1995. (1997). Washington, DC: DHHS.

P. 78. Robertson, M. (1996). *Homeless youth on their own.* Berkeley, CA: Alcohol Research Group.

P. 78. Wendell D. A., et. al. (1992, Jan.). Youth at risk. Sex, drugs, and human immunodeficiency virus. *American Journal of Diseases of Children, 146,* 76–81.

P. 78. Greene & Ringwalt, *Youth with runaway, throwaway, and homeless experiences.*

P. 78. Homeless teens at risk for severe substance abuse problems. (1997, Nov.). *The Brown University Digest of Addiction Theory and Application, 15*(11), 4.

P. 79. Shinn, M., & Weitzman, B. (1996). Homeless families are different. In J. Baumol (Ed.), *Homelessness in America.* Washington, DC: National Coalition for the Homeless.

P. 79. *Statistical abstract of the United States: The national data book.* (1997). Washington, DC: GPO.

P. 79. Rainwater, L., & Smeeding, T. M. (1995). *Doing poorly: The real income of American children in a comparative perspective.* Syracuse, NY: Maxwell School of Citizenship and Public Affairs, Syracuse University, pp. 2–22.

P. 79. Baum, D. (1996). *Smoke and mirrors: The war on drugs and the politics of failure.* Boston: Little, Brown.

P. 79. May, R. (1995). *Poverty and income trends, 1993.* Washington, DC: Center on Budget and Policy Priorities, pp. 22–23.

P. 79. Courtney, M. (1998, July). *Foster facts.* Madison, WI: Irving Piliavin School of Social Work, University of Wisconsin.

P. 79. Roman, N. P., & Phyllis, B. W. (1995). *Web of failure: The relationship between foster care and homelessness.* Washington, DC: National Alliance to End Homelessness.

P. 79. Robertson, M. (1996). *Homeless youth on their own.* Berkeley, CA: Alcohol Research Group.

P. 79. NCH Fact Sheet #11, (1998, Jan.). Available: nch.ari.net.

P. 80. Crank, J. (1999, Jan.). Personal communication.

P. 80. Robertson, M. J. (1991). Homeless youth: An overview of recent literature. In J. H. Kryder-Coe, L. M. Salamon, & J. M. Molnar (Eds.), *Homeless children and youth: A new American dilemma* (pp. 33–68). New Brunswick, NJ: Transaction.

P. 81. Tough Penalties for Guns in schools. (1998, Aug. 19). *Los Angeles Times,* p. A12.

P. 81. Kann, L., Warren, C. W., Harris, W. A., Collins, J. L., Williams, B. I., Ross, J. G., & Kolbe, L. J. (1996, Sept. 27). Youth risk behavior surveillance, 1995. Fatal firearm injuries in the United States, 1962–1994. In *CDC Surveillance Summaries* (Violence surveillance summary series, no. 3., 1997; Summary of injury mortality data, 1988–1994). Atlanta, GA: CDC, NCIPC.

P. 81. *Morbidity, Mortality Weekly Reports, 45*(SS–4), 1–83. Atlanta, GA: CDC.

P. 81. Annest, J. L., Mercy, J. A., Gibson, D. R., & Ryan, G. W. (1995). National estimates of nonfatal firearm-related injuries: Beyond the tip of the iceberg. *Journal of the American Medical Association, 283,* 1749–1754.

P. 82. Males, M. A. (1996). *The scapegoat generation: America's war on adolescence.* Monroe, ME: Common Courage Press, p. 127.

P. 82. Lotke, E. (1997, Spring). Youth homicide: Keeping perspective on how many children kill. Symposium Issue on Youth Violence. *Valparaiso Law Review, 31*(2).

P. 82. *Weapons related victimization in selected inner-city high school samples.* (1995, Sept.). NIJ Research Report Update. Washington, DC: DoJ.

P. 82. *National Summary of Injury Mortality Data, 1987–1994.* (1996, Nov.). Atlanta, GA: CDC, NCIPC.

P. 82.   Kachur, S. P., Potter, L. B., James, S. P., & Powell, K. E. (1995). *Suicide in the United States, 1980–1992* (Violence Surveillance Summary, No. 1). Atlanta, GA: CDC.

P. 82.   Donziger, S. (Ed.) (1996). *The real war on crime: Report of the National Criminal Justice Commission.* New York: HarperCollins, pp. 9, 19.

P. 82.   Fox, J. A. (1996, Mar.). *Trends in juvenile violence: A report to the United States Attorney General on current and future rates of juvenile offending.* Washington, DC: BJS.

P. 83.   Rates of homicide, suicide, and firearm-related death among children: 26 industrialized countries. (1997, Feb. 7). *Morbidity, Mortality Weekly Reports, 46*(5), 101–105. Atlanta, GA: CDC.

P. 83.   World Health Statistics. (1994). Geneva: WHO.

P. 83.   U.S. deaths by race. (1995). Hyattsville, MD: NCHS.

P. 83.   Krug, E. G., Powell, K. E., & Dahlberg, L. L. (1998). Firearm-related deaths in the United States and 35 other high and upper middle income countries. *International Journal of Epidemiology, 27*, 214–221.

P. 83.   Panpel, F. C., & Gartner, R. (1995, Dec.). Age structure, socio-political institutions and national homicide rates. *European Sociological Review, 11*(3), 243–260.

P. 84.   Gun-Free Schools Act of 1994. Public Law 103–227.

P. 84.   Friedfel, S. (1998, Aug.). Research on improving school safety: The role of technology and reduced class size (National School Board Association Survey). Washington, DC: NCES.

P. 84.   NCES, 1996–97. Available: http://www.ed.gov/stats.html

P. 84.   Inta, E. (1994, Nov. 1). The negative impact of zero-tolerance law. *Santa Barbara News Press*, p. A1.

P. 85.   Bortnick, B. (1994, June 19). Weapons on campus common, boys claim. *Santa Barbara News Press*, p. A18.

P. 85.   Zimmerman, J, M., & Coyle, V. (1997). *The way of council.* Las Vegas, NV: Bramble.

P. 86.   *A matter of time: Risk and opportunity in the nonschool hours, report of the task force on youth development and community programs.* (1992). Waldorf, MD: The Carnegie Council on Adolescent Development.

P. 86.   Cantelon, S., & LeBoeuf, D. (1997, June). *Keeping young people in school: Community programs that work.* Washington, DC: OJJDP.

P. 87.   Chaiken, M. (1996). *Youth afterschool programs and the role of law enforcement* (videotape). Washington, DC: NIJ.

P. 90.   Dryfoos, J. G. (1993). Common components of successful interventions with high-risk youth. In N. J. Bell & R. W. Bell, et al. (Eds.) *Adolescent risk taking* (pp. 131–147). Newbury Park, CA: Sage.

Chapter Five

P. 100. *Boys to men: It takes the whole village*. (1998, May 16). Annual Youth
Violence Prevention Conference of The Fatherhood Coalition, Santa Barbara
City College, Santa Barbara, CA.

P. 102. Bettleheim, B. (1976, July). Personal communication.

P. 102. Seitz, V. (1990). Intervention programs for impoverished children:
A comparison of educational and family support models (Yale Child Welfare
Research Project). *Annals of Child Development, 7*, 84–87.

P. 103. Rotramel, C. A. (1987, Apr. 30). *In an iron chain: The pursuit of
constructive juvenile corrections*. Senior Honors Thesis, Rice University,
Sociology Department, Houston, TX.

P. 103. Miller, J. (1998). Last one over the wall. *Case studies in public policy
and management: Jerome Miller and the department of youth services* (2nd ed.).
Columbus, OH: Ohio State University Press.

P. 106. Kupers, T. A. (1999). *Prison madness: The mental health crisis behind bars
and what we must do about it*. San Francisco: Jossey-Bass.

P. 106. Cart, J. (1998, Aug. 27). "Pattern of abuse" found in Arizona youth
camp. *Los Angeles Times*, p. A3.

P. 106. Torrey, E. F. (1995, Dec.). Jails and prisons: America's new mental
hospitals. *American Journal of Public Health, 85*(12), 1611–1613.

P. 106. Meyer, J. (1998, Sept. 5). [Sheriff] Block says 8 sheriff's employees
were in jail vigilante group. *Los Angeles Times*, p. B3.

P. 107. Santoro, J. A. (1998, Aug. 29). Stop using jails as mental hospitals.
Los Angeles Times, p. B7.

P. 107. Kupers, *Prison madness*.

P. 109. Gilligan, J. (1996). *Violence: Our deadly epidemic and its causes*.
New York: Grosset/Putnam.

P. 112. Horne, A. M., & Sayger, T. V. (1990). *Treating conduct and
oppositional defiant disorders in children*. New York: Pergamon, p. 34.

P. 113. Ibid., pp. 25–26.

P. 114. Ibid., p. 138.

P. 114. Goldman, D. (1989, Jan. 10). Pioneering studies find
surprisingly high rate of mental ills in the young. *New York Times*,
pp. C1, 9.

P. 114. American Psychiatric Association. (1994). *Diagnostic and statistical
manual of mental disorders* (4th ed.). Washington, DC: American Psychiatric
Association.

P. 115. Report card on the national plan for research on child and adolescent
mental disorders: The midway point. (1995, Feb.). Institute of Medicine

Committee for the Study of Research on Child and Adolescent Mental Disorders. American Academy of Child and Adolescent Psychiatry.

P. 115. NIMH. (1990). *National plan for research on child and adolescent mental disorders: A report requested by the U.S. Congress* (DHHS publication 90–1683). Rockville, MD: The National Advisory Mental Health Council.

P. 115. Metz, H. (1991, Dec.). Kids in the cuckoo's nest. *The Progressive*, pp. 12, 22–25.

P. 115. Select committee on children, youth, and families. (1985, June 6). Emerging trends and mental health care for adolescence. National Association of Private Psychiatric Hospitals. Washington, DC: U.S. House of Representatives, 99th Congress, First Session, hearings transcript, pp. 78–79.

P. 115. Ibid., pp. 78–79.

P. 115. Talan J. (1988, 7 Jan.). The hospitalization of America's troubled teenagers. *Newsday, 48*, p.1.

P. 116. Horne & Sayger, *Treating conduct and oppositional defiant disorders*, p. 31.

P. 116. Metz, Kids in the cuckoo's nest, pp. 22–25.

P. 116. Select committee on children, youth, and families, pp. 78–79.

Chapter Six

P. 119. *Addiction: A chronic brain disease*. (1998, Sept. 17). *Mayo Clinic Health Oasis* [On-line].
Available: http://www.mayohealth.org/mayo/9809/htm/addiction.htm

P. 121. Cohen, J., Nagin, D. S., Wasserman, L. A., & Wallstrom, G. L. Hierarchical Bayesian analysis of arrest rates. *Journal of the American Statistical Association, 93*(444), 1260–1270.

P. 123. Brown, J. H. (1997, Spring). Students and substances: Social power in drug education. *Educational Evaluation and Policy Analysis, 19*(1), 65–82.

P. 123. Keeping score: What we are getting for our federal drug control dollars? (1995). *Drug Strategies*, Washington, DC: RAND.

P. 123. Ennett, S. T., et al. (1994). How effective is drug abuse resistance education? A meta-analysis of project DARE outcome evaluations. *American Journal of Public Health, 84*(9).

P. 123. Substance abuse and mental health services administration. (1997, Aug.). Office of Applied Studies, Preliminary Results from DHHS, 1996 NHSDA.

P. 124. Marks, J. (1996, Spring). Mission impossible? Rescuing the Fourth Amendment from the war on drugs. *Criminal Justice, 11*(1) 16.

P. 124. Rhodes, S. (1998, Nov. 20–22). Drug-test the chess club? *USA Weekend* [On-line]. Available: http://www.usaweekend.com/98_issues/9811223/98112/nationalforum.html

P. 124. The IONSCAN® Ion Mobility Spectrometer (IMS) Detection System. *OCETA environmental technology profile*. Mississauga, Ontario: Barringer Research Limited.

P. 124. Zimring, F. E., & Hawkins, G. (1991). *The scale of imprisonment*. Chicago: University of Chicago Press, p. 174.

P. 124. Petersilia, J. (1995). Diverting non-violent prisoners to intermediate sanctions: The impact on prison admissions and corrections costs. *Californian Policy Seminar*. Berkeley, CA: Californian Policy Seminar, pp. 30–34.

P. 124. Harer, M. (1994). *Recidivism among federal prisoners released in 1987*. Washington, DC: Federal Bureau of Prisons, Office of Research & Evaluation.

P. 125. Galasyn, J. (1998, Nov. 21). Court voids Louisiana drug test law. *San Jose Mercury News*.

P. 125. Lloyd, J. (1998, Nov. 22). How drug testing has changed the job market. *Christian Science Monitor*.

P. 125. White House fact sheet on helping communities to keep kids drug-free. (1998, Sept. 12). Washington, DC: Anti-Drug Media Campaign.

P. 125. Greene, J., & Ringwalt, C., et al. (1995). *Youth with runaway, throwaway, and homeless experiences: Prevalence, drug use, and other at-risk behaviors*. Washington, DC: NCFY. Available: http://www.ncfy.com/chapt2_youth_run.htm

P. 132. Young Black men most likely to be jailed. (1990, Mar. 10). *Washington Afro-American*, p. A1.

P. 132. Mauer, M. (1995). *Americans behind bars: U.S. and international use of incarceration*. Washington, DC: Sentencing Project.

P. 132. Mauer, M., & Huling, T. (1997, Jan.). *Young Black Americans and the criminal justice system: Five years later*. Washington, DC: Sentencing Project.

P. 132. Miller, J. (1996). *Search and destroy: African-American males in the criminal justice system*. New York: Cambridge University Press.

P. 132. Mauer, M. (1997). *Intended and unintended consequences: State racial disparities in imprisonment*. Washington, DC: Sentencing Project.

P. 133. Reuter, P. H., Patrick, J. M., & Praskac, A. (1988, July). *Drug use and drug problems in the Washington metropolitan area*. Santa Monica, CA: RAND, p. v.

P. 133. Reuter, P., MaCoun, R., & Murphy, P. (1990). *Summary of money from crime: The economics of drug dealing in Washington, DC*. Washington, DC: Greater Washington Research Center, p. 2.

P. 133. Currie, E. (1998). *Crime and punishment in America*. New York: Henry Holt, p. 13.

P. 133. Ibid., p. 46.

P. 133. Campaign for an Effective Crime Policy. (1996). *The impact of "three strikes and you're out" laws: What have we learned?* Washington, DC: Campaign for an Effective Crime Policy.

P. 136. Williams, C. (1989, Spring). Personal communication. Glide Memorial Church. 330 Ellis St., San Francisco, CA 94102.

P. 137. Dolan, P. (Trans.) (1998, Nov. 13). 3500 drug experts to hold workshops. [European Cities on Drug Policy]. *Frankfurter Rundschau*, Germany.

P. 137. Dutch to extend free heroin hand-outs to addicts. (1998, Nov. 24). CNN [On-line]. Available: http://cnn.com/WORLD/europe/9811/24/BC-DUTCH-HEROIN.reut

P. 137. Posner, G. L. (1988). *The warlords of crime*. New York: Penguin, p. 184.

P. 137. Gay, L. (1990, Jan. 23). Is there a Dutch lesson on drugs? *Washington Times*, p. A11.

P. 137. Bertram, E., & Sharpe, K. (1997, Jan. 6). War ends, drugs win, resisters . say we're fighting the wrong battles. *The Nation* [On-line]. Available: http://www.thenation.com/1997/issue/970106/0106bert.htm

P. 138. Redmann, J. (1998, Nov. 20). First question: What are the implications for health? (P. Dolan, Trans.). *Frankfurter Rundschau*, Germany.

P. 138. Dolan, P. (Trans.) (1998, Nov. 15). Heroin to be distributed first in Hamburg and Frankurt. *Siegener*, Germany.

P. 138. Lusane C., with Desmond, D. (1991). *Pipe dream blues: Racism and the war on drugs*. Boston: South End Press, pp. 69, 74.

P. 138. Valentine, P. W., Miller, B., Montgomery, D., Sipress, A., Pan, P. P., & Benning, V., & the Associated Press. (1998, Dec. 2). Groups seek results of marijuana vote. *Washington Post*.

P. 138. *FY 1999 Washington, DC budget* (Sec. 171). Amendment introduced by Republican Representative Bob Barr (GA).

P. 138. Flynn, K. (1998, Nov. 17). Arrests soar in crackdown on marijuana. *New York Times*, p. B1.

P. 139. Cruel and usual: Disproportionate sentences for New York drug offenders. (1997, Mar.). *Human Rights Watch*, 9(2) (B).

P. 139. Crime in the United States, 1997. In *Statistical abstract of the United States: The national data book*. (1997). Washington, DC: GPO.

P. 139. *Behind bars: Substance abuse and America's prison population*. (1998, Jan.). Report of the National Center on Addiction and Substance Abuse. New York: Columbia University.

P. 139.   Landes, A. (1997). *Illegal drugs: American anguish*. Wylie, TX:
Information Plus, pp. 39–40.

P. 139.   Brown, L. P. (1994). *Pulse check: National trends in drug abuse* (Testimony
before the Senate Committee on the Judiciary). Washington, DC: ONDCP.

P. 139.   *1996 National Household Survey on Drug Abuse*. Available:
www.health.org/pubs/nhsda

P. 139.   Rydell, P. C., & Everingham, S. S. (1994). *Controlling cocaine:
Supply versus demand programs*. Santa Monica, CA: RAND.

P. 139.   California Department of Alcohol and Drug Programs.

P. 139.   Lipton, D. (1995, Nov.). The effectiveness of treatment for drug abusers
under criminal justice supervision (NIJ Research Report). Available:
http://www.ncjrs.org/txtfiles/drugsupr.txt

P. 139.   U.S. Substance Abuse and Mental Health Services Administration
[SAMHSA]. (1994, Mar.). *Annual emergency room data, 1992* (DHHS Pub #
SMA 94–2080). Rockville, MD: DHHS, table 2.06c.

P. 140.   Inciardi, J. A. (1996). *A corrections-based continuum of effective drug abuse
treatment*. Washington, DC: NIJ.

P. 140.   Amity Righturn program. R. J. Donovan Correctional Facility,
San Diego, CA.

P. 140.   Focus on drug treatment. (1994, June 17). *USA Today*, p. 6A.

P. 140.   *Behind bars: Substance abuse and America's prison population*.

P. 140.   Sherman, L., et. al. (1997, Feb.). *Preventing crime: What works, what
doesn't, what's promising*. Report to the United States Congress, prepared for the
NIJ by the University of Maryland.

P. 140.   Hynes, C. J., & Powers, S. A. (Oct. 1994 to Oct. 1995). *Drug treatment
alternative to prison* (Fifth Annual Report of Operations). Brooklyn, NY: Kings
County District Attorney,.

P. 140.   Caulkins, J. P., Rydell, C. P., Schwabe, W., & Chiesa, J. (1997).
Mandatory minimum drug sentences: Throwing away the key or the taxpayer's money?
Santa Monica, CA: RAND.

P. 140.   Gerstein, D. R., Johnson, R. A., Harwood, H. J., Fountain, D., Suter,
N., & Malloy, K. (1994). *Evaluating recovery services: the California drug and
alcohol treatment assessment*. Sacramento, CA: California Dept. of Alcohol
and Drug Programs.

P. 141.   *Preliminary report. The persistent effects of substance abuse treatment:
One year later*. (1996, Sept.). The National Treatment Improvement
Evaluation Study, Center for Substance Abuse Treatment. Rockville, MD:
DHHS.

P. 141.   ONDCP, 1997.

P. 141. Bancroft, A. (1997, Sept. 26). Board looks into alternative sentences for drug offenders. *Santa Barbara News Press*, p. A1.

P. 141. *Treatment works*. (1990, Mar.). Washington, DC: National Association of State Alcohol and Drug Abuse Directors, p. v.

P. 141. Young, N. K. (1994, July). *Invest in treatment for alcohol and other drug problems: It pays*. Los Angeles: University of California.

P. 141. Manville, R. P. (1998, Aug. 2). Two programs for teens help fill gap. *Santa Barbara News Press*, p. B2.

P. 141. Srinivasan, K. (1998, Nov. 12). *Drug courts get credit for cutting crime, drug abuse among offenders. Rehabilitation, not punishment, yielding results*. Available: http://www.ndsn.org/NOVDEC98/courts2.html.

P. 141. Caher, J. (1998, Nov. 18). Kaye sees drug courts as leaders. *Times Union* (Albany, NY).

P. 141. Cooper, C. S., & Trotter, J. A. Jr. (1994), *Drug case management and treatment intervention strategies in the state and local courts* (vol. 2). Washington, DC: The American University.

P. 141. Sherman, *Preventing crime*.

P. 141. Keeping score: What we are getting for our federal drug control dollars? (1995). *Drug Strategies*. Washington, DC: RAND.

P. 142. War on drugs enlists an antibody. (1998, Nov. 22). *Science News, 154*, 239.

P. 142. Dewey, S. L., et al. (1998, Oct.). A novel strategy for the treatment of cocaine addiction. *Synapse, 30*(2), 119–29.

P. 142. Bor, J. (1998, Feb. 2). The detox doc. *Los Angeles Times*, p. S7.

P. 142. Philips, C., & Hiltzik. M. A. (1998, Sept. 27). Hotel detox: For affluent addicts. *Los Angeles Times*, pp. A1, 28.

P. 143. Youth violence, guns, and illicit drug markets. (1996, June). *NIJ Research Review*.

P. 143. Sobieraj, S. (1998, July 12). States' drug programs get $32 million. *Santa Barbara News Press*, p. A3.

Chapter Seven

P. 145. Rothman, D. J. (1971). *The discovery of the asylum: Social order and disorder in the new republic*. Boston: Little, Brown, pp. 255, 257, 261.

P. 146. Lattimore, P. K, Linster, R. L., & MacDonald, J. M. (1997, May). Risk of death among serious young offenders. *Journal of Research in Crime and Delinquency, 34*(2), pp. 197–206.

P. 146. CYA Summary Fact Sheet. (1998, Oct.). Sacramento, CA: Data compiled by California Youth Authority's Communications Office, Office of Public Affairs. Available: http://www.cya.ca.gov/facts/summarys.html

P. 151. Horn, W. F. (1998). *Father facts* (3rd ed.). Gaithersburg, MD: National Fatherhood Initiative.

P. 151. Blankenhorn, D. (1995). *Fatherless America*. New York: Harper Perennial.

P. 151. Dawson, D. A. (1991, Aug.). Family structure and children's health and well-being: Data from the 1988 national health interview survey on child health. *Journal of Marriage and the Family, 53*, 573–584.

P. 151. Characteristics of at-risk students in NELS: 88. (1992, Aug.). Washington, DC: NCES.

P. 151. Marital status and living arrangements (1994, Mar.). In *Statistical abstract of the United States: The national data book*. (1996). Washington, DC: GPO, pp. 20–484.

P. 151. Donald, H. J. (1993). *America's children: Resources from family government and the economy*. New York: Russell Sage Foundation, p. 65.

P. 151. Marriage, divorce and remarriages in the 1990s. In *Statistical abstract of the United States: The national data book*. (1997). Washington, DC: GPO, tables M & N, pp. 11–12.

P. 152. Brooks, K. (1996, July 20). "Forget about the blame," gang researcher tells task force on youth violence. *Corpus Christi Caller Times* [On-line]. Available: http://www.gangwar.com/news10.htm

P. 155. Fremon, C. (1996, Oct. 6). His life is a movie. *Los Angeles Times Magazine*, pp. 7–12, 28–30.

P. 155. Mohan, G. (1994, Sept. 5). Homeboys to dough boys: Former gang members explore better living by baking. *Los Angeles Times*, pp. B1, 3.

P. 156. Violent and Juvenile Offender Act of 1997. (1997, Oct. 9). *Report of the Committee on the Judiciary*, United States Senate, Report 105–108.

P. 158. Simon, P. (1994, Dec. 21). *In new survey, wardens call for smarter sentencing, alternatives to incarceration, and prevention programs*. Washington, DC: Office of Senator Paul Simon, U.S. Senate.

P. 158. *The United States sentencing guidelines: Results of the federal judicial center's survey*. (1996). Federal Judicial Center Survey, report to the Committee on Criminal Law of the Judicial Conference of the United States.

P. 158. Police chiefs survey. (1996, Apr. 30). *Law Enforcement News*.

P. 159. Maguire, K., & Pastore, A. L. (Eds.) (1998). *Sourcebook of criminal justice statistics 1997* (NCH-1711147). Washington, DC: GPO.

P. 159. United Nations special rapporteur on torture. (1988, Apr. 17). New York: UN Document E/CN.

P. 159. Meeting the mandates. (1995, Fall/Winter). *Juvenile Justice, 2*(2). Washington, DC: OJJDP.

P. 159. Harris, R. (1993, 22 Aug.). A nation's children in lockup. *Los Angeles Times*, p. A20.

P. 165. Jackson, Jesse. (1992, Fall). Presidential campaign speech, Sonoma State University, CA.

P. 165. Money, income, and poverty status in the United States. (1997). In *Statistical abstract of the United States: The national data book*. (1997). Washington, DC: GPO, series P–60–193.

P. 165. Rainwater, L., & Smeeding, T. M. (1995). *Doing poorly: The real income of American children in a comparative perspective*. Syracuse, NY: Maxwell School of Citizenship and Public Affairs, Syracuse University, pp. 2–22.

P. 167. Hahn, K. (1991). *Readings from the Hurricane Island outward bound school*. Rockland, ME: Outward Bound.

P. 167. Male Involvement Program (MIP). Office of Family Planning, California State Department of Health Services.

P. 167. Santa Barbara Pro Youth Coalition, c/o Zona Seca, Inc. Box 1990, Santa Barbara, CA, 93102–1990.

P. 167. Boot Camp for New Dads. http://www.newdads.com

P. 167. Cypser, R. J. (1997, Oct. 21). *What works in reducing recidivism, and thereby reducing crime, and cost*. Citizens United for the Rehabilitation of Errants [On-line]. Available: http://www.bestweb.net/~cureny/payback.htm

Chapter Eight

P. 169. Western District Wisconsin. *Morales v. Schmidt*. 340 (W. D. Wisconsin, 1972), pp. 544, 548–49.

P. 170. Zimring, F. E., & Hawkins, G. (1991). *The scale of imprisonment*. Chicago: University of Chicago Press, p. 76.

P. 170. National Council on Crime and Delinquency. (1972). Institutional construction: a policy statement. *Crime and Delinquency, 18*, 331–332.

P. 170. *National moratorium on prison construction*. (1978). Washington, DC: National Advisory Commission's Task Force on Corrections.

P. 170. National Advisory Commission on Criminal Justice Standards and Goals. (1973). *Task force report on corrections*. Washington, DC: GPO, p. 597.

P. 170. Gilliard, D., & Beck, A. J. (1998, Jan.) *Prison and jail inmates at midyear 1997*. Washington, DC: BJS Bulletin.

P. 171. Walmsley, R. (1997). *Prison populations in Europe and North America*. Helsinki: HEUNI.

P. 171. Mauer, M. (1995). *Americans behind bars: U.S. and international use of incarceration*. Washington, DC: Sentencing Project.

P. 171. Currie, E. (1998). *Crime and punishment in America*. New York: Henry Holt, p. 20.

P. 171. Solzhenitsyn, A. (1973). *The gulag archipelago*. New York: Harper and Row.

P. 172. *Supermax housing: A survey of current practice.* (1997, Mar.). Washington, DC: National Institute of Corrections.

P. 173. *Cold storage: Super-maximum security confinement in Indiana.* (1997, Oct.). New York: Human Rights Watch.

P. 173. *UK special security units: Cruel, inhuman and degrading treatment.* (1997, Mar.). AI Index [On-line]. Available: http://www.amnesty.org/ailib/aipub/1997/EUR/44500697.htm

P. 173. Amensty International. (1998). *United States of America: Rights for all.* New York: AI Publications, pp. 349–353.

P. 173. Gladstone, M., & Arax, M. (1998, Sept. 30). Prison oversight agency given more authority. *Los Angeles Times*, pp. A3, 9.

P. 173. Davis, M. (1996). The politics of super incarceration. In E. Rosenblatt (Ed.), *Criminal injustice: Confronting the prison crisis* (p. 75). Boston: South End Press.

P. 174. Tashjian, H. (1997). *Racism and the California prison system.* The Prison Activist Resource Center [On-line]. Available: http://www.igc.apc.org/prisons/crisis/prison-industrial.html#racism

P. 174. Phinney, D. (1998, July 9). *Colleges or prisons? The options pose a stark contrast.* ABC News [On-line]. Available: www.abcnews.com/sections/us/DailyNews/prisoneducaton980707.html

P. 174. Connolly, K., McDermind, L., Schiraldi, V., & Macallair, D. (1996, Oct.). *From classrooms to cell blocks: How prison building affects higher education and African American enrollment.* San Francisco: CJCJ, p. 6.

P. 174. Schiraldi, V. (1998, Feb.). *Report in brief: Is Maryland's system of higher education suffering because of prison expenditures?* San Francisco: CJCJ.

P. 174. Ambrosio, T. J., & Schiraldi. V. (1997, Feb.). *From classrooms to cell blocks: A national perspective.* Washington, DC: JPI.

P. 174. Baum, N., & Bedrick, B. (1994, Apr.). *Trading books for bars: The lopsided funding battle between prisons and universities.* San Francisco: CJCJ, p. 39.

P. 174. Jacobs, J. B. (1983–1984). The politics of prison expansion. *New York University Review of Law and Social Change, 12,* 209–241.

P. 174. Zimring & Hawkins, *The scale of imprisonment,* p. 219.

P. 175. Ibid., p. 121.

P. 175. Ibid., p. 130.

P. 175. Bishop, N. (1988). Non-custodial alternatives in Europe. Helsinki: Institute for Crime Prevention and Control, p. 119.

P. 175. Petersilia, J. (1987). *Expanding options for criminal sentencing.* Santa Monica, CA: RAND, p. xi.

P. 176. *Education as crime prevention: Providing education to prisoners.* (1997,

Sept.). Occasional Paper, Series No. 2. New York: The Center on Crime, Communities, and Culture.

P. 176. Justice Department Statistics (1998, Aug. 17).

P. 176. Batiuk, M. E. (1997, June). The state of post-secondary education in Ohio. *Journal of Correctional Education*, 48(2), 70–72.

P. 176. Batiuk, M. E., Moke, P., & Rounree, P. W. (1997, Mar.). Crime and rehabilitation: Correctional education as an agent of change: A research note. *Justice Quarterly*, 14(1).

P. 176. Duguid, S. (1997, June). Cognitive dissidents bite the dust: The demise of university education in Canada's prisons. *Journal of Correctional Education*, 48(2), 56–68.

P. 176. Clark, C. H. (1991, Aug.). *Analysis of return rates of the inmate college program participants: Follow-up study of a sample of offenders who earned high school equivalency diplomas while incarcerated* (1989, July). New York: State Department of Correctional Services.

P. 176. Taylor, J. M. (1992, Sept.). Post-secondary correctional education: An evaluation of effectiveness and efficiency. *Journal of Correctional Education*, 43(3), 132–141.

P. 176. Schumaker, R., Anderson, D., & Anderson, S. (1990, Mar.). Vocational and academic indicators of parole success. *Journal of Correctional Education*, 41(1), 8–13.

P. 176. O'Neill, M. (1990, Mar.). Correctional higher education: Reduced recidivism? *Journal of Correctional Education*, 41(1), 28–31.

P. 176. Lawyer, H. L., & Dertinger, T. D. (1993, Winter). Back to school or back to jail? *ABA Criminal Justice*, p. 21.

P. 177. Tashjian, *Racism and the California prison system*.

P. 177. Shuster, B. (1998, Aug. 23). Living in fear. *Los Angeles Times*, pp. A1, 32–3.

P. 177. Lait, M. (1998, Aug. 24). Public fear of crime proves elusive enemy for L.A.P.D. Crime reports steadily increase in news but crime is less. *Los Angeles Times*, p. B1.

P. 177. Updegrave, W. L. (1994, June). You're safer than you think. *Money Magazine*.

P. 177. *Nations' probation and parole population reached new high last year.* (1998, Aug. 16). Washington, DC: DoJ. Available: http://www.ojp.usdoj.gov/bjs/pub/press/papp97.pr

P. 177. Mauer, M. (1997). *Losing the vote: The impact of felony disenfranchisement laws in the United States*. Washington, DC: Sentencing Project, p. 4.

P. 178. Richey, W. (1998, Oct. 23). Black men hit hard by voting bans for

convicts. *Christian Science Monitor* [On-line]. Available:
www.csmonitor.com/durable/1998/10/23/f-p4s1.shtml

P. 177. Wiechman, L. (1998, Oct. 19). County pleads for young males to
volunteer for jury duty. *On-line Athens*. Available:
http://www.athensnewspapers.com/1998/101998/1019.a2jurors.html.

P. 179. The Wackenhut Corporation (NYSE:WAK).
http://www.wackenhut.com

P. 179. Prison Realty Trust (NYSE:PZN). *Prospectus, shareholder reports
and press kit.* (1997, July 15). http://www.prisonreit.com/html/linkset.html

P. 180. Prisoners to share cost of health care: Idaho Board of Correction OKs
medical co-payments. (1998, Oct. 1). Associated Press [On-line]. Available:
http://www.spokane.net.

P. 180. BI Incorporated (Nasdaq: BIAC). http://www.bi.com

P. 180. Anderson, D. C. (1998). *Sensible justice: Alternatives to prison*. New York:
The New Press.

P. 180. Pharmchem (NASDAQ: PCHM). sec.yahoo.com/e/l/p/pchm.html

P. 180. National Center for Policy Analysis. (1998). Report to the House
Judiciary Committee's Subcommittee on Crime.

P. 181. 1996 [video] taken by prison guards at the Detention Center
of Brazoria County, Texas. (1997, Aug. 21). Available:
http://www.cnn.com/us/9708/25/briefs.pm/prisoner.abuse

P. 183. U.S. Constitution, Amendment 13, ratified Dec. 6, 1865.

P. 183. Browne, J. (1995). The labor of doing time. In *Criminal injustice: Confronting the prison crisis.* Prison Activist Resource Center [On-line]. Available:
http://www.igc.apc.org/prisons/crisis/labor-of-doing-time.html

P. 183. Oshinsky, D. M. (1997). *Worse than slavery: Parchman farm and the ordeal
of Jim Crow justice.* New York: The Free Press.

P. 183. Tonry, M. (1994, June). Drug policies increasing racial disparities in U.S.
prisons. *Overcrowded Times, 5.*

P. 183. Zimring & Hawkins, *The scale of imprisonment*, p. 73.

P. 184. Gilliard, D. K., & Beck, A. J. (1998). *Prisoners in 1997* (NCJ–170014,
document no. 120). Washington, DC: BJS Clearinghouse.

P. 184. *The Farm* [film]. A&E special. (1999, Jan 29).

P. 184. *Statistical Abstract of the United States*, Table No. 127, p. 94.

P. 184. Clendenning, A. (1998, Sept. 24). *27-year-old Louisiana prison
lawsuit settled.* Associated Press [On-line]. Available:
http://www.nandotimes.com

P. 184. Green, F. M. (1949). Some aspects of the convict lease system in the
southern states. *Essays in Southern History, 31,* 112. Durham, NC: University
of North Carolina Press.

P. 184. Wilson, W. (1933). *Forced labor in the United States*. New York: AMS Press, p. 63.

P. 184. California Department of Corrections, Conservation Camps Program.

P. 184. Free labor rebelled against it. (1995, Mar.). *Solidarity*, United Auto Workers.

P. 184. Lichtenstein, A. (1993). Good roads and chain gangs in the progressive south: The Negro convict is a slave. *Journal of Southern History*. Athens, GA: Southern Historical Association, p. 87.

P. 185. Oshinsky, *Worse than slavery*.

P. 186. Rikers Island guards beat inmates for years: Details emerge from NYC court settlement; reforms reported. (1998, Aug. 16). Associated Press.

P. 186. Hornblum, A. M. (1998). *Acres of skin: Human experiments at Holmesburg Prison: A true story of abuse and exploitation in the name of medical science*. Danbury, CT: Routledge.

P. 186. Bronskill, J. & Blanchfield, B. (1998, Oct. 1). Minister demands answers on prison experiments; Solicitor General upset by citizen account of inmates used as guinea pigs. *The Ottawa Citizen*. For copy call: 613-596-3744.

P. 187. Lowe, H. (1998, Nov. 6). Former inmates protest: They say they still suffer from experiments performed on them in Philadelphia prisons. *Philadelphia Inquirer*.

P. 187. Braithwaite, R. L., Hammett, T. M. & Mayberry, R. M. (1996). *Prisons and AIDS: A public health challenge*. San Francisco: Jossey-Bass.

P. 187. Kupers, T. A. (1999). *Prison madness: The mental health crisis behind bars and what we must do about it*. San Francisco: Jossey-Bass.

P. 188. Hanlon, S. M. (1993, Dec. 24). State prisons taking a hit from AIDS. *Washington Times*.

P. 188. Gordon, R. (1998, Sept. 11). S.F. may sue state over HIV prison care. Leno contends the city covers care of ex-cons with AIDS. *San Francisco Examiner* [On-line]. Available: http://www.sfgate.com/ cgi-bin/article.cgi?file=/examiner/archive/1998/09/11/news5009.dtl

P. 189. Moniz, D. (1997, Sept. 28). VA discovers many men subjected to sexual abuse. *Seattle Times* [On-line]. Available: http://archives.seattletimes.com/ cgi-bin/texis.mummy/web/vortex/display?storyID=36d4d203f

P. 189 Wooden, W. S., & Parker, J. (1982). *Men behind bars: Sexual exploitation in prison*. New York: Plenum.

P. 189. Lockwood, D. (1980). *Prison sexual violence*. New York: Elsevier.

P. 190. Scacco, A. M. Jr. (Ed.) (1982). *Male rape: A casebook of sexual aggressions* (Studies in Modern Society, No. 15). New York: AMS Press.

P. 190. Rideau, W., & Wikberg, R. (1992). *Life sentences: Rage and survival behind bars*. New York: Time Books, pp. 73, 76.

P. 190. Ibid., pp. 73, 76.

P. 190. Douglas, J. E., Burgess, A. W., Burgess, A. G., & Ressler, R. K. (1992). *Crime classification manual: A standard system for investigating and classifying violent crimes*. San Francisco: Jossey-Bass, pp. 191–246.

P. 190. Struckman-Johnson, C., et al. (1996). Sexual coercion reported by men and women in prison. *Journal of Sex Research, 33*(1).

P. 190.. Wooden & Parker, *Men behind bars*.

P. 190. Lockwood, *Prison sexual violence*.

P. 190. Donaldson, S. (1995, July). *Rape of incarcerated Americans: a preliminary statistical look* (7th ed.) [On-line]. Stop Prisoner Rape, Inc.. Available: http://www.spr.org/docs/stats.html

P. 190. Donaldson, S. (1990). Rape of males. In Wayne R. Dynes (Ed.), *Encyclopedia of homosexuality*. New York: Garland.

P. 191. Dumond, R. W. (1992). The sexual assault of male inmates in incarcerated settings. *International Journal of the Sociology of Law, 20*, 135–157, 146–47.

P. 191. Groth, N., & Burgess, A. W. (1979). *Men who rape*. New York: Plenum.

P. 191. Groth, N., & Burgess, A. W. (1980). Male rape: Offenders and victims. *American Journal of Psychiatry, 137*, 806–810.

P. 191. Kaufman, A., et al. (1980). Male rape victims: Noninstitutionalized assault. *American Journal of Psychiatry, 137*, 221–223.

P. 192. Rideau & Wikberg. *Life sentences*, p. 73, 76.

P. 192. Scacco, A. Jr. (1975). *Rape in prison*. Springfield, IL: Thomas, p. 91.

P. 192. Arax, M., & Gladstone, M. (1998, Oct. 9). Prison: 5 Corcoran guards charged. *Los Angeles Times*, pp. A1, 27.

P. 192. Arax, M., & Gladstone, M. (1998, July 6). Corcoran: Former guard tells of brutality at prison. *Los Angeles Times*, pp. A1, 14.

P. 192. Thomas, Clayton L. (Ed.) (1997). *Taber's cyclopedic medical dictionary* (18th ed.). Philadelphia: Davis, p. 1836.

P. 194. Porter, E. (1986). Treating the young male victim of sexual assault. Syracuse, NY: Safer Society Press.

P. 194. Amnesty International. (1998). *United States of America: Rights for all*. New York: AI Publications.

P. 194. Struckman-Johnson, Sexual coercion reported by men and women in prison.

P. 197. Rethinking criminal justice policy: A view from the research community. (1996, Feb.). *National Institute of Justice Journal*.

P. 197. Boyer, E. J. (1998, Nov. 18). A new drive for justice. *Los Angeles Times*, p. B2.

P. 197. Foucault, M. (1977). *Discipline and punish: The birth of the prison*. New York: Pantheon Books.

P. 197. The Church Council on Justice and Corrections. (1996). *Satisfying justice: Safe community options that attempt to repair harm from crime and reduce the use or length of imprisonment.* Ottawa, Ontario: The Church Council on Justice and Corrections. 1-800-665-8948.

Chapter Nine

P. 211. Neale, L., & Densmore, J. (Producers). *Road to Return* [film].

P. 211. Project Return: From Prison to Community. Dr. Robert E. Roberts, director. Tulane University Medical Center School of Public Health and Tropical Medicine, Applied Health Science Department.

P. 211. Roberts, R. E., Marks, N., with Parker, J. L. *Project return: A book about hope: how a black man and a white man found a path to brotherhood and built a road to hope for former offenders.* Unpublished manuscript and personal communications.

P. 214. Dr. Roger Williams, Project Director. Boys to Men. Department of Professional Development and Applied Studies at University of Wisconsin at Madison. Division of Continuing Studies Outreach Program.

P. 217. Gilmore, D. (1990). *Manhood in the making: Cultural concepts of masculinity.* New Haven, CT: Yale University Press.

P. 219. Zimmerman, J, M., & Coyle, V. (1997). *The way of council.* Las Vegas, NV: Bramble.

P. 222. Male Involvement Program (MIP). Office of Family Planning, California State Department of Health Services.

P. 224. Morton-Young, T. (1995). *After-school and parent education programs for at-risk youth and their families: Guide to organizing and operating a community-based center for basic educational skills reinforcement, homework assistance, cultural enrichment, and a parent involvement focus.* Springfield, IL: Thomas.

Chapter Ten

P. 228. Adler, S. J., & Lambert, W. (1993, Mar. 12). Common criminals: Just about everyone violates some laws, even model citizens. *Wall Street Journal,* p. A1.

Electronic Resources

Boot Camp for New Dads
http://www.newdads.com

Bureau of Justice Statistics/Sourcebook of Criminal Justice Statistics
http://www.albany.edu/sourcebook

California Youth Authority
http://www.cya.ca.gov/facts/summarys.html

Centers for Disease Control and Prevention
Youth violence: http://www.cdc.gov/ncipc/dvp/yvfacts.htm
Firearm fatalities: http://www.cdc.gov/ncipc/dvp/fafacts.htm
Firearm suicides: http://www.cdc.gov/ncipc/osp/us9592/farmsuic.htm

National Center for Injury Prevention and Control
Firearms: http://www.cdc.gov/ncipc/dvp/fivpt.htm
Suicide: http://www.cdc.gov/ncipc/dvp/suifacts.htm

Child Welfare
http://www.futureofchildren.org

Condition of Education
http://nces.ed.gov/Pubs98/condition98/index.html

Department of Health and Human Services
http://www.os.dhhs.gov

Drug Reform and Information
http://www.drcnet.org
http://www.druglibrary.org
http://www.drugsense.org

Fatherhood
http://www.fathers.com
http://www.fatherhood.org
http://fatherhood.miningco.com

Foster Care
http://www.intellectualcapital.com/issues/97/0821/icpolicy2.html

National Center for Education Statistics
http://www.nces.ed.gov
http://www.ed.gov/stats.html

National Child Abuse and Neglect Data
www.ndacan.cornell.edu/index.html
http://www.calib.com/nccanch

National Coalition for the Homeless
http://nch.ari.net

National Consortium on Alternatives for Youth at Risk, Inc.
http://www.ncayar.org

National Household Survey on Drug Abuse
http://www.health.org/pubs/nhsda

National Resource Center on Homelessness and Mental Illness
http://www.prainc.com/nrc/index.html

National School Safety Center
http://nssc1.org

Office of Justice Programs
http://www.ojp.usdoj.gov

Office of Juvenile Justice and Delinquency Prevention
http://www.ojjdp.ncjrs.org

Prison Reform and Awareness
http://www.prisonactivist.org
http://www.igc.apc.org/justice/prisons/pubs/rtw1.html

Project Return
http://www.projectreturn.com

Psychiatric Reform
http://www.breggin.com/ritalin.html

RAND Corporation
http://www.rand.org

Statistical Abstract of the United States
www.census.gov/prod/3/98pubs/98statab/cc98stab.htm

Sentencing Project
http://www.sentencingproject.org

Statistical Resources on the Web, Sociology
http://www.lib.umich.edu/libhome/Documents.center/stsoc.html

Violence and Discipline Problems in U.S. Schools
http://nces.ed.gov/pubs98/violence/index.html

Violence Prevention
http://www.pcvp.org/index.html

What Works in Reducing Recidivism
http://www.bestweb.net/~cureny/whatwork.htm

About the Author

Aaron Kipnis, Ph.D., is president of the Fatherhood Coalition, a nonprofit organization that supports positive male involvement in family planning, parenting, relationships, and community. He is author of *Knights Without Armor*, coauthor of *What Women and Men Really Want*, and contributor to many anthologies.

As codirectors of the Gender Relations Institute, Aaron and his wife, Liz Herron, facilitate male-female communication workshops nationwide and hold private consultations with couples in Santa Barbara, California. Dr. Kipnis is on the faculty of Pacifica Graduate Institute, where he trains graduate students in counseling, clinical, and depth psychology. He is an international speaker and consultant on male psychology to professional organizations, governmental agencies, universities, treatment facilities, and training institutes. He enjoys fishing, smoking cigars, and talking to old men.

Please visit *www.kipnis.com* for updates, conferences, links, and other resources. Dr. Kipnis's travel and speaking schedule, e-mail link, and downloadable articles are also found here.

For correspondence:
Box 4782
Santa Barbara, CA 93140

Index

Date Due

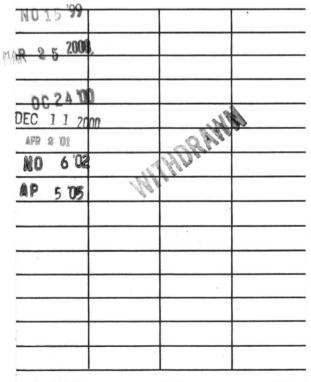